W9-BWA-804

LIBERAL EDUCATION
AND THE CANON

LIBERAL EDUCATION AND THE CANON

FIVE GREAT TEXTS SPEAK TO
CONTEMPORARY SOCIAL ISSUES

Laura Christian Ford

CAMDEN HOUSE

Library of Congress Cataloging-in-Publication Data

Ford, Laura Christian, 1948-
    Liberal Education and the canon : five great texts speak to contemporary
social issues / Laura Christian Ford.
    p.   cm.
    ISBN: 1-57113-013-6 (alk. paper)
    1. Education, Humanistic--United States. 2. Canon (Literature) 3. Criti-
cism--United States. 4. Education, Higher--Social aspects--United States. 5. Social problems in literature. I. Title.
LC1011.F65 1994
370.11'2--dc20   94-21298
                                                                        CIP

To my teachers

Contents

Note on Sources

THIS BOOK WAS intended to be accessible to a broad audience. For that reason I have identified canonical works by unabbreviated title and/or author each time they are mentioned in the text. Numerical citations have been given following quoted passages using the Modern Language Association's suggested format.

I have avoided the temptation to use my own translation of Greek passages lest the choice of words be unduly influenced by my desire to make a point in the argument. I have therefore used only standard published translations. For Homer and Plato, I have relied upon the translations of the Loeb Classical Library (Cambridge, Mass.: Harvard University Press) unless otherwise indicated in the notes. The Loeb translations of the *Iliad* and the *Odyssey* are by A. T. Murray. The Loeb translations of Plato's dialogues are by Harold N. Fowler, W. R. M. Lamb, Paul Shorey, and R. G. Bury.

For the works of Shakespeare, I have used *The Annotated Shakespeare,* edited by A. L. Rowse (New York: Greenwich House, 1984). The text used in this edition is that of the Globe Edition, edited by William Aldis Wright and William George Clark (New York: Macmillan, 1900). Bibliography for the King James Bible and the American founding documents is not given. Citations of the decisions of the Supreme Court of the United States and lower courts are in the standard legal format.

Preface

MODERN SCHOLARSHIP IN many fields has come to regard the personal characteristics of the investigator as relevant to the substance of his or her work in ways not previously considered. As one recent blue-ribbon committee of scholars put it, "The best contemporary work in the humanities strives to make clear both its critique of the ideologies of previous work, and its own inevitable ideological blindspots."[*] Without committing myself to total agreement with this assertion, but in a spirit of cooperativeness, I shall reveal enough about myself to enable readers to identify blind spots and compensate for biases. In fact, I welcome the opportunity to do so, because this book had its genesis in a troubling personal conflict that I have been unable to resolve.

I was born an Anglo-American female in 1948, which means that I am a baby boomer and an approximate contemporary of our nation's newly-elected leaders. I became involved in politics through the influence of John F. Kennedy. In 1963 I organized and headed a local teenage Democrats club that shocked the central Virginia city in which I lived by electing a racially integrated slate of officers. My college years in the mid-to late 1960s were consumed by Vietnam and the counterculture. Following law school in the early 1970s, I specialized in labor and equal employment opportunity law, which was then in its formative years, working first at a private law firm and next at the American Council on Education.

In the late 1970s I returned to the academic world, where I completed a doctorate and entered a career that has combined university administration with some teaching. A single professional woman and a registered Democrat, I supported the equal rights amendment and am strongly pro-choice. I am committed to protection of every minority's right to dissent and to academic freedom. Although I was raised in the

[*] American Council of Learned Societies, "Speaking for the Humanities," Occasional Paper No. 7, reprinted in the *Chronicle of Higher Education* (January 11, 1989), p. A14.

Methodist denomination, my Christian background has been tempered with that basically secular humanistic outlook common to many members of university communities.

Lest the picture I have painted so far seem to categorize me too handily, there is another important aspect of my personal history that is even more relevant to the writing of this book. I have had a lifelong fascination with the great books philosophy of higher education. I majored in Greek and Latin at a college with traditional course offerings, although I sometimes longed for a curriculum structured more like the great books program of St. John's College. I studied classics and philosophy in graduate school at Harvard and later at Princeton, from which I hold a Ph.D. in classics. My dissertation dealt with classical educational theory, and my teaching experience has been either in a classics department or in interdisciplinary humanities courses. Through the years, I have never wavered from my dedication to studying those few supremely brilliant works that have constituted the Western tradition. Encountering the searing white light of true genius, whether in literature, music, or elsewhere, can be a transforming intellectual and aesthetic experience. It has always been difficult for me to imagine any other basis for a liberal education worthy of the name.

Now, as an academic administrator at a selective private university, I am daily confronted with various manifestations of current curricular controversies. I support the interesting work that is being done in my own university's programs in gender and cross-cultural studies. And yet I find that many of the faculty members doing this creative work, often my contemporaries, seem alienated from the very works that I have always regarded as most important. This perplexes me and has led me to wonder whether my own values – as a feminist and social progressive on one hand and a classical humanist and great books enthusiast on the other – are hopelessly in conflict. This book was conceived as an attempt at reconciliation.

As a high school student in the mid-1960s, I loved to read Kenneth Rexroth's column "Classics Revisited" in the *Saturday Review of Literature*.* Somehow, in my young imagination, the intellectual enjoyment of Rexroth's column about great books and the political excitement of the brain trust President Kennedy had assembled in Washington seemed

---

* A collection of Kenneth Rexroth's columns has been published as *Classics Revisited* (New York: New Directions, 1986).

connected. After all, weren't most of those brainy intellectuals — magazine columnists and government officials alike — liberal Democrats? To me, they personified that era's great optimism that the application of informed intelligence to the nation's social problems could and would solve them. The rationality, tolerance, and open-mindedness that characterized prominent liberals of the time seemed to go naturally with an intellect cultivated by reading great books.

It is hard to imagine a column like Rexroth's appearing in a major magazine today. The only mention of classical literary works one is apt to find in current publications is in articles depicting the recent assaults on them as relics from an elitist, patriarchal culture whose days are numbered. While columnists and journalists are not always sympathetic with such characterizations of the canon, they nevertheless have allowed the tone of their writing to be dictated by those who view these works as sources of oppression rather than inspiration.

There is a touch of irony in the current state of affairs on campus. Many humanities professors routinely lament the fact that today's students have not developed the habit of reading, have not acquired a taste for literature, and are not majoring in literary fields to the extent they used to. And yet, in their scholarly writings and in the classroom, these same faculty members will find every possible means to diminish the literary canon, as by formulating theories — often brilliantly and creatively — to show that the claimed greatness of these works is either an illusion or evidence of a sinister plot foisted upon the unsuspecting for political reasons. One cannot but sympathize with the students, who must ask why they should bother to become conversant in a tradition that has been presented to them in this fashion. Surely a better balance can be struck between the need for infectious enthusiasm for what is best in the literary heritage of the West and the need for detached and highly critical scrutiny to improve our understanding of what works have been valued and why.

These personal reflections were intended to provide information some scholars think necessary to decode what follows. If I have made such decoding more, rather than less, difficult, I apologize in advance.

Introduction

THE HEADLINE FOR an October 1992 article in the *New York Times* was typical of many in recent years: "At Columbia, Classics Are Attacked as Old Deities."[1] The article described the debate that was then in progress at Columbia, as at many colleges and universities, about curricular reform in response to criticism that the traditional course offerings are dominated by authors and works that do not reflect America's increasing cultural diversity and are not relevant to the concerns of today's students. As the article's inset asked, "Is the dead hand of history white, male, and European?"

In the early 1990s this controversy moved into the limelight of media attention. A flood of newspaper and magazine articles, scholarly and popular books, and even television reports has emerged explaining to the sophisticated and unsophisticated alike what it is all about. A whole new vocabulary has developed to enable those engaged in the debate to use shorthand. In the popular literature, such phrases as DWEMs (Dead White European Males), the P.C. (political correctness) movement, and multiculturalism have been adopted.[2] In the scholarly literature, one regularly encounters terms such as Western cultural hegemony, radical social transformation, marginalization, and phallocentrism.

As the conflict has escalated, the language of war — language everyone can understand — has been used with unsettling frequency. Among the book titles that have recently appeared are W. B. Carnochan's *The Battleground of the Curriculum,* Henry Louis Gates, Jr.'s, *Loose Canons: Notes on the Culture Wars,* and Gerald Graff's *Beyond the Culture Wars: How Teaching the Conflicts Can Revitalize American Education.* Our colleges and universities and even our public education systems have become the principal combat zones of this civil, but increasingly uncivil, war.

Whether or not the language of war is justified depends on what is at stake — if one is to believe the traditionalists, nothing less than the future of Western civilization. Charles Sykes advises us that "the battle for the soul of American education is just beginning." Hilton Kramer tells us, "It is our civilization that we believe to be at stake in this struggle." Roger Kimball opines that "what is at stake is nothing less than the traditional liberal understanding of democratic society and the place of education and high culture within it." Feminist Elizabeth Fox-Genovese, although speaking from a different perspective, concurs that the stakes are high: "the struggle over the canon is emerging as a struggle for our present and future – for the contemporary interpretation of an individualism that has ruthlessly excluded countless numbers of our people, even as it offered them their highest aspirations."[3] With so many voices speaking at such a high level of rhetorical intensity, there is little wonder that the controversy has captured the attention of the general public.

Much of the debate thus far has tended to conflate two different questions: what is the best way for students to learn about the Western tradition, and what is the appropriate blend of learning about the Western tradition and learning about non-Western traditions?[4] By "the Western tradition" I mean the Western tradition in general and the American version thereof in particular (much of which is embraced also by Western Europe).[5] By "non-Western traditions" I mean all traditions that are not Western, including certain minority traditions within American society (that is, those that have non-Western roots, such as African-American and Asian-American).

This book will address the first of these two questions. It will argue that immersion in the literary works of the traditional canon is the best way for students to learn about Western culture and thus the best means of preparing them to deal with many of the complex human problems our society will face in coming decades. I am fully aware that the second question is receiving – and for the foreseeable future will likely continue to receive – greater attention. However, conflation of the two questions has tended to muddle debate about the first.

State of the Debate

Motivation for writing this book stems from my perception that recent defenses of the traditional canon have been largely ineffective. This is partly because this side of the debate has come to be identified with political conservatives such as William Bennett, Lynne Cheney, and the late Allan Bloom, who do not represent the mainstream of American higher education. It is also due to the baffling silence of the moderate to liberal professoriate, many of whom were drawn into the academic profession by their love for the great works of the Western tradition. Some maintain that the prevailing campus climate has become so radicalized that nonradical faculty members are actually intimidated from expressing their true beliefs.[6] Whatever the explanation, the debate so far has been dominated by the neoconservatives on one side and the radical leftists on the other, with precious little contributed by those in between.

For convenience, I will refer to the canon's defenders as traditionalists and to its detractors as revisionists, meaning the loose coalition of radical feminists, black activists, multiculturalists, Marxists, deconstructionists, and other members of what has been called the cultural left.[7] Revisionists come in so many varieties that it sometimes seems their primary commonality is having a shared enemy in the traditionalists. To convey the flavor of revisionists' rhetoric, I offer a representative sampling from writings that have appeared in recent years (italics have been added to highlight specific imagery).

From a 1990 essay by Henry A. Giroux on the role of liberal arts education in a democracy: [8]

> The university is not ... a place whose purpose is merely to cultivate the life of the mind or reproduce *the cultural equivalent of "masterpiece theater"*.... They [the new elitists] disdain the democratic implications of pluralism and argue for a form of cultural uniformity in which difference is consigned to the margins of history or to the museum of the disadvantaged. From this perspective, culture, along with the authority it sanctions, becomes merely *an artifact, a warehouse of goods,* posited either as a canon of knowledge or a canon of information that simply has to be transmitted as a means for promoting social order and control.

From a 1991 book by James A. Winders concerning gender, theory, and the canon:[9]

> The logic of the canon is one of *hoarded capital,* with academic humanists living on the accumulated interest.... My own use of these texts assumes that they are not about to be tossed out of their *cultural bank vault.* In fact, I assume that they will continue to yield something new to us. I also do not assume that one can simply behave as if the canon did not exist. It is just that I do not accept the dubious notion that these texts are inherently more worthy of *canonical enshrinement* than others that might be located.

From a 1993 book by Peter N. Stearns about recasting the teaching of culture and history: [10]

> For at base, the canonists seek *an appreciation of eternal truths* — for their own sake and for their potential utility in taming suspect hordes — rather than active analysis.... The canon favors *the status quo;* it promotes *catechisms*; it divides its students from the excitement of research.... The canon, as it has evolved to survive, *has shot its bolt.*

All of the emphasized words and phrases evoke images of the out-of-date, the useless, the stored away, that to which we pay homage for what it used to be but no longer is, that which is revered but remote from today's needs and concerns. Such imagery might be expected from the revisionist camp. What is surprising, however, is that the rhetoric used by many of the canon's defenders does not differ substantially from that of its detractors. Witness the following excerpts from a representative sampling of recent writings of the traditionalists (again, italics have been added to highlight specific imagery).

From Allan Bloom's 1987 book *The Closing of the American Mind,* about students who no longer read works of the canon:[11]

> It is not merely the tradition that is lost when the voice of civilization *elaborated over millenia* has been stilled in this way. It is *being itself* that vanishes beyond the dissolving horizon.... Thus, the failure to read good books both enfeebles the vision and strengthens our most fatal tendency — the belief that the here and now is all there is.... We are long past the age when *a whole tradition could be stored up in all students, to be fruitfully used later by some.*

From Dean Eva T. H. Brann's opening convocation address at St. John's College in Annapolis, Maryland, in September 1991:[12]

> To begin with, I want to prognosticate that the more books you read, the more you will find that *there is greatness, that it is an emergent quality that some books just have,* and that each reading confirms. The community that has in common the reading of these books and the acknowledgment of their greatness is bound by two powerful bonds: first, the fact of a shared judgment, competently come by and continually confirmed, and second the fact of a practical willingness to *revere what is high,* a willingness expressed in a daily schedule of study.

From a 1992 book by James Atlas on the ramifications of the current debate on the literature curriculum:[13]

What do the Great Books have to do with *the fragile edifice of culture*? Doesn't it always need shoring up against the forces of barbarism? To my mind the connection isn't fanciful.... Only a nation *schooled in its own past* can grasp the negotiation between personal freedom and collective self-interest that is *the essence* of our American democracy. Those ideas are learned in books. The Great Books. The best that is known and thought in the world. The canon.

Again, the emphasized words and phrases evoke images of accumulated capital and of arbitrary standards of value established by our forebears; they point to a realm of eternal essences that are to be exalted but not used, and to a past that is to be honored for what it once was rather than for what it has now become. There is little wonder that such imagery has failed to elicit more than yawns from audiences both on and off campuses.

The similarity between imagery used by the revisionists to criticize the canon and that used by the traditionalists to praise it is puzzling. Does the traditionalists' use of this imagery, connoting remoteness, mean they have conceded that the works of the canon do not have any particular relevance to the needs and concerns of today's world? Or have they simply failed to find appropriate imagery to convey a sense of these works' immediacy and resilience as a complement to their claimed timelessness and transcendence? Do the kinds of argument that the traditionalists have been making ironically increase the risk that the works they praise will eventually become cultural relics of antiquarian interest only? With such vital questions at stake, it is incumbent upon the moderate to liberal majority of the American professoriate who believe in the continuing importance of the canon for the education of today's students to step forward and make a more effective case for it.

An Experiment

Before the current "culture wars" erupted, there was an era, stretching roughly from the mid-1930s to the mid-1960s, in which substantial agreement prevailed among both educators and literary critics about what were the great books of the Western tradition and the reasons for their educational efficacy. Prominent among spokesmen of that era were John Erskine, Robert Maynard Hutchins, Mortimer Adler, Mark Van Doren, and Jacques Barzun, who joined forces with such classicists as Gilbert Highet and Moses Hadas to imbue two generations of students with the idea that there are certain books with which every college-educated man or woman should have some acquaintance.[14] To be sure, there has never been unanimity on an exact list of the great books, and the reputation of some has risen and fallen. Still, substantial consensus was melded during the decades in question that certain works are at the core of the Western tradition and thus indispensable for a liberal education. This consensus gave rise to a presumption in favor of these works that challengers ever since have sought to dispel.

In recent years there has been a proliferation of challenges to the traditional canon. (It has been said that one can no longer use the phrase "great books" with a straight face in the academic world; the more neutral "canon" has become standard.) The most prominent assaults have received wide attention through the media's use of the acronym DWEMs. Because the allegations of obsolescence (Dead), racism (White), Eurocentrism (European), and sexism (Males) are separate and distinguishable, and because each is a complex subject in its own right, this book will focus on only one strand of the overall controversy, namely the allegation of obsolescence. While the other three charges will enter into the discussion from time to time, detailed treatment of each must be left for its own day. If the challenge of obsolescence is rebutted and these works are shown to have continuing centrality to Western culture, then the presumption in their favor as the centerpiece of a liberal arts education remains intact (unless and until some other challenge succeeds in overriding it).

To assess the seriousness of the allegation of obsolescence, I decided to undertake an experiment. I wanted to make my own evaluation of how the works of the canon relate to various contemporary social issues. It seemed to me that many of the participants in the ongoing debate have a pronounced tendency to cite each other, often to the neglect of the literary works in question. Why not examine the canonical texts themselves and make one's case by specific reference to them? If there are passages that speak in an immediate and forceful way to contemporary concerns, then the case against obsolescence is made. The fact that such passages might be intermixed with other, less immediately relevant material need not deter.

Selecting the Texts

Obviously, the first obstacle to such an experiment was to select a group of canonical texts to be examined. I sought a short list that would be both manageable and as nearly indisputable as anything can be in the current tendentious climate. Everyone's list of a hundred or fifty or even twenty-five great books differs. And yet there are certain works that are at the top of virtually everyone's list. These are the works to which Roger Shattuck referred when he said, "Even a randomly picked group of intelligent and educated people will agree on a handful of books that everyone should read at some point, in some form."[15] These are the works that constitute what Elizabeth Fox-Genovese calls "the uncontested great texts of our tradition."[16] And these are among the small number of writers that the late Irving Howe allowed to be "of such preeminence that they must be placed at the very center of [the classical heritage of mankind]," while acknowledging that "beyond that, plenty of room for disagreement remains."[17]

In his controversial 1984 report entitled *To Reclaim a Legacy,* William J. Bennett, then chairman of the National Endowment for the Humanities, went so far as to make a partial listing of these preeminent works. Bennett invited several hundred educational and cultural leaders, as well as the general public, to recommend ten books that any high school graduate should have read. When the results were compiled, although hundreds of different texts and authors were listed, there were four that were cited by at least fifty percent of the respondents: the Bible, Shakespeare's plays, the American founding documents, and *The Adventures of Huckleberry Finn.*[18] The seven most frequently mentioned authors (in order of rank) were Shakespeare, the American founding documents, Twain, the Bible, Homer, Dickens, and Plato.[19] (The surprisingly high ranking of Twain is no doubt attributable to the way the question was worded, focusing on the high school rather than the college graduate.)

Of course there are many ways other than public surveys for selecting the works to be used in an experiment such as this. For example, one might look at the frequency with which the names of various canonical writers are used by both sides in the current debate as an indicator of presumed status. A survey of the index of a 1992 volume of essays first presented at a highly publicized North Carolina conference on the canon wars reveals the following number of references to authors or works that would be likely candidates for inclusion on a very short list: Shakespeare (7), Plato (6), Homer (4), the Bible (3), Aristotle (3), Virgil (3), and Dante (2).[20] This unscientific method yields results that might have been predicted, regardless of the ideology of those who wrote the essays. It would be inconceivable for the defining works of the Western tradition to be enumerated without including those of such stature and influence.

In light of all these considerations, I arrived at a list of five great texts for use here: Homer, Plato, the King James Bible, Shakespeare, and the American founding documents. I will refer to this list hereafter as the Canon, while using the lower case when the word "canon" is used in its more general meaning.

The choice of the American founding documents requires some elaboration. While not a great book, strictly speaking, the various documents that have spelled out evolving concepts of democratic government and individual freedoms constitute an essential part of Western culture's doctrinal canon if not its literary canon (although some of the doctrinal writings of Jefferson and Lincoln have considerable literary merit).[21] Among those documents that are crucial in defining our ideals of liberty, justice, and equality under the law are the Declaration of Independence, the Federalist Papers, the U.S. Constitution, the Bill of Rights, the Emancipation Proclamation, and the Gettysburg Address.

In drawing upon this tradition, I have often turned to the reported decisions of the Supreme Court of the United States interpreting the Constitution and its various amendments. These decisions focus clearly on the cutting-edge issues of contemporary American life and also provide well-reasoned and articulate analyses of where we are as a society in dealing with them. In fact, the Court's major constitutional decisions often provide the truest intersection between a canonical text and a contemporary social issue. Thus it is not unusual to read a comment like that of Columbia history professor J. W. Smit, who said in the October 1992 *New York Times* article mentioned above that he routinely ends his Western civilization course with decisions of the U.S. Supreme Court.

Choice of Contemporary Social Issues

The social issues that are matters of concern in the United States and much of the West today are familiar, ranging from abortion to xenophobia. Some problems, such as global warming, nuclear proliferation, and gun control, are peculiarly modern phenomena. Others, such as child abuse, prostitution, and homelessness, have been with humankind for millenia. One of the strengths of the canonical works selected for discussion here is their focus on fundamental human concerns, and a wide range of such concerns finds expression in them, though the list of works is short. By the same token, problems arising out of the industrial revolution or technological advances could not be expected to be represented.

In selecting the issues to be considered in this book, I sought subjects of intense current interest which are of sufficient importance to human experience to be somehow reflected in most of the works of the Canon. I arrived at a list of six such issues: sexual harassment, rape, homophobia, abortion, the right to die, and the death penalty. I believe that I could have written just as convincingly about a dozen others.

Three of the selected issues are related to gender (sexual harassment, rape, and homophobia), and three deal with matters of life and death (abortion, the right to die, and the death penalty). Two of these issues, though not new to human experience, have only recently become the focus of controversy in our legal system (sexual harassment and the right to die); two deal with very old subjects that are as problematic today as ever (rape and the death penalty); and two are topics about which our society is vexed and deeply divided (abortion and homophobia). All six are matters of intense public interest, with which students are daily bombarded by the media, and yet few attempts seem to be made to engage student interest in great literary works by making meaningful connections between the texts and these issues.

Gerald Graff has correctly pointed out that canons have always been subject to revision because of their claimed failure to engage student interest.[22] The current situation is no different, although the reasons offered for the alleged lack of engagement this time are. Some revisionists say motivation for revision stems primarily from students' alienation from an elite culture that appears remote from them.[23] Others argue that the impetus for revision is actually coming from baby-boomer faculty, whose own alienation from the elitism of canonical works has rendered them unable to teach those works in enthusiastic and imaginative ways that link the texts to students' experience.[24] In either event, there seems to be universal agreement that today's students are situated in "a present-oriented media culture" that fails to examine critically connections to the past. [25]

One of the most disturbing commentaries on this issue may be found in the 1989 report "Speaking for the Humanities," written by a committee of prominent humanities professors and issued by the American Council of Learned Societies. The report recommends that popular culture, instead of being "excoriated" as the source of the degeneracy of youth, be made a definitive element in contemporary education: "The study of the history of, and competing theories about, popular culture provides students with a framework in which to criticize the materials they consume daily and unthinkingly."[26] Would it not be preferable to use the greatest works of the Western tradition to provide just such a framework? That is essentially what this book attempts to do. While popular culture need not be shunned, it should not be expected to fill the pivotal role that the ACLS report implies.

Finally, although the works selected for discussion here contain much material that speaks directly to questions of gender and matters of life and death, I must acknowledge the absence of comparable material that speaks in an immediate and meaningful way to questions of race. The American experience of having a substantial minority population with a history of enslavement and consequent social and economic disadvantage is unprecedented in the West. The challenge to overcome that history and provide economic opportunity and social equity for all citizens regardless of race has posed difficult problems that were not confronted by the societies represented in these works. I am unable to say where we should turn for guidance in dealing with the plague of racism in our society. I would only hazard the observation that, if we had the advantage of two and a half millenia of the best thinking of others seeking to overcome a comparable past and to put all citizens on an equal footing, perhaps we would be better able to deal with the race-related problems that now afflict us.

The Approach Taken

Yet another aspect of the current debate is the quarrel between practitioners and opponents of literary theory. Opponents of literary theory often overlap with the traditionalists, who see attention to theory as supplanting attention to literary works themselves.[27] Practitioners of literary theory respond that such objections are occasioned by their opponents' worries that the specific theories now current in literary criticism are too reformist or too radical in nature; in fact, all interpretations of literary works reflect one theory or another, even if the interpreter is unaware of, or unwilling to acknowledge, his or her own.[28]

The practitioners of literary theory are undoubtedly correct that theoretical stances, like political stances, are omnipresent, whether or not acknowledged. There is also considerable practical wisdom, however, in an observation by University of Chicago professor Leon Kass: "Teaching is all too often filling empty vessels with information *about,* rather than initiating the young into thinking and feeling *with,* the books they read. Students are drawn into second-order scholarly concerns even before they have directly experienced the texts and the *human concerns* that moved authors to write them."[29]

This book is written without attention to "second-order scholarly concerns" and with no pretense to sophistication in literary criticism. It was written by one who is foremost interested in the "human concerns" to which Kass referred. The primary focus here is on what these texts might mean to typical undergraduate students or casual adult readers who read with shared knowledge of today's problems and ample common sense, but little else. If at times interpretations are suggested that would have been unimaginable to their authors, that is taken as a tribute to their vitality and resilience. My reliance on published research in law and the social sciences, rather than on literary criticism, has enabled me to remain unencumbered by these complications and has helped to assure that at least one foot remains firmly planted on the ground. This approach is consistent with my belief that the complexities of human motivation are endlessly fascinating, and a specialized vocabulary is not required to explore them.

The back cover of the 1992 volume of essays from the North Carolina conference states, "Responding to attacks on contemporary humanities teaching by government officials, journalists, and academic traditionalists, the authors argue that educational methods and materials cannot remain the same while social, technological, and intellectual conditions change significantly." Teachers of the humanities especially should be wary of this statement, because it overlooks what should be obvious to them of all people. As a college Latin teacher of this writer used to ask whenever a classical author exposed the frailties and foibles of people in ancient times, "Have human beings really changed that much?"

This book is intended as a response to one particular challenge to the traditional canon, namely the argument that social and intellectual conditions have changed so dramatically that the canon has become obsolete and no longer addresses our contemporary problems in a meaningful way. This challenge fails to recognize that the great writings of the past continue to be central to Western culture. Nothing shows this more clearly than the light they shed on some of the most heated social issues of our time. This book will demonstrate how five canonical texts illuminate six such issues, each of which is the subject of deep and ongoing controversy. This demonstration will provide compelling evidence that the allegation of obsolescence is unfounded, leaving the presumption in the canon's favor intact.

To ensure that this presumption will survive future challenges, traditionalists should become more attentive to the need vigorously to assert the continuing centrality of these texts to contemporary Western culture. Effective demonstration of this point can complement other arguments customarily made by traditionalists in the canon's defense. Because these works are at the core of the Western tradition, they are indispensable for a liberal education as that concept has evolved in the West; their future and that of liberal education are inextricably intertwined, and the survival of neither can be taken for granted.

Notes

1. Mervyn Rothstein, October 10, 1992, p. 10.

2. The acronym DWEMs has become so standard that the derivative DWAMs for such authors as Thoreau, Emerson, and Twain has been adopted. See Bernard Knox, *The Oldest Dead White European Males and Other Reflections on the Classics* (New York: Norton, 1993), pp. 25-26.

3. Quoted passages are from the following works: Charles J. Sykes, *The Hollow Men: Politics and Corruption in Higher Education* (Washington, D.C.: Regnery Gateway, 1990), p. 67; Hilton Kramer, "The Prospect Before Us," *New Criterion* (September 1990), quoted by James Atlas, *Battle of the Books: The Curriculum Debate in America* (New York: Norton, 1992), p. 70; Roger Kimball, *Tenured Radicals: How Politics Has Corrupted Our Higher Education* (New York: Harper & Row, 1990), p. 2; and Elizabeth Fox-Genovese, *Feminism Without Illusions* (Chapel Hill: University of North Carolina Press, 1991), p. 198.

4. I have avoided use of the phrase "our own culture" and "other cultures" because this usage is considered troublesome by some. For example, in commenting on Lynne Cheney's use of such phrases in her report *Humanities in America,* Stanley Fish wrote, "The number of questions begged here is large and familiar: what about the students for whom the word 'our' in 'our society' is problematical, students for whom the culture made up of texts from fifth-century Athens, first-century Rome, and sixteenth century England is decidedly 'other'? What happens to *their* concerns, perspectives, values, heritages?" "The Common Touch, or, One Size Fits All," in *The Politics of Liberal Education,* ed. Darryl J. Gless and Barbara Herrnstein Smith (Durham: Duke University Press, 1992), p. 259.

The contrary view is well stated by James Atlas, who wrote, "To someone brought up on the idea that assimilation was an essential component of the American experience – that what established one's identity was the convergence, after several generations, of one's particular heritage and the generic American traits of tolerance, optimism, belief in opportunity – this insistence upon celebrating what could almost be described as a kind of ethnic tribalism is bewildering." *Battle of the Books,* p. 62.

5. E. D. Hirsch, Jr., speaks in terms of "layers" of cultural literacy but says that for the purposes of educational policy, cultural literacy has a decidedly national character. *Cultural Literacy: What Every American Needs to Know* (Boston: Houghton Mifflin, 1987), p. 17. Certainly where the law and matters of social policy are concerned, cultures must be considered on a national basis.

6. See, for example, Peter Shaw, *Recovering American Literature* (Chicago: Ivan R. Dee, 1994), p. 16; Dinesh D'Souza, *Illiberal Education: The Politics of Race and Sex on Campus* (New York: Free Press, 1991), p. 247; and Sykes, *The Hollow Men,* p. 35.

7. This nomenclature originated at a 1988 conference jointly sponsored by Duke University and the University of North Carolina at Chapel Hill. See Richard Rorty, "Two Cheers for the Cultural Left," in *The Politics of Liberal Education,* pp. 233-240.

8. Henry A. Giroux, "Liberal Arts Education and the Struggle for Public Life: Dreaming about Democracy," in *The Politics of Liberal Education,* pp. 120 and 125.

9. James A. Winders, *Gender, Theory, and the Canon* (Madison: University of Wisconsin Press, 1991), p. 17.

10. Peter N. Stearns, *Meaning over Memory: Recasting the Teaching of Culture and History* (Chapel Hill: University of North Carolina Press, 1993), p. 94.

11. Allan Bloom, *The Closing of the American Mind: How Higher Education Has Failed Democracy and Impoverished the Souls of Today's Students* (New York: Simon & Schuster, 1987), pp. 63-64.

12. Eva T. H. Brann, "What Is a Book?" *St. John's Review,* vol. 41, no. 1, 1991-92, p. 87.

13. James Atlas, *Battle of the Books,* p. 136.

14. See Erskine, *My Life as a Teacher* (Philadelphia: J. B. Lippincott, 1948); Hutchins, *The Higher Learning in America* (New Haven: Yale University Press, 1936); Adler, *How to Read a Book* (New York: Simon & Schuster, 1940); Van Doren, *Liberal Education* (New York: Henry Holt, 1943); Barzun, *Teacher in America* (Boston: Little, Brown, 1945); Highet, *The Art of Teaching* (New York: Vintage, 1950); and Hadas, *Old Wine, New Bottles* (New York: Trident Press, 1962).

15. From a talk delivered in 1987 to the American Council of Learned Societies, quoted by Atlas, *Battle of the Books,* p. 130.

16. Fox-Genovese, *Feminism Without Illusions,* p. 169.

17. Irving Howe, "The Value of the Canon," *New Republic,* February 18, 1991, p. 42.

18. William J. Bennett, *To Reclaim a Legacy* (Washington, D.C.: National Endowment for the Humanities, 1984), reprinted in *Chronicle of Higher Education,* November 28, 1984, p. 18.

19. These tabulated results were supplied in private correspondence dated March 24, 1993, from John Agresto, president of St. John's College in Santa Fe, New Mexico, who was formerly a member of the NEH staff.

20. *The Politics of Liberal Education,* pp. 295-305.

21. George Kennedy states that the neoconservatives often seem to blur the distinction between literary and doctrinal canons. "Classics and Canons," in *The Politics of Liberal Education,* p. 226. However, much of Plato and the Bible, as well as parts of the American founding documents, might be classified both ways.

22. Gerald Graff, *Beyond the Culture Wars: How Teaching the Conflicts Can Revitalize American Education* (New York: Norton, 1992), p. 95.

23. See Stearns, *Meaning over Memory,* p. 93; Fish, "The Common Touch," pp. 259-260; and Fox-Genovese, *Feminism Without Illusions,* p. 191.

24. This is one of the main premises of Roger Kimball's book *Tenured Radicals.* Henry Louis Gates, Jr., admits as much: "Ours was the generation that took over buildings in the late sixties and demanded the creation of black and women's studies programs, and now, like the return of the repressed, has come back to challenge the traditional curriculum." Quoted by John Searle, "The Storm over the University," *New York Review of Books,* December 5, 1990, p. 38.

25. Winders, *Gender, Theory, and the Canon,* p. 22.

26. American Council of Learned Societies. "Speaking for the Humanites," Occasional Paper No. 7, reprinted in *Chronicle of Higher Education,* January 11, 1989, p. A16.

27. See, for example, Kimball, *Tenured Radicals,* pp. 10-15.

28. See, for example, Graff, *Beyond the Culture Wars,* pp. 52-56.

29. Quoted in Cheney, as reprinted in *Chronicle of Higher Education,* September 21, 1988, at p. A19.

1: Sexual Harassment

THE CONCEPT OF sexual harassment is so new that there is still uncertainty about what it is and even how to pronounce it. The phrase began to appear in the opinions of federal courts in the mid-1970s. Only in 1986 did the U.S. Supreme Court formally accept the concept as constituting a violation of federal law. Given the novelty of the terminology and the legal sanctions that attach to it, sexual harassment would seem to constitute a special challenge to the Canon. How could these literary works from bygone eras possibly treat such a new and emerging development in the interaction between men and women and between both genders and the state? Before this question can be answered, some brief background on the history and definition of sexual harassment is in order.

An Emerging Concept

In a paraphrase of a frequently quoted description of the discipline of psychology, sexual harassment has been said to have had "a long past but a short history."[1] Of course, women have been familiar for a long time with the practices that are now said to constitute sexual harassment. It was not until the mid-1970s, however, that the term "sexual harassment" was coined to embrace a variety of objectionable practices in the workplace, including pressure for sexual favors, unwanted romantic attention, unwelcome physical contact, verbal abuse of a sexual nature, vulgar or obscene jokes, and the like. Before that time, these practices persisted within a system that condoned them by failing to recognize their offensiveness to working women. As one feminist legal scholar put it, "Much of what women suffered remained unnamed, unreported, unchallenged, and unchanged.... The injuries stemming from harassment were internalized, institutionalized, and, for the most part, inaudible."[2]

In the late 1970s the first cases were decided in federal courts holding that sexual harassment violates the provisions against sex discrimination in federal civil rights laws. In 1979, an influential book by feminist legal scholar Catharine MacKinnon offered a coherent and compelling legal theory of sexual harassment as violating the law prohibiting sex discrimination in employment.[3] About the same time, the agency charged with enforcing that law, the Equal Employment Opportunity Commission, issued guidelines stating that the following kinds of conduct constitute sexual harassment, a form of unlawful discrimination on the basis of sex:[4]

> Unwelcome sexual advances, requests for sexual favors, and other verbal or physical conduct of a sexual nature constitute sexual harassment when (1) submission to such conduct is made either explicitly or implicitly a term or condition of an individual's employment, (2) submission to or rejection of such conduct by an individual is used as the basis for employment decisions affecting such individual, or (3) such conduct has the purpose or effect of unreasonably interfering with an individual's work performance or creating an intimidating, hostile, or offensive working environment.

The next major step in establishing sexual harassment as a legal concept came in 1986, when the U.S. Supreme Court unanimously concluded in *Meritor Savings Bank v. Vinson* that sexual harassment is a violation of Title VII of the Civil Rights Act of 1964.[5] Factually, the case was a compelling one: a woman who was employed as an assistant branch manager of a bank testified that her supervisor fondled her in front of other employees, followed her into the women's restroom when she went there alone, exposed himself to her, and even forcibly raped her on several occasions. In an opinion by Chief Justice William Rehnquist, the Court interpreted the statute as covering both *quid pro quo* cases (harassment that conditions employment benefits on sexual favors) and "hostile environment" cases, thus endorsing the interpretation of the EEOC guidelines quoted above. Rehnquist concluded that the EEOC had been correct in holding that Title VII affords employees "the right to work in an environment free from discriminatory intimidation, ridicule and insult."[6]

Even though the prohibition of sexual harassment became the settled law of the land with the *Meritor* decision, five more years elapsed before the concept exploded into the public's consciousness with the hearings before the Senate Judiciary Committee in October 1991 concerning Clarence Thomas's confirmation as an associate justice of the U.S. Supreme Court. A national television audience was transfixed for one long weekend as Anita F. Hill, a law professor at the University of

Oklahoma and former member of Thomas's staff at the EEOC, testified that he had sexually harassed her. According to Hill, Thomas had repeatedly pressured her to go out with him on a social basis, had described his sexual prowess and parts of his anatomy to her, and had discussed pornographic videos in her presence.[7]

When Thomas vehemently denied these charges, the situation became a classic one of "her word against his." The Judiciary Committee was evenly divided. The nomination was eventually approved by the full Senate, but in the closest vote on a Supreme Court confirmation in over a century.[8] For weeks thereafter, the entire nation indulged in a frenzy of speculation over who had been telling the truth. Many women regarded Anita Hill as a hero, and the political consequences of her treatment by some of the senators continued long after the hearings ended.[9] As one senator who had participated put it, "Out of the Clarence Thomas/Anita Hill confrontation came a totally unplanned and unexpected cultural earthquake on sexual harassment. Like all earthquakes, it shook everything. How much lasting damage or improvement it will bring about is not yet certain, but after every serious earthquake, things never are completely the same again — and this one was serious."[10]

In November 1993 the Supreme Court rendered its second decision in a sexual harassment case, providing further refinement of the legal concept. In *Harris v. Forklift Systems, Inc.,* the Court addressed the question of whether plaintiffs in hostile environment cases must prove that they were not only offended but also psychologically injured by verbal abuse in the workplace. In a unanimous decision, the Court concluded that psychological injury need not be a factor in order for a plaintiff to prevail. Justice Sandra Day O'Connor wrote, "So long as the environment would reasonably be perceived, and is perceived, as hostile or abusive, there is no need for it also to be psychologically injurious."[11]

Because of the intense media attention given to the Thomas-Hill matter and a few other celebrated cases, a general awareness of the concept of sexual harassment has developed in American culture in a brief time. All of the proffered definitions refer to unwanted sexually-related conduct in an inappropriate context. Among the types of offense now understood to constitute sexual harassment are explicitly bartered sex, abuse of authority to obtain sexual favors, and conduct which creates a hostile environment (unwelcome sexual advances, unwanted touching, and verbal abuse of a sexual nature). Examples of each type of behavior abound in the Canon.

Instances of Sexual Harassment in the Canon

Many commentators have observed that sexual harassment has been prevalent at least since women entered the workplace. One obstacle to finding instances of sexual harassment in the Canon is the absence of women from the workplace in the eras in which these texts were written. However, one can find plentiful instances of harassing conduct in contexts other than employment. Women have long been present in churches, schools, judicial tribunals, public accommodations, and so on, and in all of these settings, the male-dominated social structure has provided ample opportunity for incidents of sexual harassment. The eventual entry of women into the workplace changed only the location, not the fundamental nature, of such conduct. It was only when women's need for employment as a means of livelihood became common in the last decades of the twentieth century that laws to combat sexual harassment became socially mandated.

Explicitly Bartered Sex

One of the most easily recognized kinds of sexual harassment is explicitly bartered sex in a context in which the harassed party is in a subordinate position that makes it difficult for her or (occasionally) him to refuse. In the *Meritor* decision, the Supreme Court identified this type of case as constituting *quid pro quo* sexual harassment. The *pro quo* in such cases might be a promotion or a raise where sexual bribery is involved, or it might be merely retaining one's job where sexual coercion is used. Outside the employment context, the *pro quo* might be anything of significant economic or psychological value to the harassed person.

Some early examples of explicit bargaining over sex are found in the *Odyssey*. During his ten years of travels on his way back to Ithaca after the Trojan War, Odysseus became sexually involved with two female figures, the nymph Calypso and the sorceress Circe, both of whom sought to marry him.[12] The usual relationship between the sexes was inverted in these cases because both female figures were superhuman and therefore in a more powerful position than Odysseus, a mere mortal. They both had it within their power to detain him on their respective islands and deny him the freedom to continue his journey home, which was what his heart desired. In both cases, it was only with help from Zeus, who dispatched his messenger Hermes, that Odysseus was able to gain release from the female figures' clutches.

Early in the poem, Odysseus is spending his days sitting on the shore of the nymph Calypso's island, Ogygia, weeping and longing to return home to Ithaca and his wife Penelope. Calypso is in love with Odysseus, but he no longer delights in seeing her. Homer says that by night he sleeps by her side under compulsion, "unwilling Odysseus beside willing Calypso" (5.155). When she announces to him that, at the direction of Zeus, she intends to let him leave the island on a raft, he is suspicious and refuses to go unless she first swears an oath that she is not plotting to do him further harm. She so swears.

That evening, after a meal in her cave, Calypso tries to change Odysseus's mind by warning him of the many travails he will yet have to endure before reaching home. She declares herself more attractive than Penelope and questions his decision to return to his wife when he could stay with her and even have immortality. Odysseus quickly realizes that he is not in a position to alienate Calypso. He is still dependent upon her for the raft, for provisions, and for counsel to continue his journey home. He therefore tells her that she is more attractive than his aging wife, and he goes to bed with her in the innermost recess of the cave. The next day she carries through on the promised arrangements for his departure from Ogygia.

Odysseus's other involvement is with the sorceress Circe, who has used magical herbs to turn some of his men into swine. Hermes has given Odysseus an antidote to the magical herbs and has told him how to gain the release of his men. When Circe raises her magical wand, Odysseus follows Hermes' instructions by drawing his sword and rushing upon her as if to kill her. She then bids him to put up his sword and come to bed with her so they can make love and learn to trust each other. Odysseus, having been forewarned by Hermes that he must not refuse Circe's proposition, first extracts a promise from her that she is not intending him any new harm:

"Circe, how canst thou bid me be gentle to thee, who hast turned my comrades into swine in thy halls, and now keepest me here, and with guileful purpose biddest me go to thy chamber, and go up into thy bed, that when thou hast me stripped thou mayest render me a weakling and unmanned? Nay, verily, it is not I that shall be fain to go up into thy bed, unless thou, goddess, wilt consent to swear a mighty oath that thou wilt not plot against me any fresh mischief to my hurt." (10.337-344)

When she so swears, Odysseus goes to bed with her. After his bath, she offers him food and drink, but he refuses until she agrees to release his men, a promise she immediately fulfills. Odysseus ends up spending a full year with Circe before finally demanding that she keep another promise she has made to send him and his men home. She responds that he should stay no longer in her house against his will and proceeds to give him instructions for his forthcoming travels. Thus Odysseus finally receives the freedom he longs for.

During his encounters with Calypso and Circe, Odysseus is depicted as persistently wanting to return home to Ithaca and his wife Penelope. He is aware that both Calypso and Circe are divine and therefore beyond his power to overcome. The gods are in control of his destiny, and he is wily enough to realize that he must play by their rules and within their system to survive (much like the plight of women in male-dominated social systems). He is compelled by circumstance to submit to sexual liaisons that he does not desire but that he cannot refuse without jeopardizing the chance to continue his journey home.

Far removed from enchanted isles and nymphs with magical powers, the setting of *Measure for Measure* is characterized by harsh reality. The prim and self-righteous deputy Angelo is substituting as ruler of Vienna while the duke takes a brief leave from his onerous responsibilities. Wishing to enforce the state's criminal laws strictly, he sentences a young man, Claudio, to death for violating the law against fornication. Claudio's sister, Isabella, comes before Angelo to plead for her brother's life. Angelo immediately takes a fancy to Isabella and decides on a strategy for seducing her: he will spare Claudio's life if she will go to bed with him. Initially, he states his proposition hypothetically:

> ANGELO: Then I shall pose you quickly.
> Which had you rather, that the most just law
> Now took your brother's life; or, to redeem him,
> Give up your body to such sweet uncleanness
> As she that he hath stain'd?
>
> (2.4.51-55)

Isabella in her naiveté does not get Angelo's drift, and she continues to urge him to find a way to show her brother mercy. Exasperated, Angelo says, "Nay, but hear me. /Your sense pursues not mine: either

you are ignorant, /Or seem so craftily; and that's not good" (2.4.73-75).
When Isabella openly admits her ignorance, Angelo tries again:

ANGELO: But mark me;
          To be received plain, I'll speak more gross:
          Your brother is to die.
          . . . .
          Admit no other way to save his life, —
          As I subscribe not that, nor any other,
          But in the loss of question, — that you, his sister,
          Finding yourself desired of such a person,
          Whose credit with the judge, or own great place,
          Could fetch your brother from the manacles
          No earthly mean to save him, but that either
          You must lay down the treasures of your body
          To this supposed, or else to let him suffer;
          What would you do?

                                        (2.4.81-83, 88-98)

Isabella now understands, and she reacts with shock and horror to
Angelo's words. She proclaims that she would rather have her brother
die than yield her body up to such shame. Their conversation escalates
into a heated quarrel, and Angelo declares his love for her. When she
steadfastly refuses his demand for her love in return, he threatens not
only to execute Claudio but to give him a slow, lingering death. Angelo
asks for her answer the following day, thus giving her an opportunity
to talk with her brother and, with help from the duke (who is disguised
as a friar), to formulate a strategy for dealing with Angelo.

Angelo represents a character in the supremely ironic position of
succumbing to an offense for which he, as judge, has sentenced another
to die. Even though he recognizes this sin in himself, he is powerless to
resist, and at the same time he shows no mercy to the man he has condemned. The parallel with Clarence Thomas's alleged sexual harassment of Anita Hill is striking. In that case, Thomas was accused of violating the very law (Title VII of the Civil Rights Act of 1964) that he,
as chairman of the Equal Employment Opportunity Commission, was
charged with enforcing. This irony was apparently not lost on Thomas
himself, who said at the confirmation hearing that Hill's charges
"shocked, surprised, hurt and enormously saddened me.... For almost
a decade my responsibilities included enforcing the rights of victims of
sexual harassment."[13] The conduct of anyone occupying that position

might reasonably be expected to be beyond reproach for him or her credibly to pass judgment on others accused of sexual harassment in violation of the law.

A third instance of explicitly-bartered sex is found in *III Henry VI*. Sir Richard Grey has been killed in the battle at Saint Albans, and his widow, Lady Elizabeth Grey, appears before King Edward IV to ask for the return of his lands, which had been seized by conquering forces. King Edward acknowledges the legitimacy of her request, her husband having fought valorously for the House of York. Nevertheless, he pauses noticeably before granting her claim, prompting his brother Richard to comment in an aside, "I see the lady hath a thing to grant, /Before the King will grant her humble suit" (3.2.12-13). This comment is a classic formulation of the *quid pro quo* type of sexual harassment cases.

King Edward begins to question Lady Grey about her children, and she tells him that she would be willing to endure harm to herself in order to secure her husband's lands for them. The king proceeds to ask her what service she would be willing to do him, if he should grant her claim. She naively responds that she would be willing to do anything within her power. He says that she can do what he intends to ask. "An easy task; 'tis but to love a king" (3.2.53). Again naively, she responds that that is easy, because she is a loyal subject. The king is forced to try again, more bluntly. He says that he was referring to the "fruits of love." She says that this is what she too meant. Her interpretation is different from his, however; to her, the phrase means "my love till death, my humble thanks, my prayers; /That love which virtue begs and virtue grants" (3.2.62-63).

Lady Grey is finally beginning to understand the king's meaning, although her mind rejects the notion that he would ask such a thing. He then blurts out, "To tell thee plain, I aim to lie with thee." She responds, "To tell you plain, I had rather lie in prison" (3.2.69-70). He then states his intention to deny her claim to her husband's lands. She replies that her chastity is more important to her than any dower. She curtly asks him for an "ay" or "no" as an official dismissal of her claim. He responds, "Ay, if thou wilt say 'ay' to my request;/No, if thou dost say 'no' to my demand" (3.2.79-80). She then concludes that her suit is at an end.

The king so much admires Lady Grey's spirit that he concludes that he must have her, if not as a lover, then as his queen. She accepts this proposal, thus demonstrating that her strong objection was to the impropriety of his original proposition, not to him personally. Thereupon, her suit for her husband's lands is granted.

The preceding are all instances in which a person with power over another person solicits sex inappropriately in a context in which it is very difficult for the solicited person to refuse. In each case, the subordinate person has a vital interest of his or her own (freedom to return home, a brother's life, lands that constitute the children's birthright) to protect. In each case, the superior power of the harassing party (a pair of goddesses, a ruler acting in a judicial capacity, and a king) seems insuperable. While the male victim, who is known for surviving by his wits, submits and eventually escapes with divine help, the two female victims steadfastly resist. One eventually prevails in her resistance through some theatrical trickery at the end of the play; the other succumbs to the sexual demands only when the soliciting party elevates her to his equal in status. While none of these resolutions is true to life, the moral dilemmas in which the characters are cast are both realistic and contemporary.

Abuse of Authority

Another kind of conduct has only recently come to be recognized in the scholarly literature as constituting a form of sexual harassment. That is sex within the context of professional relationships in which a presumption of trust between the two parties is violated. An important recent book has referred to such conduct (for example, between therapist and patient, clergyman and parishioner, teacher and student) as "sex in the forbidden zone."[14] While some might attempt to defend sex under such circumstances as "consensual," the power differential and sexual disequilibrium between the parties often precludes genuine consent. Rather, there is an abuse of authority by the professionals involved and inherent exploitation of the trust of the individuals under their care. This has been held to be unethical (if not illegal) conduct by many official certification bodies in the various professions.[15]

Because women have needed the professional services of the physician, the clergyman, and other such professionals for much longer than they have been in the workplace, one might expect this form of sexual harassment to be relatively prevalent in the Canon. While some instances of such conduct can be identified, there is also a countervailing factor — the code of silence that has traditionally kept conduct of this nature out of view. That aspect of the problem will be discussed more fully below.

All in the Family

The prototype of all relationships in which one's well-being is entrusted to a trained professional is that of the parent and child.[16] The parent is presumed not only to have superior knowledge and experience but also to have the best interests of the child at heart. Even when a child is required to endure something unpleasant or painful in the short term, it is presumed to be for a greater long-term good. A healthy parent-child relationship requires trust that these presumptions obtain.

In *Pericles,* Shakespeare broached one of the most taboo subjects of any era — a father's sexual abuse of his young daughter. This theme is set in the prologue to the play (at 21-30), where it is said that King Antiochus, a widower, took a liking to his fair daughter "and her to incest did provoke." This practice is condemned ("to entice his own to evil should be done by none"), but it is also recognized that what has become long custom eventually is not regarded as sin. Even though the initiative for the incestuous relationship clearly lay with the father (he "provoked" and "enticed" her), the prologue holds both parties culpable: "Bad child; worse father!"

Pericles, the hero of the play, visits Antioch and solves a supposedly unsolvable riddle, devised by King Antiochus to ward off his daughter's suitors, which reveals the nature of his relationship with her. Pericles, who was originally attracted to the young woman, is disgusted by this revelation. He renounces any interest in her:

> PERICLES: You are a fair viol, and your sense the strings;
> Who, finger'd to make man his lawful music,
> Would draw heaven down, and all the gods, to hearken:
> But being played upon before your time,
> Hell only danceth at so harsh a chime.
> Good sooth, I care not for you.

(1.1.81-86)

In a soliloquy, Pericles voices the same sentiment as the speaker of the prologue does, that both father and daughter are blameworthy for their mutual sin. He addresses King Antiochus:

> PERICLES: If it be true that I interpret false,
> Then were it certain you were not so bad
> As with foul incest to abuse your soul;

Where now you're both a father and a son,
By your untimely claspings with your child,
Which pleasures fits a husband, not a father;
And she an eater of her mother's flesh,
By the defiling of her parent's bed;
And both like serpents are, who though they feed
On sweetest flowers, yet they poison breed.

(1.1.124-133)

Pericles seems oblivious to the fact that he is characterizing the daughter at the same time as a child within the grasp of her father and an autonomous individual capable of free moral choice. Although her age is not revealed, it is known that she has endured sexual abuse for a long time and from an early age. She can hardly be seen as her father's consensual lover in any meaningful sense. Her father has betrayed her trust in a horrible way, taking advantage of her dependent status and the absence of a mother from the scene. Divine punishment is eventually inflicted upon both father and daughter, who are killed simultaneously when their chariot is struck by a thunderbolt from the gods.

In Protective Custody

The relationship of child to parent is a paradigm for the relationship of the mentally retarded to their custodians. The potential for abuse of authority in this realm is demonstrated by a passage from *All's Well That Ends Well*. Parolles has been tricked into believing that he has been captured by the enemy. He shows himself a faithless coward by telling his interrogators what he knows in an effort to save his own life. In addition, he embellishes his testimony with malicious gossip and lies about his former colleagues Bertram and Captain Dumaine, who — hidden nearby — are listening. When asked whether Captain Dumaine is in the camp and how he is regarded by the troops, Parolles responds with the most scurrilous story he can think up. He says that he used to know the captain in Paris, when Dumaine was a mender's apprentice. He alleges that Dumaine got into trouble and was whipped when it was discovered that he had impregnated "the shrieve's fool," a mentally retarded young woman placed under the sheriff's charge. Parolles describes her as "a dumb innocent that could not say him nay" (4.3.213-214).

Parolles's words demonstrate the conceptual underpinning of this kind of sexual offense. There can be no meaningful consent from significantly retarded persons, and officials to whom their care is entrusted violate basic expectations of human decency by taking advantage of their position over such charges. Public outrage was recently elicited in a highly publicized case in Glen Ridge, New Jersey, in which three high school boys were convicted of having sexually abused a teenaged girl who was mentally retarded and therefore legally incapable of consenting to the sexual acts that were performed upon her.[17]

In School

The educational environment provides another important setting in which the potential for abuse of authority exists. After the workplace, the second largest and most important area in which sexual harassment is now forbidden by federal law is within schools. Title IX of the Education Amendments of 1972 prohibits discrimination on the basis of sex in federally assisted educational programs and activities,[18] and this law has been interpreted as prohibiting sexual harassment along the same lines as Title VII of the Civil Rights Act of 1964. Given the number of years most people spend in school and the profound influence teachers have upon their lives, this emphasis of the law seems appropriate. Most colleges and universities now have formal sexual harassment policies, many of which address the sensitive issue of "consensual" amorous relationships between professors and students.[19]

In *Love's Labour's Lost,* Holofernes, a comically pedantic schoolteacher, and his obsequious companion Nathaniel are discussing a recent deer hunt. When Holofernes interjects a ridiculous, lengthy description of his own rhetorical talents, Nathaniel responds with the expected reverence: "Sir, I praise the Lord for you: and so may my parishioners; for their sons are well tutored by you, and their daughters profit very greatly under you: you are a good member of the commonwealth" (4.2.75-79). Holofernes picks up the sexual innuendo and responds, "Mehercle, if their sons be ingenuous, they shall want no instruction; if their daughters be capable, I will put it to them" (4.2.80-83). He then cautions silence because a woman is approaching.

The attitude presented in this passage, although intended for comic effect, nevertheless demonstrates much of what feminists have argued about the "chilly climate" for women in classrooms where male teachers treat male students with more seriousness of purpose than female students. In a worst-case scenario, as here, the female students are treated as sex objects. Such an attitude undermines any semblance of trust between teacher and student and almost ensures that daughters will profit less from their schooling than sons. For all his learning, Holofernes is a caricature of some of the least admirable traits of teachers through the ages.

In the Temple

Of all the professional roles in which men function with power over women, one might reasonably expect that of clergyman (used generically to refer to all faiths) to be the most immune to charges of sexual misconduct. However, recent scandals involving high-profile televangelists have shown otherwise, and there is evidence from the Hebrew scriptures to indicate that men acting under color of religious authority have been known to abuse their positions since biblical times.

The story of Eli is told in the second chapter of I Samuel. He was a descendant of Aaron and a priest, serving in the house of the Lord at Shiloh, which was likely the intertribal sanctuary where the ark was kept. Because the priestly tradition was hereditary, Eli's sons, Phinehas and Hophni, were expected to carry on that role. They were, however, "sons of Belial" who did not know the Lord. They departed from the sacred tradition concerning the priests' portion of food by demanding more than their rightful share and trying to use force to get it. They came to typify the declining Shilonite priesthood, which is starkly contrasted with the exemplary conduct of the young Samuel.

When Eli was very old, he heard some disturbing rumors about the conduct of his sons at the temple, "how they lay with the women that assembled at the door of the tabernacle of the congregation" (2.22). The sons were rebuked by their father: "Nay, my sons; for it is no good report that I hear: ye make the Lord's people to transgress" (2.23-24). Eli seems to have realized that it was his sons who were responsible for the conduct in question; it was they who led the women astray. As members of the priesthood, they had a professional responsibility to lead the people of the congregation in the ways of the Lord, and they had shirked that responsibility in an egregious way. Nevertheless, Eli's rebukes were ineffective, and he failed to remove his sons from their sacred office. As a result, a doom was pronounced upon them and their descendants.

With the Help

A final instance of abuse of authority is somewhat different in that it does not, strictly speaking, involve a professional relationship. However, it does involve betrayal of trust and disequilibrium of power and status. That is the sexual involvement of some of the suitors with the housemaids in Odysseus's palace during his prolonged absence in the *Odyssey*.

Odysseus has been away for twenty years, the first ten fighting in the Trojan War and the second ten wandering in his quest to return home. His palace in Ithaca has become overrun with suitors eager to marry his wife Penelope. The suitors are all members of the nobility and thus of the same social class as Odysseus and Penelope. Initially they were treated as guests in Odysseus's palace, but as the years have passed, they have gradually worn out their welcome and become a nuisance. Their eating and drinking habits have begun to exhaust the considerable resources of Odysseus's household, and in addition some of the suitors have entered into secret sexual liaisons with the housemaids. Secrecy would have been necessitated by the sacred bonds of trust that existed between hosts and guests in Greek culture of the time.

It is difficult to view the housemaids as in a position to give meaningful consent to these liaisons. The master of their household had been away for twenty years, and his son — only recently having reached manhood — was not allowed to supervise the women servants. The mistress of the house was no longer able to control the riotous conduct of the suitors, all of whom were socially superior to the servant class. The housemaids must have been fearful of what the future held for them and eager to be favored by whichever of the suitors might become their new master. It is little wonder that twelve of the fifty have become disloyal to Penelope and have "gone the way of shame" with the suitors.[20]

Odysseus, however, shows no compassion for the women's plight. He has them led outside the main hall and orders his son Telemachus and two herdsmen to "strike them down with your long swords, until you take away the life from them all, and they forget the love which they had at the bidding of the wooers, when they lay with them in secret" (22.443-445).

Hostile Environment

The Supreme Court's decision in the *Meritor* case is most important for establishing the principle that sexual harassment is discrimination on the basis of sex in violation of Title VII of the Civil Rights Act of 1964. Interestingly, *Meritor* was a hostile environment case, which many regarded as a weaker kind of test case than the more flagrant *quid pro quo* cases. In fact, one of the points argued before – and rejected by – the Court was that there must be some kind of detrimental economic effect (rather than a merely psychological effect) on the victim for legal relief to be available under Title VII.[21]

The guidelines of the EEOC provided an early formulation for hostile environment cases. It defined sexual harassment as encompassing conduct that has "the purpose or effect of unreasonably interfering with an individual's work performance or creating an intimidating, hostile, or offensive working environment."[22] Opponents were quick to point out that what is "intimidating, hostile, or offensive" is a subjective judgment about which opinions will surely differ.[23] As the courts have wrestled with this issue, some have adopted a new standard for sexual harassment cases by adapting the traditional common-law notion of the "reasonable man" into the "reasonable woman." This makes allowance for the fact that the sensibilities of men and women differ concerning sexual matters. As one appeals court that adopted the reasonable woman standard noted, "Conduct that many men consider unobjectionable may offend many women."[24] A hostile environment for women can be created by unwelcome sexual advances, unwanted touching, or verbal abuse, and instances of each are found in the Canon.

Unwelcome Sexual Advances

Women have been vulnerable to unwelcome sexual advances in public settings in ancient times, in Shakespeare's era, and today. Travel in isolated areas, especially unaccompanied by a man, and the use of public accommodations have often been regarded as especially risky for women, because they are likely to come into contact with various people of uncertain character.

Women's concern about ogling or leering by unknown men in public places is captured in the *Odyssey*. Odysseus has finally reached Ithaca and, disguised as a tattered beggar, is observing the outrageous conduct of the suitors in his own palace. He sits on the doorsill, then lurks on the periphery of the giant hall (where a great feast has just been consumed) and eats the morsels that the banqueters throw his way. One of the serving women, Melantho, casts him in a lurid light when she chides him as follows: "Stranger, night through, must we still suffer you? Will you roam through this house and ogle women? Be off, you oaf; be glad you've grabbed a meal – or else we'll fling a torch to clear you out" (19.65-69).[25]

In *The Two Gentlemen of Verona,* Julia misses her boyfriend Proteus, who has been forced by his father to leave Verona and go to Milan to pursue his education. Julia discusses with her maidservant Lucetta her plan to travel to Milan to visit Proteus. When Lucetta asks what she will wear, Julia says, "Not like a woman, for I would prevent the loose encounters of lascivious men" (2.7.40-43).[26] She disguises herself as a boy so she can travel without the obvious dangers an unprotected female faces on the highway. Her caution proves to have been well advised, for later in the play she encounters outlaws whose treatment of women travelers is questionable.

In *II Henry IV,* women are seen working at the Boar's Head Tavern, one of the wayside drinking establishments depicted in several of Shakespeare's histories. The Ancient Pistol shows up and is greeted by his friend Sir John Falstaff. The hostess (Mistress Quickly) and Doll Tearsheet both react strongly against Pistol, who is well known to them as a rogue and a cutpurse. When Falstaff and Pistol employ sexual innuendo in urging the hostess to be the subject of their toast, she retorts, "Come, I'll drink no proofs nor no bullets: I'll drink no more than will do me good, for no man's pleasure, I" (2.4.127-129). Clearly the hostess has been around and is aware of the dangers inherent in consuming alcohol while she is at the tavern, given the obvious sexual aggressiveness of her patrons. She intends to keep her wits about her as the best defensive strategy against unwelcome sexual attentions. Perhaps the eighty-three women who were sexually assaulted by Navy aviators at a Las Vegas hotel in September 1991 in the so-called Tailhook scandal would understand her predicament.[27]

Unwanted Touching

Touching is an ambiguous form of interpersonal communication. What seems a normal expression of human warmth to one person might be highly offensive to another. Especially where men touching women is concerned, almost any touching runs the risk of being interpreted as sexually suggestive. In the workplace, the proverbial pat on the back has had to be replaced by the safer and more appropriate verbal expression of congratulation or encouragement. Touching that is clearly unwanted is universally held to be unacceptable as an offense against the bodily integrity and fundamental dignity of a person.

One of the Canon's most sensitive portrayals of the quandary over touching is found in the sixth book of the *Odyssey*. Odysseus has left the island of the nymph Calypso on a raft and is blown off course by a terrible storm. He is washed ashore on the island of the Phaeacians, where – exhausted by his frantic struggle to stay afloat – he enters a thicket, covers his naked body with leaves, and falls asleep. He is awakened by the sounds of the young princess Nausicaa and her maidservants playing ball on the shore, where they have come to do the royal laundry. Odysseus comes out from beneath the bushes, having first broken off a leafy branch to hold around him to hide his nakedness. All of the maidens except Nausicaa are frightened by the sight of him befouled with brine. Only the princess stands her ground and faces him.

The ordinary means for a Greek in Odysseus's plight to seek help from a stranger was by a traditional ritual known as supplication. A person in need, known as a suppliant, would essentially throw himself on the mercy of the person being petitioned by falling at his feet and clasping his knees or, alternatively, reaching up and touching his chin. The person thus supplicated came under a special obligation from Zeus to protect the suppliant from whatever exigencies had befallen him. This ritual was as well known to Greeks of the time as the custom of clasping one's hands in prayer is today.[28]

As Odysseus stands facing Nausicaa, his first impulse is naturally to fall at her feet and supplicate her for assistance. Even in his traumatized state, however, he realizes the delicacy of the situation:

> She fled not, but stood and faced him; and Odysseus pondered whether he should clasp the knees of the fair-faced maid, and make his prayer, or whether, standing apart as he was, he should beseech her with gentle words, lest the maiden's heart should be wroth with him if he clasped her knees; so straightway he spoke a gentle word and crafty. (6.141-148)

Odysseus's diplomatic skills serve him well, and he convinces Nausicaa to lead him to the royal palace, where he might seek the aid of her parents in resuming his journey home to Ithaca. When he enters the royal palace of the Phaeacians, he proceeds enshrouded in a wondrous mist until he comes upon the royal couple, King Alcinous and Queen Arete, who have been holding court. He immediately places his hands around the knees of the queen and makes his prayer of supplication to her, which she eventually grants.[29]

One might ask why Odysseus so freely touched the knees of Queen Arete after having been so hesitant with respect to her daughter Nausicaa. Several differences might be cited: they are in the royal palace with many witnesses present, rather than unchaperoned on the seashore; Queen Arete is a mature matron, while Nausicaa is a young maiden; and Odysseus now has clothes on. A more important explanation, however, might be that Odysseus has been instructed by Athena to seek out Queen Arete. He therefore feels more confident of a sympathetic reception than he did with Nausicaa.

Unwanted touching can also be offensive among people who know each other very well. An instance in the *Symposium* involves two men who are romantically linked. Socrates and the brilliant but unstable young man Alcibiades are said to be in love, in keeping with the tradition of affairs between men of the Greek aristocracy in Plato's era.[30] When Alcibiades, already uproariously drunk, arrives late at Agathon's house for a drinking party, he proceeds to pick a quarrel with Socrates. He claims that Socrates has managed to sit beside the handsomest person in the room. Socrates responds playfully that Alcibiades is filled with "a spiteful jealousy which makes him treat me in a monstrous fashion, girding at me and hardly keeping his hands to himself" (213d). Alcibiades subsequently tries to turn the tables on Socrates when he says, "It is he who, if I praise any god in his presence or any person other than himself, will not keep his hands off me" (214d).

It is unclear from the context whether the alleged laying on of hands is in the form of fondling or of force; force, in turn, might be used either to separate the beloved from any third party in whom he is showing inordinate interest or to punish him for it. Both fondling and force attend situations involving what Socrates calls "amorous frenzy" (at 213d), and both kinds of touching characterize domestic disputes today. Unwanted touching can be offensive at times even to persons who are on good terms, and sensitivity on this score is apparent in the comments of Socrates and Alcibiades about who is the initiator of physical contact.

Verbal Abuse

Many feminists now argue that the fundamental nature of sexual harassment has more to do with power and the degradation of women than with sexual desire.[31] It has been described as a tactic to control or frighten women, a way to keep them in their place, and a means of

scaring them off a male preserve.[32] Hostile environment cases involving verbal abuse often arise when a woman has intruded into a male
environment such as a bar, a poolroom, or a male workplace. This is
the kind of harassment inflicted upon female cadets at the U.S. Naval
Academy, who are routinely subjected to humiliating rituals and verbal
debasement,[33] and upon a professor of neurosurgery at the Stanford
University Medical School, who resigned to protest the persistent
abuse to which she was subjected by male surgeons.[34]

Through harassment men are said to devalue women's role in the
workplace by inappropriately calling attention to their bodies or their
sexuality.[35] This tactic can be seen in one of the few settings in the
Canon in which women are in the workplace, the tavern. At the beginning of *The Taming of the Shrew*, Christopher Sly is portrayed as a
drunken beggar outside a rural alehouse. The hostess of the establishment is pursuing him and demanding payment for the glasses he has
broken. He responds, "No, not a denier. Go by, Jeronimy: go to thy
cold bed and warm thee" (Ind.1.9-10). The hostess is forced to rely on
her only remedy under the circumstances, summoning the constable.
Sly's reference to her cold bed appears to be a gratuitous insult; the
hostess speaks only three lines, and her personal life is not relevant to
the scene. The audience knows nothing about her, nor is there any reason to think that Sly does. His allegation of frigidity has meaning only
as a form of verbal abuse.

Not surprisingly, Sir John Falstaff and his followers were prone to
similar encounters with hostesses of the taverns they frequented. In *I
Henry IV,* after an extended argument between Falstaff and the hostess
at the Boar's Head Tavern over nonpayment of a debt, Prince Hal enters. The hostess tells the Prince that the "foulmouthed" Falstaff has
spoken most vilely of him; when Falstaff denies it, the hostess swears
by the "faith, truth and womanhood" in her (3.3.121). Falstaff seizes
this opportunity to claim, in most colorful terms, that she is a sexually
disreputable woman. He tries to shift the focus of the discussion from
his integrity, which is the source of the dispute, to her sexual reputation, which is irrelevant to it.

In *II Henry IV,* the same hostess is trying to have Falstaff arrested
for his usual nonpayment. While the page, a young boy loaned to Falstaff by Prince Hal, is helping the fat knight resist arrest, he directs a
stream of verbal abuse in the worst possible street language at the hostess: "Away, you scullion [kitchen servant]! You rampallian [scoundrel]!

You fustilarian [untidy fat woman]! I'll tickle your catastrophe [whip your backside]" (2.1.65-66). Although, in this case, there was underlying affection in spite of the abuse,[36] a tavern clearly could be a hostile and threatening environment for women who had to earn their livelihood in this way.

A final passage depicts the rare case of a woman verbally abusing a man by inappropriately commenting on his body. Like the situation of Odysseus with Calypso and Circe, however, this case involves the atypical circumstance of the woman's being in a position of superior power. In *I Henry VI*, the Countess of Auvergne tries to capture the English warrior Talbot by seductively inviting him to dinner. He is suspicious, however, and arranges a signal to his bodyguards, who are posted nearby. When the countess thinks she has him as her prisoner, she insults him because of his unimposing physical appearance: "Alas, this is a child, a silly dwarf! It cannot be this weak and writhled shrimp/Should strike such terror to his enemies"(2.3.22-24). When Talbot gives the signal and his men arrive, the countess changes her tune: "Victorious Talbot! pardon my abuse: /I find thou art no less than fame hath bruited/And more than may be gathered by thy shape" (2.3.67-69). The countess's behavior demonstrates how easy it is to be abusive when one is in a position of power over the person being abused. When there is a sudden reversal of fortune, the hostile environment often becomes instantly friendlier.

The Code of Silence

If sexual harassment is as prevalent as feminists assert and the Canon seems to indicate, why has it taken so long for it to come to public attention in a concerted way? One factor contributing to this oversight is society's unwritten rule against talking about matters of this kind. Women who are victims of sexual harassment often keep silent because they fear losing their jobs; because they think that they will not be believed anyway; or because they think that talking about it will only cause more trouble, and they prefer to avoid conflict.

One authority on sexual harassment has written, "Sexual abuse mutes victims socially through the violation itself. Often the abuser enforces secrecy and silence; secrecy and silence may be part of what is so sexy about sexual abuse."[37] Dictates of secrecy and silence are prevalent in cases of sexual harassment in the Canon and can be seen in some of the passages already discussed. Other instances may be described as those in which the perpetrator orders or recommends that his conduct not be talked about and those that demonstrate the deleterious effects of rumors and gossip on everyone involved in such cases.

Don't Tell Anyone

In the *Odyssey*, once again a god acts in an unseemly manner. Odysseus has traveled to the underworld and is about to view the shades of several Greek women which now reside there. The first one he sees is Tyro, a mortal woman of noble ancestry. Although she was married to Cretheus, she was in love with a river god, divine Enipeus, and was accustomed to resort to his fair waters. One day Poseidon, disguised as Enipeus, lay with her at the outpouring of the eddying stream. The upheaving water covered them, and Poseidon loosed her girdle. He cast a sleep on her and consummated his desire for her. Then he told her to expect to bear offspring as a result, because sex acts of the gods never fail to bear fruit. He added, "But now go to thy house, and hold thy peace, and tell no man; but know that I am Poseidon, the shaker of the earth" (11.251-252).[38] The reason for this admonition to silence is not clear from the context. One might posit either Poseidon's sensitivity to the fact that Tyro was a married woman or his wish not to antagonize his colleague Enipeus.

Another instance of cautioning to silence is found in *Love's Labour's Lost*. Mention has already been made of the abuse of authority by the pedantic schoolteacher Holofernes, who speaks to his fawning companion Nathaniel with sexual innuendo about his treatment of girls in his schoolroom. He has just told Nathaniel that, if the daughters are capable, he will "put it to them." Just then, a woman approaches, and Holofernes switches immediately to Latin, as a kind of secret code known only to men: "But *vir sapit qui pauca loquitur* [the man is wise who speaks few things]; a soul feminine saluteth us" (4.2.85-86).[39] Holofernes seems to be adept at keeping his dirty practices hidden from public view.

Angelo and Isabella of *Measure for Measure* were left at a point where Angelo was pressuring Isabella for an answer to his offer to spare her brother's life in exchange for her sexual favors. She is outraged and threatens to use Angelo's misconduct as the basis for some extortion of her own:

ISABELLA: I will proclaim thee, Angelo; look for't:
            Sign me a present pardon for my brother,
            Or with an outstretch'd throat I'll tell the world aloud
            What man thou art.

                                                    (2.4.151-154)

Angelo predictably responds with a reminder of their relative status:

ANGELO: Who will believe thee, Isabel?
            My unsoil'd name, the austereness of my life,
            My vouch against you, and my place i' the state,
            Will so your accusation overweigh
            That you shall stifle in your own report
            And smell of calumny.
            . . . .
            Say what you can, my false o'erweighs your true.

                                              (2.4.154-159, 170)

As Angelo exits, Isabella voices her dilemma in a soliloquy : "To
whom should I complain? Did I tell this,/Who would believe me?"
(2.4.171-172). She is brought to the brink of silence by her sinking feeling that Angelo is right in saying she will not be believed.

Like the passages discussed earlier, these also resonate themes from
the Clarence Thomas-Anita Hill confirmation hearings. In the play, the
official who is responsible for dispensing justice is accused of having
violated the very law he is entrusted with enforcing. Because he is of
high station and repute, and because the woman whom he is accused
of having sexually harassed is of neither, he presumes that she will not
be believed. He astutely observes that, if she does make any public accusations against him, this will likely be held more against her than
against him. Tragically, she too senses that she will not be believed,
and this perception clouds her judgment about whether to go public
with revelations of his misconduct.

In the confirmation hearings, Anita Hill similarly had reservations
about whether or not to come forward with her accusations.[40] Her critics have charged that her credibility was damaged by the passage of a
decade before she decided to do so and by her apparent good relations
with Thomas after the alleged harassment (including following him to
another job). Her supporters point to the very factors enumerated by
Angelo above, along with career considerations, as sufficient explanation for her prolonged silence.

Rumors and Gossip

Sometimes, in spite of the best attempts to keep sexual harassment secret, it nevertheless becomes public knowledge. The more titillating the secret, the harder it is to prevent its coming out. Our earlier discussion of *Pericles* showed Pericles learning of the incest between King Antiochus and his daughter by solving a riddle posed by the king. As soon as he has guessed the nature of the king's secret, Pericles realizes the danger this knowledge poses for him. He observes in a soliloquy that men who "blush not in actions blacker than the night, /Will shun no course to keep them from the light" (1.1.135-136). This observation is confirmed when King Antiochus counters in his own soliloquy, "He must not live to trumpet forth my infamy, /Nor tell the world Antiochus doth sin in such a loathed manner" (1.1.145-146).

The tendency of rumors about sexual harassment to be trumpeted forth is demonstrated in I Samuel. In the case of the priest Eli's sons, who were abusing their authority by lying with the women who assembled at the door of the tabernacle of the congregation, their father became aware of their misconduct through the bad reports he heard. Eli himself was very old at the time and might be presumed not to have gotten out much. Nevertheless, he says that he has heard about his sons' misconduct from many people: "And he said unto them, Why do ye such things? for I hear of your evil dealings by all this people. Nay, my sons; for it is no good report that I hear; ye make the Lord's people to transgress" (2.23-24). Eli's sons appear not to have been aware of how their recklessness might harm their future. A modern assessment of the situation might be that, however one views their offense, they certainly showed poor judgment.

The opposite extreme, excessive concern over the possibility of generating rumors, can be seen in the *Odyssey*. Odysseus's conduct with respect to Nausicaa and her maidservants was shown earlier to have been above reproach. The Phaeacian princess has agreed to lead Odysseus into town from the seashore where they first met. However, she advises him to follow them closely only until they reach the outskirts of town. There she tells him to stop in a park alongside the road and wait until the women have reached their destination. Then he should ask a passerby for directions to the royal palace, which any child could give.

Nausicaa is straightforward about her reasons for this devious strategy. She wants to avoid the rude talk of the sailors and workers in the shipyards they must pass by:[41]

Now the rude talk of such as these I would avoid, that no one afterwards may give me blame. For very forward persons are about the place, and some coarse man might say, if he should meet us: "What tall and handsome stranger is following Nausicaa? Where did she find him? A husband he will be, her very own. Some castaway, perhaps, rescued from his vessel, some foreigner.... The people of our own land here, Phaeacians, she disdains, though she has many highborn suitors." So they will talk, and for me it would prove a scandal. I should myself censure a girl who acted so, who, heedless of friends, while father and mother were alive, mingled with men before her public wedding. (6.273-288)

A short time later, after Odysseus has reached the royal palace and related to King Alcinous how he got to Phaeacia, the king apologizes for his daughter's rudeness in not having brought him to the palace personally. Odysseus responds graciously, if not entirely truthfully, by defending Nausicaa: "Sire, do not reproach the blameless girl. For she instructed me to follow with the maids; but I would not, for fear and very shame, lest possibly your heart might be offended at the sight. Suspicious creatures are we sons of the earth" (7.303-307).[42] One might well imagine a modern royal family envying King Alcinous for having offspring as sensitive to the damaging effects of scandal as Nausicaa was.

Sexual relations by their very nature are presumed to be private, and privacy in such matters is generally regarded as healthy. On the other hand, when unhealthy or even damaging situations exist, as in cases of sexual harassment, victims are confronted with a strong societal predisposition not to address them openly. In the past, such situations have often been relegated to the realm of rumor and gossip, where victims stood to lose more than they would gain by airing their grievances. Only in recent years has contemporary society encouraged victims of sexual harassment to adjudicate their claims and seek justice through courts of law. Even there, they face an uphill battle.

"Her Word Against His"

When sexual matters become public and conflicting claims need to be resolved, there is often no evidence of what transpired other than the word of the two persons involved. In the past, the traditional requirement of corroborating evidence in rape cases essentially stacked the deck against women. In 1983 the EEOC abandoned such a requirement in cases of sexual harassment, leading Catharine MacKinnon to observe pungently, "Perhaps they recognized that women don't choose to be sexually harassed in the presence of witnesses."[43]

When cases of sexual harassment must be adjudicated, they very often come down to "her word against his," and many feminists believe that, under such circumstances, women tend to be disbelieved more often than men. As one legal scholar has written, "Feminist scholars and activists have long criticized the way the adjudication of sexual aggression is animated by myths about women, by assumptions regarding their veracity and their integrity, and by doubts about their grasp on reality."[44] It is no surprise that the roots of such myths, assumptions, and doubts can be found in the Canon.

Strange Antecedents from Ancient Lore

True to the tradition that began with Adam and Eve, the Canon contains many instances of women acting in treacherous or deceitful ways in sexual matters. They have been depicted as less than truthful in making false allegations of attempted rape, arranging for wrong or substitute partners to sleep with unsuspecting men, and using sex for the purpose of trickery.

In Genesis (at 39.1-20), the story is told of Joseph's sojourn in Egypt after his brothers sold him into servitude. He is a servant to the captain of the guard, and he has come to wield great influence because his master trusts him utterly. His master's wife finds Joseph attractive and repeatedly tries to seduce him. Because of his loyalty to his master, he always refuses and tries to avoid her. One day when they are alone in the house, she tries again to persuade him to lie with her. As he flees from her grasp, he leaves his garment behind in her hand. When the men of the house return, she tells them that Joseph tried to rape her and that only her scream prevented him from succeeding. Moreover, she has his garment to corroborate her claim. She is believed, and Joseph is imprisoned.

A strikingly similar story is told about another attractive young man, this one in the *Iliad* (at 6.156-170). The Greek warrior Diomedes and his Trojan counterpart Glaucus are about to engage in combat when, in the course of identifying themselves to each other, they discover that an ancient hospitality bond exists between their families. This discovery is made when Glaucus tells the story of his ancestor Bellerophon: the gods endowed Bellerophon with such great beauty that Anteia, the wife of the king, tried to seduce him. The king was Bellerophon's overlord, and he therefore rejected her advances. In revenge, Anteia told her husband that Bellerophon had nearly succeeded in raping her. The king believed her but in spite of his anger could not bring himself to kill a guest. Instead, he sent him across the sea bearing a sealed tablet asking Anteia's father to exact vengeance on the bearer.

Both of these stories might also be examples of "explicitly bartered sex," for they involve situations in which a sexual proposition is made to a subordinate by the wife of a man in power. When the subordinate refuses, the wife seeks vengeance by falsely accusing him of attempted rape. In both cases the wife is believed, and the subordinate is unjustly punished (although, interestingly, neither meets the punishment of death that might be expected). In both cases the subordinate ultimately prevails in spite of his unjust punishment, largely because of divine protection. The fate of the lying women remains untold.

A strangely prevalent theme throughout the Canon is that of men being tricked by women into having sex with the wrong partner or a substitute one. This scenario is presented three times in Genesis.

The first story in Genesis (at 19.31-36) concerns Lot and his two daughters, who have left Sodom just before its destruction. (The daughters' husbands refused to heed Lot's warning to flee, and Lot's wife was turned into a pillar of salt when she looked back at the destruction.) The three refugees are living together in a cave in the mountains when the two daughters scheme to become pregnant by their father to perpetuate their clan. They conspire to make him drunk with wine so he will not realize what is happening. The elder and the younger daughter take turns on succeeding nights, and both become pregnant as a result. It is unclear from the passage why it was necessary for the two daughters to trick Lot by making him drunk. One might have conjectured that he would be as desperate as they to preserve the family line.

Some aspects of the foregoing story are paralleled in a mythological account of the birth of the god Eros in Plato's *Symposium* (at 203b-c). Socrates gives an account of his interaction with the Mantinean priestess Diotima, who related the following fable to explain Eros's parentage. The gods gave a feast to celebrate the birth of Aphrodite, and the god Resource — having consumed too much nectar — lay down to sleep in Zeus's garden. The goddess Poverty then schemed to have a child by Resource, so she lay down beside him and seduced him in his drunken stupor, becoming pregnant with the god Eros as a result. This story differs from that about Lot in that Resource was responsible for his own inebriation. Getting him drunk was not a part of Poverty's scheme; she simply took advantage of the situation when it arose.

A second story in Genesis (at 29.20-30) concerns Jacob's courtship of Rachel, for whom he served her father Laban faithfully for seven years. At the end of the seven years, Jacob asks Laban for Rachel so they can consummate the marriage. Laban hosts a large wedding feast, and in the evening he takes his elder daughter Leah to Jacob, who has intercourse with her. (Although it is not stated, one might surmise that wine was served at the wedding feast.) In the morning, he realizes that he has slept with Leah rather than Rachel. When he protests to Laban, the father explains that it is the custom in his country not to give a younger daughter in marriage before an older one. After allotting Leah her "bridal week," Jacob is allowed to marry Rachel as well, but he has to serve Laban an additional seven years for the second daughter. Responsibility for the deceitful plan to substitute Leah for Rachel apparently lies with Laban rather than his daughters, although they are at least willing to go along with its execution.

Judah is the subject of the third story in Genesis (at 38.6-26). He has three sons, of whom the eldest, Er, dies childless. The middle son refuses to fulfill his responsibility under Hebrew law to father a child with Er's widow Tamar.[45] The middle son then dies, and Judah declares that Tamar will have to wait for the third son until he reaches manhood. In the meantime, she is compelled to live in her father's house. When time passes and she is not given to the third son, Tamar puts on a veil and sits at the crossroads in the manner of a prostitute. Judah solicits her services, not recognizing her as his daughter-in-law. After negotiating the price and a pledge for security, she lies with him and becomes pregnant. Later, when Judah learns that Tamar is pregnant by whoredom, he directs that she be put to death as punishment. Only when she reveals that she has Judah's pledged property does he realize the prostitute's identity. He then admits that she has been more in the right than he, because he failed to give her to his third son.

While male colleagues are sometimes as involved in planning these schemes as the women who carry them out, nevertheless it is uniformly women who end up being the unintended partners in bed, and it is uniformly men who end up unintentionally sleeping with them. (A similar substituting of one woman for another in bed would later be used by Shakespeare as a means of resolving the central problem of two plays.[46]) The message that these passages send is a clear one: men must be careful to avoid the treachery of the women with whom they sleep.

Another strand of ancient lore depicts women as sometimes using sex for ulterior motives rather than for the presumed purposes of love, pleasure, or procreation. This strand began early and at the top, with Zeus and Hera, the king and queen of the gods. In the *Iliad,* Hera is portrayed as plotting to divert Zeus' attention from the battlefield on the plains of Troy, where his brother Poseidon is giving undue aid to the Greeks. Zeus will certainly turn the tide of battle in favor of the Trojans unless Hera, who supports the Greeks, can find a way to distract him. "And this plan seemed to her mind the best — to go to Ida, when she had beauteously adorned her person, if so be he might desire to lie by her side and embrace her body in love, and she might shed a warm and gentle sleep upon his eyelids and his cunning mind" (14.161-165). Having enlisted the help of Aphrodite and Sleep, Hera seduces Zeus; while he is in a deep slumber, Poseidon can assist the Greeks on the battlefield without opposition from his more powerful brother.

In the *Republic* (at 390c), Plato singles out the foregoing passage of the *Iliad* for especially harsh denunciation, although he levels his criticism more at Zeus for allowing his passions to overrule his judgment than at Hera for her manipulative conduct and exploitation of marital love. Hera's strategy would later be replicated by one of Shakespeare's most despicable villainesses. In *Titus Andronicus,* Titus Andronicus describes Tamora, the captive queen of the Goths who becomes the wife of the Roman emperor Saturninus, as follows: "She's with the lion deeply still in league,/And lulls him whilst she playeth on her back,/And when he sleeps will she do what she list" (4.1.98-100).

Another deceitful woman is presented in the story of Samson and Delilah in Judges. Samson had already had trouble with his first wife, a Philistine woman, who — by incessant weeping — wheedled from him the solution to a riddle he had posed and then revealed it to the Philistine men with whom Samson had a wager. Delilah was Samson's subsequent lover; she conspired with the Philistine lords to discover the secret of his strength. Three times he gave her wrong answers, and three times she tested the information and found it to be fallacious. Finally she lamented, "How canst thou say, I love thee, when thine heart is not with me? Thou hast mocked me these three times, and hast not told me wherein thy great strength lieth" (16.15). He relented and told her the secret of his uncut hair. Delilah sent this information to the Philistines, and then "she made him sleep upon her knees" (16.19). While he was asleep, she cut off his seven locks and thus incapacitated him. Although there is no explicit description of how she made him sleep, the passage is highly suggestive of the nature of her tactics.

A final instance of sexual trickery by a woman involves a situation in which the woman herself did not have sex for ulterior motives but rather induced another person to do so on her behalf. In the *Iliad,* Achilles' venerable tutor, Phoenix, is sent as part of a deputation to persuade the sulking warrior to return to the battle. Phoenix relates the circumstances of his having come into the service of Achilles' father, Peleus. Phoenix's father, Amyntor, had a beautiful slave girl, Clytia, whom he cherished more than his wife. His wife, feeling wronged, formulated a devious strategy: she pleaded with her son (even using the rite of supplication by grasping his knees) "to have dalliance with that other first" himself so that his father would seem repulsive to her (9.451-452). Phoenix agreed, and when Amyntor heard what his son had done, he cursed him with childlessness. Phoenix thereupon decided that he could not stay in the palace of his angered father any longer, so he emigrated to Phthia. Whether King Amyntor knew of his wife's role in the matter is not known.

Why are women so often depicted as perpetrators of various kinds of sexual trickery? If one subscribes to the view that biology is destiny, one might surmise that this is because of physiological factors that make women's sexuality more subtle and susceptible to misinterpretation than men's. Whatever the reason, there are certainly abundant instances in the Canon of this kind of behavior by women of the ancient world.

Whether one is talking about false allegations of attempted rape, about wrong or substitute sexual partners foisted upon unsuspecting men, or about the use of sex for the purpose of trickery, women were often depicted in the ancient world as unreliable when it came to sexual matters. Together, all these instances of sexual dishonesty, from both the Hebrew and the Greek traditions, have created a strong cultural bias that calls into question women's trustworthiness in sexual matters. It is not merely paranoia on the part of feminists when they say that women tend to be disbelieved in these matters and that the expectation not to be believed has discouraged many women from coming forward with complaints of sexual harassment. Nor is there any wonder that, when women have finally come forward to make charges of long-standing sexual harassment against powerful politicians such as Senators Brock Adams and Robert Packwood, they have done so in groups sufficiently large to counter the societal tendency to disbelieve.[47]

Somebody Is Lying

In spite of all the cultural baggage cited above, demonstrating society's strong predisposition to disbelieve women where sexual matters are concerned, Shakespeare shows a marked preference for his innocent heroines. He usually portrays the man as the liar and the woman as an innocent victim in cases pitting her word against his before impartial hearers.[48] In some cases Shakespeare portrays the guilty man as assuming in advance that he will be able to take advantage of the known cultural predisposition to disbelieve women. Three instances of sexual harassment discussed earlier involve direct conflict between a man's and a woman's word about what has transpired between them in private.

In *Measure for Measure,* Lord Angelo, filling in for the Duke of Vienna, demanded sex from Isabella in exchange for clemency for her brother. Isabella pretended to go along with this deal, but in fact she arranged for Mariana, Angelo's spurned fiancée, to substitute for her in the dark. Angelo believes that he has deflowered Isabella, and he has reneged on their agreement by ordering her brother put to death so that he cannot seek revenge. When the Duke of Vienna returns from his leave of absence, Isabella steps forward during the welcoming celebration and appeals to him for justice. (She has been forewarned by "Friar Lodowick," who was actually the duke in disguise and knows all, to expect her pleas to be rejected initially.)

The duke at first tries to send Isabella to Angelo for a hearing of her complaint, but she protests vigorously, implying that Angelo is the problem. She readily acknowledges that she is running the risk of not being believed but insists that the duke himself must hear her story. Angelo steps in at this point and makes his first counterpoint, that Isabella's wits are infirm. As a second defensive strategy, he offers her motivation to lie about him:

> ANGELO: My lord, her wits, I fear me, are not firm:
> She hath been a suitor to me for her brother
> Cut off by course of justice, —

ISABELLA: By course of justice!

ANGELO: And she will speak most bitterly and strange.

ISABELLA: Most strange, but yet most truly, will I speak:
             That Angelo's forsworn; is it not strange?
             That Angelo's a murderer; is't not strange?
             That Angelo is an adulterous thief,
             An hypocrite, a virgin-violator;
             Is it not strange and strange?
             . . . .

DUKE: Away with her! Poor soul,
             She speaks this in the infirmity of sense.

                                        (5.1.33-42, 46-47)

Isabella feels compelled to defend herself against the allegation of mental impairment. She then presents her complaint against Angelo in a rational, coherent way. The duke comments upon her persuasive manner of presenting her case but continues to appear incredulous. He then suggests a third defensive strategy for Angelo, asking who put her up to making these charges:

DUKE: By heaven, fond wretch, thou know'st not what thou speak'st,
             Or else thou art suborn'd against his honour
             In hateful practice. First, his integrity
             Stands without blemish. Next, it imports no reason
             That with such vehemency he should pursue
             Faults proper to himself: if he had so offended,
             He would have weigh'd thy brother by himself
             And not have cut him off. Some one hath set you on:
             Confess the truth, and say by whose advice
             Thou camest here to complain.

                                        (5.1.105-114)

Once again there are remarkable parallels with the Clarence Thomas-Anita Hill confirmation hearings. In both cases the woman who brought charges of sexual harassment was accused of suffering from a mental disorder: in Isabella's case the terminology was "infirm wits"; in Anita Hill's it was "psychic fantasies" and "delusional erotomania."[49] Both women's motivation to lie was explored: Isabella was said to be motivated by the desire for revenge over denial of clemency for her brother, while various conjectures were made about Anita Hill's motivation (a book contract, revenge as "a woman scorned," and so on).[50] And in both cases allegations were made that the woman was put up to making her complaint by an unnamed conspiracy to discredit an honorable man for political purposes.[51]

In the Shakespearean drama, the "impartial hearer" is the duke, who must temporarily hide the fact that he actually knows which party is telling the truth. The question of which party was telling the truth in the Thomas-Hill matter remains unresolved. Much has been made of the difficulty in presenting precisely accurate testimony about conversations and events that took place over a decade ago. [52] Moreover, recent publicity surrounding a retracted accusation of sexual abuse against Cardinal Joseph Bernardin of Chicago has underscored the trickiness of problems of proof when one person's word is pitted against another's about what transpired between them many years before. [53] Resolution of the Thomas-Hill enigma may ultimately depend upon whether or not lost memories are recaptured by one or more of those involved.

Another case of her word against his is presented in *All's Well That Ends Well*. Bertram has been compelled to marry Helena against his will by the king of France, who gave Helena her choice from among his knights because of a debt of gratitude to her and her father. Bertram leaves for the war in Italy without consummating the marriage, and he sends Helena a message that he will have nothing to do with her until she meets two conditions that are intended to be impossible: she must show him a certain ring that she must take from his finger and also a child she has borne by him. Helena disguises herself and journeys to Florence to try to fulfill Bertram's conditions.

Meanwhile, Bertram has fallen in love with the virgin Diana, daughter of a Florentine widow, and tries to seduce her. Helena plots with Diana to substitute for her in bed. During the sexual encounter that follows, Helena exchanges rings with Bertram and also conceives a child. He remains unaware of her identity throughout.

At the end of the play, after the war, Bertram is confronted with Diana's allegation of seduction, with the king of France as the impartial hearer. Bertram admits that he knows Diana and that he had sex with her. He counters, however, that she was a common prostitute in the military camp and that he therefore could not have had any intent to marry her. She, in turn, produces the ring he relinquished, which had been in his family for six generations and which he clearly would not have given to a prostitute. Bertram then elaborates upon his defense:

KING: She hath that ring of yours.

BERTRAM: I think she has: certain it is I liked her,
           And boarded her i' the wanton way of youth:
           She knew her distance, and did angle for me,
           Madding my eagerness with her restraint,
           As all impediments in fancy's course
           Are motives of more fancy; and, in fine,
           Her infinite cunning with her modern grace,
           Subdued me to her rate: she got the ring;
           And I had that which any inferior might
           At market-price have bought.

                                                   (5.3.209-219)

Even though Diana is able to present further evidence in support of her version of the facts, the king is on the verge of sending her to prison as a common prostitute. At this point, Helena enters and reveals the whole truth. Bertram, having been taught a lesson, has the good grace to admit his offenses and finally accepts Helena as his wife.

Bertram's defense against the charge of seduction is of interest because it represents a strategy sometimes used by men to avoid responsibility for a sexual encounter: first, the woman's sexual reputation is attacked by the allegation that she is a slut or even a prostitute. Second, it is alleged that he merely liked her, while she used a cunning means of angling for him; thus she, not he, is said to be the responsible party. The technicality that Bertram was in fact innocent and that Diana was making an untrue allegation may be attributed to dramatic irony. The human truth of the scene derives from Bertram's intention to lie about his misconduct and from Diana's courageous plot to expose him.

In *II Henry IV,* familiar characters present another case of her word against his The hostess of the Boar's Head Tavern has entered a suit against Sir John Falstaff for a large debt he owes her, and several officers accost him and attempt his arrest. Two of Falstaff's followers are defending him when the lord chief justice arrives and restores order. The hostess explains to the chief justice the reasons for her suit, and almost as an afterthought she includes an allegation that Falstaff had once promised to marry her. When she challenges him to deny it, he makes his appeal directly to the chief justice:

FALSTAFF: My lord, this is a poor mad soul; and she says up and down
            the town that her eldest son is like you: she hath been in good
            case, and the truth is, poverty hath distracted her. But for

these foolish officers, I beseech you I may have redress against
them.

(2.1.103-108)

The chief justice as impartial hearer is not fooled by Falstaff's allegation
of mental impairment, and he places greater trust in the hostess's cre-
dulity than in that of the fat knight: "You have, as it appears to me,
practiced upon the easy-yielding spirit of this woman, and made her
serve your uses both in purse and in person" (2.1.114-117).

Thus, in all three instances of an impartial party's hearing conflicting testimony of a man and a woman about what has transpired between them in private, Shakespeare portrays the woman as more
reliable. These portrayals run counter to a strong cultural tradition that
the word of women concerning sexual matters cannot be trusted. The
women prevail before impartial hearers in spite of defenses by the men
that question their mental balance, impugn their sexual reputation, and
offer up their motivation to lie.

One might expect skeptics to ask how the Canon, comprised of traditional literary works from bygone eras, could possibly treat such a
new and emerging development as sexual harassment. In answer, it has
been shown that virtually every aspect of the concept of sexual harassment as defined by the law today can be found in the Canon. Nor is
the approach taken by those who produced these works monolithic;
the perspectives of men and women, masters and servants, perpetrators
and victims are all well represented.

While it is accurate to say that these texts preceded women's entry
into the workplace on a large scale, a sociocultural system that kept
women in a subordinate position presented many contexts other than
employment in which men and women interacted, with men holding
the power (in a king's court, in the halls of justice, in the church, and
so on). Furthermore, one can see in the passages cited here the antecedents of women's role in the workplace — women working as harlots in
brothels, as house servants in Homeric palaces, and as hostesses in taverns frequented by the lower classes in Shakespearean times. Women
throughout the ages have been vulnerable to what is now called sexual
harassment, and these basic works provide many illustrations of the
dynamics of this conduct.

The students in our classrooms will no doubt encounter the problem of sexual harassment during their lifetimes. If they are fortunate enough not to be directly involved, they will likely be affected as supervisors in their workplaces, as jurors in their local communities, or as citizens watching a Senate confirmation hearing on television. They must be prepared to understand and deal with this conduct wherever it occurs. A thorough grounding in the works of the Canon provides ample exposure to the problem of sexual harassment, and it does so through the medium of the finest and most influential literature of the Western tradition.

Notes

1. Louise F. Fitzgerald, "Sexual Harassment: The Definition and Measurement of a Construct," in *Ivory Power: Sexual Harassment on Campus,* ed. Michele A. Paludi (Albany: State University of New York Press, 1990), p. 41.

2. Deborah L. Rhode, *Justice and Gender: Sex Discrimination and the Law* (Cambridge, Mass.: Harvard University Press, 1989), pp. 230-231.

3. Catharine A. MacKinnon, *Sexual Harassment of Working Women: A Case of Sex Discrimination* (New Haven: Yale University Press, 1979).

4. 29 C.F.R. § 1604.11 (1981), implementing 42 U.S.C. § 2000e, 2(a)(1) *et seq.*

5. *Meritor Savings Bank, FSB v. Vinson et al.,* 477 U.S. 57, 106 S. Ct. 2399, 91 L. Ed. 2d 49 (1986).

6. 477 U.S. at 65.

7. Two recent books give similar detailed accounts of the Hill-Thomas hearings but reach different conclusions concerning who was telling the truth. For the pro-Hill version, see Timothy M. Phelps and Helen Winternitz, *Capitol Games: Clarence Thomas, Anita Hill, and the Story of a Supreme Court Nomination* (New York: Hyperion, 1992). For the pro-Thomas version, see David Brock, *The Real Anita Hill: The Untold Story* (New York: Free Press, 1993). Also, see generally Toni Morrison, ed., *Race-ing Justice, En-gendering Power: Essays on Anita Hill, Clarence Thomas, and the Construction of Social Reality* (New York: Pantheon, 1992).

8. Paul Simon, *Advice and Consent: Clarence Thomas, Robert Bork and the Intriguing History of the Supreme Court's Nomination Battles* (Washington, D.C.: National Press Books, 1992).

9. Brock, *The Real Anita Hill,* pp. 9-13.

10. Simon, *Advice and Consent,* p. 122. See also Stephen Labaton, "For Oklahoma, Anita Hill's Story Is Open Wound," *New York Times,* April 19, 1993, pp. A1 and A9.

11. *Harris v. Forklift Systems Inc.,* 114 S. Ct. 367, 371, 126 L. Ed. 2d 295 (November 9, 1993). See Linda Greenhouse, "Court, 9-0, Makes Sex Harassment Easier to Prove," *New York Times,* November 10, 1993, pp. A1 and A14.

12. Odysseus emphasizes the desire of both female figures to marry him, and his resistance, in his account of his travels to King Alcinous (at 9.29-33). He might have been attempting to preempt any attempt by the king to interest him in marrying his daughter Nausicaa.

13. Quoted by Simon, *Advice and Consent*, p. 108.

14. Peter Rutter, *Sex in the Forbidden Zone: When Men in Power — Therapists, Doctors, Clergy, Teachers and Others — Betray Women's Trust* (Los Angeles, Calif.: Jeremy P. Tarcher, 1989).

15. See, for example, Glen O. Gabbard, *Sexual Exploitation in Professional Relationships* (New York: American Psychiatric Association, 1989). Because such conduct does not occur in the context of an employer-employee relationship, it is generally not covered by sex discrimination laws; an exception is the teacher-student relationship, which is covered by the federal law against discrimination on the basis of sex in federally assisted educational programs and activities.

16. Rutter, *Sex in the Forbidden Zone*, p. 42.

17. Robert Hanley, "Three Are Sentenced to Youth Center for Sexual Abuse of Retarded Girl," *New York Times*, April 24, 1993, pp. 1 and 8.

18. 20 U.S.C. § 1681 *et seq.*

19. See generally Michele A. Paludi and Richard B. Barickman, eds. *Academic and Workplace Sexual Harassment: A Resource Manual* (Albany: State University of New York Press, 1991), pp. 99-114.

20. At 22.421-425. The verb used at 18.325 indicates that the housemaid Melantho in particular has become "sexually involved" with the suitor Eurymachus.

21. 477 U.S. at 67-68.

22. 29 C.F.R. § 1604.11(a)(3).

23. A representative of this point of view is Michael Weiss, who has written that, under the hostile environment theory of sexual harassment, whether one thinks Anita Hill told the truth or not, Clarence Thomas's crime was "all in her mind." See "Crimes of the Head: Feminist Legal Theory Is Creating a Government Not of Laws but of Women," *Reason*, vol. 23, no. 8 (January 1992), p. 30.

24. *Ellison v. Brady*, 924 F. 2d 872, 878 (9th Cir. 1991). In its 1993 decision *Harris v. Forklift Systems, Inc.,* the Court left unexamined whether the standard should be that of a "reasonable person" or that of a "reasonable woman," but applied the former.

25. Translated by Allen Mandelbaum (Berkeley: University of California Press, 1990).

26. Obviously the treatment of women travelers by the outlaws is on everyone's mind. When Valentine is accosted by the outlaws, they ask him to become their leader; he agrees provided that they agree to "do no outrages on silly [defenseless] women or poor passengers." The outlaws respond that they detest such "vile base practices" (4.1.70-73). Later, when Valen-

tine's girlfriend Silvia is captured, the outlaws assure her that they "will not use a woman lawlessly" (5.3.12-14). When Proteus rescues Silvia from the outlaws, he claims that they "would have forced your honour and your love" (5.4.21-22).

27. See Office of the Inspector General, Department of Defense, *The Tailhook Report: The Official Inquiry into the Events of Tailhook '91* (New York: St. Martin's Press, 1993).

28. See Agathe Thornton, *Homer's Iliad: Its Composition and the Motif of Supplication* (Göttingen: Vandenhoeck & Ruprecht, 1984), pp. 117-118.

29. At 7.139-152. There are some indications that Phaeacian society may have been fundamentally matriarchal, and that explains why Odysseus – on the advice of Athena - supplicates the queen rather than the king. See 7.48-77.

30. At 213c. Alcibiades admits later (at 218c - 219c) that his attempt to seduce Socrates failed.

31. See generally chapter 3, "Desire and Power, " of Catharine A. MacKinnon, *Feminism Unmodified: Discourses on Life and Law* (Cambridge, Mass.: Harvard University Press, 1987).

32. Jill L. Goodman, "Sexual Harassment: Some Observations on the Distance Travelled and the Distance Yet to Go," *Capital University Law Review*, vol. 10 (1981), pp. 454-456.

33. See Carol Burke, "Dames at Sea: Life in the Naval Academy," *New Republic,* August 17, 1992, p. 20.

34. Elizabeth L'Hommedieu, "Walking Out on the Boys," *Time,* July 8, 1991, pp. 52-53.

35. MacKinnon, *Sexual Harassment,* p. 41.

36. As the hostess makes her complaint to the chief justice, she recalls that Falstaff had once promised to marry her so that he could borrow money (at 2.1.92-112). In *Henry V,* she tenderly attends Falstaff's deathbed (at 2.3.10-28).

37. MacKinnon, *Feminism Unmodified,* p. 104.

38. Translated by Mandelbaum.

39. Holofernes' use of the gender-specific noun *vir* rather than the gender-neutral noun *homo* (which might have been expected in a maxim of this kind) is revealing.

40. Phelps and Winternitz, *Capitol Games,* pp. 230-236; and Brock, *The Real Anita Hill,* pp. 125-131.

41. Translated by George Herbert Palmer (Boston: Houghton Mifflin, 1894), who captures well the overtones of sexual scandal.

42. Translated by Palmer.

43. MacKinnon, *Feminism Unmodified*, p. 113.

44. Kimberle Crenshaw, "Whose Story Is It, Anyway? Feminist and Antiracist Appropriations of Anita Hill," in *Race-ing Justice, En-gendering Power*, ed. Morrison, p. 408.

45. The duty of a brother to a childless, widowed sister-in-law is set forth at Deuteronomy 25. 5-10.

46. See *All's Well That Ends Well* 3.7.1-48 and *Measure for Measure* 3.1.200-281 and 4.1.1-76. In both cases, even after having had sex, the men were not aware of the substitution.

47. In 1992 a group of eight women made charges against Adams (D., Washington) that led to his retirement from the Senate. See Patricia King, "The Senator, the Sex Stories," *Newsweek*, March 16, 1992, p. 64. An even larger group (twenty-four) made charges against Packwood (R., Oregon), which led to an investigation by the Senate Ethics Committee. See Trip Gabriel, "The Trials of Bob Packwood," *New York Times Magazine*, August 29, 1993, p. 32.

48. This generalization does not apply, of course, to cases of her word against his in which the perspective is intentionally that of an impassioned or irrational hearer, such as Othello or King Leontes.

49. Phelps and Winternitz, *Capitol Games*, pp. 323-324 and 361-362.

50. See generally chapter 8, "The Search for a Motive," of Brock, *The Real Anita Hill.*

51. Simon, *Advice and Consent*, p. 138; and Phelps and Winternitz, *Capitol Games*, p. 244.

52. See Jane Mayer and Jill Abramson, "The Surreal Anita Hill," *New Yorker*, May 24, 1993, p. 92.

53. See Kenneth L. Woodward, "Was It Real or Memories?" *Newsweek*, March 14, 1994, pp. 54-55.

2: Rape

U NLIKE SEXUAL HARASSMENT, rape has been condemned as a crime by virtually all civilized societies for millenia. Because the legal systems that have condemned rape have been male-dominated, the law of rape has developed from a male perspective. Only in recent years have there been arguments for change that would make this body of law more reflective of women's experience.[1] The subject of rape therefore poses a different kind of challenge to the Canon. This chapter will show that the profiles of rapists in the Canon correspond closely to taxonomies developed in the current scholarly literature. Further, the dilemmas and ordeals faced by rape victims in the Canon will be shown not to differ substantially from those that have become the focus of feminists' concern in recent years. The patterns that have emerged from our new understanding of rape turn out to be patterns with a long history.

A New Understanding of Rape

Within the Anglo-American judicial system, rape has been defined by the traditional common law as occurring when a man engages in intercourse with a woman not his wife, by force or threat of force, against her will and without her consent.[2] Before the U.S. Supreme Court invalidated most death penalty statutes in 1972, rape was punishable by death in sixteen states plus federal jurisdictions.[3] When state legislatures reformed their statutes to comply with the Court's 1972 requirements, only a few southern states reenacted the death penalty for rape.

In *Coker v. Georgia* (1977), the U.S. Supreme Court heard an appeal by a defendant who had been sentenced to death by the state of Georgia for raping an adult woman.[4] (The defendant was an escaped convict who broke into the home of a Georgia couple at night, tied up and robbed the husband, raped the wife at knifepoint, and stole the family car, taking the wife with him; when the police stopped the car, she was released "unharmed."[5]) Because Georgia had reformed its statutes, the only basis for the defendant's appeal was that the death penalty for raping an adult woman is per se cruel and unusual punishment in violation of the Eighth Amendment. The Court's divided decision (7 to 2) reveals a spectrum of views on the nature of rape and its gravity as a crime.

Seven justices concurred in the Court's judgment that imposition of the death penalty in the *Coker* case would constitute cruel and unusual punishment in violation of the Eighth Amendment. Two justices who opposed the death penalty in all cases (William Brennan and Thurgood Marshall) were joined by four who believed that the rape of an adult woman is not a crime of the same gravity as murder. A seventh justice (Lewis Powell) concurred in the result in the *Coker* case but was unwilling to extend the principle to rape cases committed with "excessive brutality" or inflicting serious or lasting injury. Two justices (Warren Burger and William Rehnquist) dissented, arguing that the Georgia court's death sentence should have been upheld.

In writing for the four justices who drew the line between rape and murder, Justice Byron White stated, "We do not discount the seriousness of rape as a crime. It is highly reprehensible, both in a moral sense and in its almost total contempt for the personal integrity and autonomy of the female victim and for the latter's privilege of choosing those with whom intimate relationships are to be established. Short of homicide, it is the 'ultimate violation of the self.'" However, he went on to draw a crucial distinction: "Life is over for the victim of the murderer; for the rape victim, life may not be nearly so happy as it was, but it is not over and normally is not beyond repair."[6]

Justice Powell, who drew the line between simple rape and aggravated rape, wrote, "The deliberate viciousness of the rapist may be greater than that of the murderer. Rape is never an act committed accidentally. Rarely can it be said to be unpremeditated. There is also wide variation in the effect on the victim." Citing the plurality's passage quoted above, Powell answered, "Some victims are so grievously injured physically or psychologically that life *is* beyond repair."[7]

Chief Justice Burger, in dissent, responded to the same passage more strenuously: "A rapist not only violates a victim's privacy and personal integrity, but inevitably causes serious psychological as well as physical harm in the process. The long-range effect upon the victim's life and health is likely to be irreparable; it is impossible to measure the harm which results.... To speak blandly, as the plurality does, of rape victims who are 'unharmed,' or to classify the human outrage of rape, as does Mr. Justice Powell, in terms of 'excessively brutal' versus 'moderately brutal,' takes too little account of the profound suffering the crime imposes upon the victims and their loved ones."[8]

The public perception of these nine male justices arguing over what it means to be raped and deciding to restrict the range of available penalties contributed to pressure for reexamination of rape from a woman's perspective. In the years since the *Coker* decision, feminists have made rape a focus of special concern. As a result, police departments and hospitals have instituted new procedures for dealing with rape cases, hot lines have been made available to counsel victims, and legislatures have reformed antiquated rape statutes. The recognition of the prevalence of "date rape" among high school and college students has prompted many educational institutions to offer programs to reduce the number of incidents on their campuses and provide assistance to those affected.

Concurrently, a growing literature on rape, much of it generated by feminist scholars, has altered our understanding of the phenomenon. The long standing debate over whether rape is about sexuality or about violence is now said to be based on a false dichotomy.[9] Most researchers have come to agree that rapists are motivated by many different combinations of sexuality and violence or aggression. Current theories about the cause of rape differ primarily in the degree of emphasis on one element or the other. As one psychologist whose clinical practice is noted in the field has said, "We look at rape as the sexual expression of aggression, rather than as the aggressive expression of sexuality."[10]

The study of rape has been characterized by two primary approaches, the psychodynamic and the sociocultural.[11] In the past, the traditional psychodynamic approach regarded the rapist as essentially a deviant personality whose actions resulted from thwarted psychosexual development or mental illness. Rapists – as aberrants – were said to be relatively rare within the general population. More recent psychodynamic research views rapists as overcompensating for low sex drives or inadequate self-esteem. Rape is seen as an expression of violent behavior, and research undertakes to explain why it is used as an outlet for aggression. This contemporary view allows for many more potential rapists within the population at large. As one scholar observed concerning psychodynamic studies in general, "Regardless of emphasis, psychologists link so many different mental and emotional abnormalities to rapists that it is difficult to distinguish between offenders and nonoffenders."[12]

Sociocultural approaches, including most feminist theories, view rape as an extension of ordinary social interaction between men and women. As one scholar has put it, "According to this perspective, rape is not an isolated act of a sick, sexually deprived, or inadequately developed male; it is aggressive behavior that is an inevitable part of the social milieu. Males are socialized into the role of aggressive seducer while females are socialized into the role of passive prey."[13] Our society is said to condone the sexual coercion of women by keeping them in a subordinate and disempowered status. Rape is said to be one of society's more violent means of keeping women in their place. Radical feminists would add that much that passes as "normal sex" is in fact a form of rape, because it is coercive or nonconsensual.[14]

Throughout this chapter, both the psychodynamic approach and the sociocultural approach to understanding rape will be invoked. Instances of rape from the Canon will be cited that comport with both approaches.

Profiles of the Rapist

Myths about rape and rapists have always existed and persist to this day. A prominent one about rapists is that they are oversexed men who have uncontrollable sex urges.[15] Although modern research indicates the contrary, this myth has had an everlasting life. Plato seems to accept it in the *Timaeus* when he offers a physiological explanation for men's inappropriate or excessive conduct in sexual matters:

> And the marrow [seed], inasmuch as it is animated and has been granted an outlet, has endowed the part where its outlet lies with a love for generating by implanting therein a lively desire for emission. Wherefore in men the nature of the genital organs is disobedient and self-willed, like a creature that is deaf to reason, and it attempts to dominate all because of its frenzied lusts. (90b)

Plato's description of the male sex organs brings to mind the debate over castration as a penalty or legally sanctioned remedy for rape. In the past, castration of rapists was routinely ordered by courts, but this practice has been discontinued. In a well-publicized 1992 case, castration was requested by a Texas prisoner as an alternative to life imprisonment, and the court's approval of the request elicited a public outcry.[16] Critics have likened castration as a penalty for rape to cutting off a hand that steals or a tongue that commits perjury. As one expert put it, "We believe that what's wrong with a sex offender is what's between his ears, not his legs."[17] Feminists, too, have generally not favored the castration option, on both practical and theoretical grounds.[18] On practical grounds, a rapist who is deprived of one weapon often simply uses another, possibly inflicting greater injury; bottles and sticks are said to be popular with rapists.[19] On theoretical grounds, castration implicitly accepts the myth that rape is a problem solely of excessive, abnormal sexual desire.[20]

In Plato's defense, it can be said that his characterization of the male sex organs as "attempting to dominate all" anticipates one of the primary motivations for rape recognized today: power. His ascribing this motivation to the genital organs rather than the brain might simply be poetic license, not unlike contemporary feminists' use of the phrase "testosterone poisoning" to describe peculiarly male forms of objectionable behavior. In any event, Plato may not have been totally removed in this thinking from A. Nicholas Groth, an expert on rape, who has written, "Rape, then, is a pseudosexual act, a pattern of sexual behavior that is concerned much more with status, hostility, control, and dominance than with sensual pleasure or sexual satisfaction."[21]

Elaborate and comprehensive psychodynamic taxonomies have been developed from the substantial recent research on rape. These classify rapists as belonging to at least four well-distinguished types: the power rapist, the anger rapist, the sadistic rapist, and the impulsive rapist.[22] Each type can be defined by reference to the current scholarly literature and then illuminated by instances from the Canon.

The Power Rapist

The power rapist is one for whom aggression in the offense "either serves to enhance the offender's sense of power, masculinity, or self-esteem, or enables him to express feelings of mastery and conquest."[23] This kind of rapist often suffers from feelings of inferiority or low self-esteem. He is particularly subject to peer pressure and can be influenced by situations that emphasize male competitiveness. The power rapist may commit his offense either alone or in groups or gangs.

Acting Alone

The rape of Lucretia was one of the most notorious sex offenses of all time, a crime that was recorded by Livy, used by Ovid, and later adopted by Shakespeare as the basis for his long poem *The Rape of Lucrece*. Lucretia (Lucrece) was a chaste Roman woman and the wife of Collatine, a distinguished general who was away with the army. She was raped in her own bed by her houseguest Tarquin, son of the Roman king of the same name. According to Roman legend, this crime contributed to the downfall of the monarchy and establishment of the Roman republic.

What could have motivated a prince to commit such a shocking crime? He was hardly the overcompensating, disempowered figure one might expect to commit a power rape. And yet, early in the poem Shakespeare hints at Tarquin's discontent, in spite of his lofty political status, and at its source. While in camp with the army, Collatine one evening had bragged about his wife to a group that included Tarquin. He told them of her beauty, her chastity, and her fidelity to him. He even went so far as to claim to be more fortunate than a king:

> For he the night before, in Tarquin's tent,
> Unlock'd the treasure of his happy state;
> What priceless wealth of the heavens had him lent
> In the possession of his beauteous mate;
> Reckoning his fortune at such high-proud rate,
>   That kings might be espoused to more fame,
>   But king nor peer to such a peerless dame.
>
>   (15-21)

While there seems to have been no particular animus between Collatine and Tarquin, Collatine should have realized that this direct comparison would be likely to evoke resentment. It is soon revealed that Collatine had indeed touched upon a sensitive point, for in one respect Tarquin's life was lacking:

> Perchance his boast of Lucrece' sovereignty
> Suggested this proud issue of a king;
> For by our ears our hearts oft tainted be:
> Perchance that envy of so rich a thing,
> Braving compare, disdainfully did sting
>   His high-pitch'd thoughts, that meaner men should vaunt
>   That golden hap which their superiors want.
>
>   (36-42)

Love and happiness were what Tarquin's life lacked, and not even a king's son could command them. Perhaps Tarquin's feelings of inadequacy would not have spurred him on to action had Collatine not brought up the matter in such a challenging fashion.

An instance of more explicit male competitiveness almost leading to rape is found in *Cymbeline*. Posthumus, a banished Englishman, goes to Rome, where – in the company of men of various nationalities – he makes elaborate boasts about his wife Imogen's beauty, her chastity, and her fidelity to him. Iachimo, an unscrupulous Italian, makes a wager with Posthumus that he can seduce Imogen back in England. When Imogen rejects Iachimo and he seems about to lose the wager, he hides in a trunk in her bedroom and emerges in the middle of the night. His intent is to use his observations concerning the surroundings – along with a bracelet he removes from Imogen's arm as she sleeps – as evidence to support his false claim that he succeeded in seducing her.

Iachimo delivers a soliloquy while standing over Imogen's bed. He compares himself to Tarquin and Imogen to Venus. He longs to touch and kiss her but restrains himself. Having memorized the furnishings and decorations, he turns his attention to Imogen herself:

> IACHIMO: Ah, but some natural notes about her body,
> Above ten thousand meaner movables
> Would testify, to enrich mine inventory.
> . . . .
> On her left breast
> A mole cinque-spotted, like the crimson drops
> I' the bottom of a cowslip: here's a voucher,
> Stronger than ever law could make: this secret
> Will force him think I have pick'd the lock and ta'en
> The treasure of her honour.
>
> (2.2.28-30, 37-42)

Iachimo has violated Imogen's privacy if not her honor, and the image of him standing lustfully over her bed is haunting. However, unlike Tarquin, he is able to control his physical impulses. Instead of indulging himself sexually, he derives his pleasure from anticipating the reaction of Posthumus to the false report that he, Iachimo, has won the wager.

Lucrece and Imogen were unavailable to Tarquin and Iachimo because they were both married. More to the point, both women became targets precisely because they were unavailable and therefore presented a challenge to their assailants (with the witting or unwitting complicity of their husbands). In II Samuel, a man is portrayed as desiring a woman who is unavailable to him for a different reason — because they are too closely related. Amnon, the eldest son of David, has fallen in love with his half-sister Tamar, the daughter of David by a different mother. His longing for her is so acute that it has made him sick. As a virgin, Tamar is closely guarded, and Amnon thinks it impossible for him "to do anything to her" (13.1-2).

Amnon's friend Jonadab, "a very subtil man," asks Amnon why he is so "lean" day after day. When Amnon tells him the reason, Jonadab suggests a scheme to give Amnon access to Tamar: Amnon should pretend that he is sick and stay in bed. He should ask his father David to send his sister Tamar to prepare food for him. Amnon follows Jonadab's advice, and when he is alone with Tamar, he takes hold of her and says, "Come lie with me, my sister." She answers him, "Nay, my brother, do not force me; for no such thing ought to be done in Israel: do not thou this folly" (13.11-12). Amnon, however, will not listen and, being stronger than she, forces her and lies with her. Then Amnon hates her exceedingly and sends her away, in spite of her protestation that his sending her away under the circumstances is a greater evil than what he has already done to her.

Amnon obviously felt disempowered by a system that would not permit him to have sexual relations with the woman he desired because she was his half-sister. He chose to assert himself by gaining physical mastery over her through rape, since he could not possess her under the religious laws of Israel at the time. He decided to take this action only after it was suggested by a male friend who obviously had influence over him. Because this plausible suggestion removed Amnon's flimsy excuse that he could not gain access to Tamar, he must have felt pressure to follow it. The only alternative would have been to admit to Jonadab that he was powerless to have the woman he desired.

An instance of attempted rape by a powerless creature who is unwilling to accept his station in life is found in *The Tempest*. Caliban, the illegitimate son of a witch and a devil, is a native of the remote island to which the magician Prospero is driven in exile from his post as Duke of Milan. Prospero initially befriends the beastlike Caliban and allows him to live in his house. Prospero's maiden daughter Miranda teaches him to speak and function as a human being, but Caliban responds by trying to rape her. Prospero therefore has Caliban enslaved and treats him as the brutish creature he has shown himself to be. Caliban remains unremorseful: "Would't had been done!/Thou didst prevent me; I had peopled else/This isle with Calibans" (1.2.349-351). He later plots unsuccessfully with some shipwrecked sailors to overthrow Prospero and rule the island.

Caliban had no more hope of becoming the lover of Miranda than Tarquin had of the married Lucrece, Iachimo of the married Imogen, or Amnon of his half-sister Tamar. The unavailability of these women became a symbol of failure to these men, who sought to prove their virility and overcome the futility of their situations by resorting to rape. Competitiveness with other men is a motivating factor for all except Caliban, who has not enjoyed the "benefits" of male social interaction.

In Groups or Gangs

Power rapists often commit their offenses in groups or gangs, and such rapes are motivated by an extension of the male competitiveness among solo rapists described above. Gang rapes are the product of both internal motives and group dynamics.[24] Some feminists have termed such group dynamics a form of male bonding.[25] The phenomenon has been described as follows: "One of the unique dynamics in gang rape is the experience of rapport, fellowship, and cooperation with the co-offenders. The offender is not only interacting with the victim, he is also interacting with his co-offenders. In fact, it appears that he is using the victim as a vehicle for interacting with the other men. He is behaving, or performing, in accordance with what he feels is expected of him by them."[26]

Antisocial gangs engaging in crime sprees will be considered in the section on impulsive rapists below. Our concern here is with power rapists for whom the gang rape takes on a sportive atmosphere. Ordinarily the victim in such cases is not brutally beaten, and no permanent physical injuries are inflicted. Thus the perpetrators may feel justified in viewing their own behavior as less than heinous.

A scene from the *Odyssey* often expurgated from school texts depicts the gods as cavorting in an atmosphere conducive to gang rape. In book 8, Hephaestus has learned of the adulterous affair between his wife, Aphrodite, and Ares. He devises a scheme to catch them in the act by dropping a net over them from which they cannot escape. When the trick works and word of it spreads on Mount Olympus, the gods (but not the goddesses) gather to get a look:

> Now the goddesses abode for shame each in her own house, but the gods, the givers of good things, stood in the gateway; and unquenchable laughter arose among the blessed gods as they saw the craft of wise Hephaestus. (8.324-327)

Apollo then asks Hermes whether he would be willing, although he is ensnared in a net, to lie with golden Aphrodite. To be sure, Apollo's question is a hypothetical one rather than an invitation.[27] Nevertheless, when Hermes responds enthusiastically that he would be thrilled at the prospect, even if he were tied up three times and all the goddesses were looking on, Poseidon steps in to put a stop to the fun and sternly orders Hephaestus to set Ares free.

The "unquenchable laughter" of the gods in this scene sounds much like the atmosphere that might obtain when things get out of hand in a bar or pool room. A celebrated 1983 episode in which a woman was repeatedly raped on a pool table at Big Dan's Tavern in New Bedford, Massachusetts – while at least fifteen male patrons looked on and cheered – occurred in just such an environment.[28]

Another scene with overtones of gang rape is found in *Troilus and Cressida*. Cressida, lover of the Trojan prince Troilus, has been given to the Greeks in exchange for a prisoner. The Trojan warrior Diomedes takes her to the Greek camp, where she is welcomed by Agamemnon. When Nestor observes that their general has saluted her with a kiss, Ulyssess responds, "Yet is the kindness but particular. 'Twere better she were kissed in general" (4.5.20-21). Nestor takes Ulysses' advice by kissing Cressida himself, followed by Achilles, who says that he will take that winter (the elderly Nestor's kiss) from her lips. Patroclus and Menelaus follow in turn. Ulysses then banters with Cressida about the terms of his kiss before Diomedes breaks in to spirit her away. Given the location of the scene (in a military camp) and the well-known practices of both armies with respect to captive women, the passage has clear overtones of gang rape.

The Anger Rapist

A second type of rapist recognized in the psychodynamic literature is the anger rapist. This type commits rape out of anger toward women and seeks in his offense to hurt, humiliate, and degrade his victim.[29]

While a rapist in this category may be generally misogynistic, his specific crime is often motivated by anger at a particular woman. He may be seeking revenge against a woman who has spurned him as a suitor or shown a preference for another man. In today's world, a woman who is raped by an ex-husband or a former boyfriend is typically the victim of this type of rapist. Unlike the power rapist, the anger rapist tends to be a man who might have been a lover of his victim had the woman not chosen otherwise; in contrast, the power rapist is typically responding to a societal situation that has rendered the woman unavailable to him by any legitimate means, regardless of her personal choice.

In *The Two Gentlemen of Verona,* Valentine has left Verona and is pursuing his education in Milan, where he has fallen in love with Silvia. Valentine's close friend Proteus at first remains in Verona because of his reluctance to leave his girlfriend, Julia, but on orders of his father he eventually travels to Milan to join Valentine. The unscrupulous Proteus takes a liking to Silvia and tries to seduce her. She resists and chastises him for his faithlessness to both his love for Julia and his friendship with Valentine. This exchange then follows:

PROTEUS: Nay, if the gentle spirit of moving words
Can no way change you to a milder form,
I'll woo you like a soldier, at arms' end,
And love you 'gainst the nature of love, – force ye.

SILVIA: O heaven!

PROTEUS: I'll force thee yield to my desire.

(5.4.55-59)

At this point Valentine enters and orders Proteus to let Silvia go. He denounces his friend's treachery in such heartbroken terms that Proteus is reduced to begging for forgiveness.

Why does Proteus attempt to rape Silvia? He is obviously competing with Valentine for her affection, even though he already has a secure relationship with Julia. This competitiveness seems to have originated with his father's having compelled him to go away to school as Valentine did, in spite of Proteus's reluctance. (An uncle's words of disdainful comparison of the two young men at 1.3.1-44, although not directly heard by Proteus, must have reverberated in Veronese gossip.) In any event, Proteus is angered by Silvia's continuing preference for Valentine, and the only way for him to succeed in this competition –

while also punishing Silvia for her uncooperativeness — is to take her by force.

An anger rapist with a more explicit grievance against his victim is found in *Cymbeline*. Imogen, the king's daughter, has rejected Cloten, the queen's son, and has instead married Posthumus, a poor but worthy nobleman. When Posthumus is exiled to Italy, Cloten hires musicians to serenade Imogen, and he professes his love to her. When he goes so far as to malign Posthumus's low station, she responds derisively:

> IMOGEN: Profane fellow!
> Wert thou the son of Jupiter and no more
> But what thou art besides, thou wert too base
> To be his groom.
> . . . .
> He never can meet more mischance than come
> To be but named of thee. His meanest garment,
> That ever hath but clipp'd his body, is dearer
> In my respect than all the hairs above thee,
> Were they all made such men.
>
> (2.3.129-132, 137-141)

Cloten is stunned by Imogen's scornful comparison. In a daze, he repeats her allusion to Posthumus's garment four separate times. Imogen dismisses him as a fool and prattles on about a bracelet she has lost. He finally recaptures her attention:

> CLOTEN: You have abused me:
> "His meanest garment!"
>
> IMOGEN: Ay, I said so, sir:
> If you will make't an action, call witness to't.
>
> CLOTEN: I will inform your father.
>
> IMOGEN: Your mother too:
> She's my good lady and will conceive, I hope,
> But the worst of me. So I leave you, sir,
> To the worst of discontent.
>
> CLOTEN: I'll be revenged:
> "His meanest garment!" Well.
>
> (2.3.155-161)

Cloten is so enraged by Imogen's insult that it comes as no surprise when the revenge he later plots is almost comically malevolent. Having dispatched his servant Pisanio to acquire one of Posthumus's garments, he recalls the sting he felt ("the bitterness of it I now belch from my heart") and muses aloud about his plan for revenge:

CLOTEN: With that suit upon my back, will I ravish her: first kill him, and in her eyes; there shall she see my valour, which will then be a torment to her contempt. He on the ground, my speech of insultment ended on his dead body, and when my lust hath dined, – which, as I say, to vex her I will execute in the clothes that she so praised, – to the court I'll knock her back, foot her home again. She hath despised me rejoicingly, and I'll be merry in my revenge.

(3.5.137, 141-150)

This passage demonstrates a confluence of violent elements ("I'll knock her back, foot her home again") and sex ("when my lust hath dined"). Cloten seems to want to please Imogen sexually, and he quirkily believes that he might attain this goal by wearing Posthumus's clothes "that she so praised." And yet he abruptly shifts to threats of violence and ends on a note of revenge. Cloten's intent to degrade and humiliate Imogen as retaliation for having been spurned makes him a good example of an anger rapist.

The Sadistic Rapist

According to the psychodynamic literature, the third type of rapist, the sadistic rapist, "is easily identified by his sexual arousal in response to violence and the very brutal, and possibly bizarre, nature of his assaults."[30] Crimes of this kind may not be so easy to identify in the prudish literary works of the past, which do not ordinarily describe the perpetrator's sexual arousal or specifics of the sex act in the graphic detail to which modern audiences have become accustomed. Nevertheless, one rape in Shakespeare appears to have been committed with sadistic motivation.

In *Titus Andronicus,* Tamora, the queen of the Goths who has been captured by the Romans, vows revenge against Titus Andronicus, the Roman general who ordered that one of her sons be killed. Even though she is a captive, Tamora marries the new Roman emperor Saturninus and thus gets an opportunity to plot her revenge. Tamora is advised by the black Moor Aaron, with whom she is having an adulterous affair. She has two vicious grown sons, Chiron and Demetrius, whom she employs in her plot.

Both Chiron and Demetrius claim to be in love with Titus's only daughter, Lavinia, who has wed the emperor's younger brother, Bassianus. When they argue over her in Aaron's presence, he suggests that they collaborate rather than compete, so that both can get what they desire:

> AARON: 'Tis policy and stratagem must do
> That you affect; and so must you resolve,
> That what you cannot as you would achieve,
> You must perforce accomplish as you may.
>
> (2.1.104-107)

Aaron notes that the emperor and his party are planning a hunt, which will provide a good setting "for rape and villainy":

> AARON: Single you thither then this dainty doe,
> And strike her home by force, if not by words:
> This way, or not at all, stand you in hope.
>
> (2.1.117-119)

Aaron plants the idea of raping Lavinia in the brothers' minds, but what they eventually do goes far beyond a simple sex offense. During the hunt, Lavinia and Bassianus have the misfortune to come across Aaron and Tamora lying together in the woods. When Tamora's sons arrive on the scene, she instructs them to kill Lavinia and Bassianus, lest they tell what they have seen. The sons kill Bassianus forthwith, but they prefer to rape Lavinia first. Tamora agrees to this plan but cautions them to be sure to kill Lavinia thereafter in order to silence her. Lavinia is last seen being dragged away by Chiron and Demetrius, to Tamora's pronouncement, "Let my spleenful sons this trull deflower" (2.3.191). At the beginning of the following scene, when the three reappear, Lavinia has been not only raped, but mutilated: both of her hands and her tongue have been chopped off. Chiron and Demetrius taunt her and seem confident that she will not be able to communicate to anyone the identity of her assailants.

Because the actual rape and mutilation are not described, it is impossible to assess the brothers' mental state while they committed the crimes. More specifically, it is not known whether they were sexually aroused by doing violence to the victim before raping her. Evidence for sadistic motivation must be sought in comments made in scenes before and after the rape. For example, when Aaron first suggests that the brothers rape Lavinia, Demetrius says, "*Sit fas aut nefas,* till I find the stream/To cool this heat, a charm to calm these fits,/*Per Styga, per manes vehor"* (2.1.133-135).[31] These lines suggest that he is overcome by fits of uncontrollable sexual passion. After the brothers have killed Bassianus, Chiron adds a touch of the bizarre by suggesting that they "make his dead trunk pillow to our lust" (2.3.130). And their taunting Lavinia after the mutilation is cold-blooded. These bits of circumstantial evidence are compatible with a conclusion of sadistic motivation.

Sadistic rapists ordinarily commit their crimes alone rather than in pairs or groups.[32] However, Chiron and Demetrius do not have well-developed separate personalities, and they seem to act in concert in an undifferentiated way. It would not seem inappropriate, therefore, to ascribe the same sadistic motivation to the two brothers acting in tandem.

The mutilation of Lavinia was intended to shock and horrify the audience in Shakespeare's time. Even in our own shockproof age, cutting off parts of a victim's body is almost too horrible to imagine. In an infamous California case, Lawrence Singleton was convicted of having raped a teenage hitchhiker and hacked off both her forearms during the attack. So outraged were the surrounding communities in northern California that, when Singleton was paroled in the mid-1980s, he was literally driven out of town after town when his presence became known. Authorities were unsuccessful in relocating him in California, Florida, and Nevada. He eventually returned to the prison and spent his remaining time on parole in relative peace behind the walls of San Quentin.[33]

The Impulsive Rapist

A final type of rapist described in the psychodynamic literature is the impulsive rapist, for whom sexual offenses are only one component of an impulsive, antisocial lifestyle resulting in a long criminal record.[34] The impulsive rapist does not ordinarily set out specifically to harm his victim, but he may do so in connection with other offenses. An impulsive rapist often commits his offenses as part of a marauding gang.

One might expect to find antecedents of this kind of rape in the wartime practices of pillaging soldiers, and the *Iliad* is replete with examples. In book 2, the Greek forces are debating whether to give up the campaign against the Trojans and return home. Nestor attempts to rally the troops by making reference to the divine signs of ultimate victory that were given when the Greeks first set sail. He concludes by alluding to two grievances that he knows will especially motivate them:

"No one should therefore think of returning until he has avenged Paris the Trojans' theft of Queen Helen, and whatever personal discomfort he may have experienced, by enjoying the wife of some Trojan enemy" (2.354-356).[35] Captive women were viewed as part of the spoils of war.

A different kind of violence manifesting itself in gang rape can be seen in Judges. A Levite and his concubine are traveling home to the hills of Ephraim from the house of her father. They decide to seek shelter for the night in Gibeah, a town of the tribe of Benjamin. As they are standing in the town plaza, an old man passes by and learns that they are journeying to the hills of Ephraim, his own homeland. He invites them to his house for the evening and treats them as his guests.

Soon a gang of ruffians ("sons of Belial") surround the house and demand that the old man send out the Levite "that we may know him." The Hebrew verb used in this expression (yd') is often used euphemistically for sexual intercourse.[36] That this is the intended meaning here becomes obvious when the old man responds: "Nay, my brethren, nay, I pray you, do not so wickedly; seeing that this man is come into mine house, do not this folly. Behold, here is my daughter, a maiden, and his concubine; them I will bring out now, and humble ye them, and do with them what seemeth good unto you; but unto this man do not so vile a thing" (19.22-24).

When the ruffians will not listen, the Levite brings forth his concubine and turns her over to them. "And they knew her, and abused her all the night until the morning: and when the day began to spring, they let her go" (19.25). The concubine makes it back to the doorstep of the house where the Levite is staying but collapses there. When the Levite comes out the next morning to leave, he orders her to get up, but she is dead. He carries her body home with him and hacks it into twelve pieces, which he sends throughout Israel as a call for vengeance against the Benjaminites. The incident is presented as the spark that sets off a civil war. Nuances concerning the ruffians' grievances against the old man (a resident alien who lived among the Benjaminites but did not belong to that tribe) and the Levite are beyond the scope of this work. What is important in this context is that those grievances provoked violence of which a brutal gang rape was but one manifestation.

An instance of anticipated rape by a an antisocial group who live beyond the reaches of the law is found in *Pericles*. Diozyma, who raised Pericles' daughter Marina but later turned against her, has dispatched Leonine to kill her. Leonine leads Marina to the seashore to carry out his assignment, for which he has obvious distaste. He is momentarily relieved when she is kidnapped by a band of pirates. He then ruminates aloud about the consequences for him:

LEONINE: These roguing thieves serve the great pirate Valdes;
            And they have seized Marina. Let her go:
            There's no hope she will return. I'll swear she's dead,
            And thrown into the sea. But I'll see further:
            Perhaps they will but please themselves upon her,
            Not carry her aboard. If she remain,
            Whom they have ravish'd must by me be slain.

                                                   (4.1.97-103)

Marina is in fact carried away by the pirates, thus relieving Leonine of his nefarious duty. Contrary to his not unreasonable expectation, however, the pirates do not rape her. Instead, they sell her into prostitution.

American society is no longer threatened by pillaging soldiers, ruffians from competing tribes, or marauding bands of pirates. Nevertheless, the public is not free from criminals who are antisocial and prone to outbreaks of random violence. Such violence can victimize men as well as women. When women are the victims, gang rape is often one vicious form of the group violence. When a gang of teenagers went on a "wilding" attack in Central Park in April 1989, a young woman jogger was gang-raped and savagely beaten almost to death. The same gang also victimized men and vandalized property — whatever lay in their path. These were impulsive rapists of the crudest sort.[37]

"Against Her Will and Without Her Consent"

According to the traditional legal formulation, for a sexual act to constitute rape, it must have been committed against the woman's will and without her consent. Examining the issue of consent requires that the focus be shifted from the rapist to the victim. Therefore, psychodynamic theories will be less relevant than sociocultural theories, which treat rape as the consequence of women's subordinate role in society generally. Among the rape-related issues that have concerned sociocultural theorists in recent years has been "date rape" or "acquaintance rape." In such cases, the woman's consent, or lack thereof, is ordinarily the sole issue in dispute. According to feminist critics, men who commit date rape are too often viewed as merely having acted opportunistically or having been more aggressive than they normally are, rather than as being criminals deserving of punishment.[38]

Examination of the issue of consent must begin with recognition that the Canon contains some material dating from archaic eras in which women had no right to self-determination in sexual matters. The following discussion of the issue of consent must be viewed against the backdrop of ancient patriarchal cultures whose mores with respect to women's sexuality are shocking to modern sensibilities. Much of the ancient Hebrew law of rape developed around violation of the father's or husband's property right in a woman's chastity rather than around the woman's right to give or withhold consent to sexual relations.[39] For example, in Deuteronomy the law provides that, if a man rapes a virgin who is not betrothed, he must make payment to her father and marry her: "Because he hath humbled her, he may not put her away all his days" (22.28-29). In two separate places in the Hebrew scriptures, there are similar stories of fathers who offer virgin daughters to a gang of ruffians ("to do with as they wished") in lieu of houseguests.[40] In these passages, the issue of the daughters' consent is not even mentioned.

With Shakespeare, one is much closer to the modern era, in which women have autonomous choice in romantic and sexual matters, with all the attendant complications. The following sections will examine several Shakespearean passages that relate to the difficult questions of how women communicate their consent or nonconsent to sex and how men interpret those communications. A tradition that encouraged women to "play hard to get" during courtship led to misinterpretation of women's stated wishes concerning sex, which in turn has contributed to the contemporary problem of date rape.

Playing Hard To Get

The traditional expectation that women should play hard to get with potential suitors seems not far removed from the era in which women were viewed as their father's property. A young woman who teased and put off her suitors was likely to be more highly valued than one who was easy or even loose. And a father's role in such matters was to coach his daughter to act in a way that would further his economic interests.

In *The Tempest*, Prospero has used his magical powers to have his daughter Miranda and the shipwrecked young nobleman Ferdinand fall in love at first sight. Although he is delighted by the success of his efforts, Prospero pretends to be harsh with the young couple. In an aside, he gives his reason for this apparent grumpiness: "They are both in either's powers; but this swift business/I must uneasy make, lest too light winning/Make the prize light" (1.2.450-452). Later in the play, when Miranda finally professes her love to Ferdinand, she hesitates when she remembers the instructions she has been given by her father:

MIRANDA: But, by my modesty,
            The jewel in my dower, I would not wish
            Any companion in the world but you,
            Nor can imagination form a shape,
            Besides yourself, to like of. But I prattle
            Something too wildly and my father's precepts
            I therein do forget.

                                                    (3.1.53-59)

Juliet, on the other hand, rebels against her father's precepts. Her father has arranged for her to marry Paris, a nobleman considerably her elder. Juliet appears obedient until she attends a masked ball and becomes enamored of Romeo. Later that evening, she goes out on her balcony and speaks aloud her new infatuation, when suddenly Romeo steps out of the dark and addresses her. Juliet is both exhilarated that Romeo has sought her out and embarrassed that he heard her earlier pronouncements:

JULIET: O gentle Romeo,
            If thou dost love, pronounce it faithfully:
            Or if thou think'st I am too quickly won,
            I'll frown and be perverse and say thee nay,
            So thou wilt woo; but else, not for the world.
            . . . .
            I should have been more strange, I must confess,
            But that thou overheard'st, ere I was ware,
            My true love's passion: therefore pardon me,
            And not impute this yielding to light love,
            Which the dark night hath so discovered.

                                            (2.2.93-97, 102-106)

Even though Juliet does not accept her father's choice for her husband, at the age of fourteen she has obviously been well coached in how a young woman should deal with suitors. Yet she also has trouble following these precepts, which she violates even as she gives voice to them.

Troilus and Cressida presents not virginal young daughters but a mature and jaded woman of wiles. Cressida is able to speak from experience and calculates her every move in her relationship with men. Early in the play, her uncle Pandarus visits Cressida to speak on behalf of the Trojan prince Troilus as a potential lover. When he leaves, Cressida says in a soliloquy that she is interested but will not show it. She knows from experience that men's treatment of women differs greatly before and after they have won what they desire. She reasons that it is therefore in a woman's interest to hold off for as long as possible: "Then though my heart's content firm love doth bear,/Nothing of that shall from mine eyes appear" (1.2.320-321). Later in the play, when she submits to Troilus and confesses that she has loved him for many months, he asks why she was so hard to win. Her explanation is so confused that it seems almost designed to negate any argument that women should have the right to consent:

> CRESSIDA: Hard to seem won: but I was won, my lord,
> With the first glance that ever – pardon me –
> If I confess much, you will play the tyrant.
> I love you now; but not, till now, so much
> But I might master it: in faith, I lie;
> My thoughts were like unbridled children grown
> Too headstrong for their mother. See, we fools!
> Why have I blabb'd? who shall be true to us,
> When we are so unsecret to ourselves?
>
> (3.2.125-133)

Cressida's conflict over revealing her true feelings to Troilus is obviously so great that she is unable to offer a coherent response to his simple question.

Cressida's duplicity gets her into further difficulties later in the play when the Greek warrior Diomedes tries to seduce her while she is being held in the Greek camp. Cressida shows Diomedes a sleeve Troilus gave her and says that the man who gave her the sleeve loved her. Thersites, the coarse common soldier who was fond of ridiculing the Greek leaders, is eavesdropping on the conversation. When Cressida announces that she will not meet Diomedes the following night and asks him to visit her no more, Thersites comments, "Now she sharpens: well said, whetstone!" (5.2.75). Thersites not only realizes that Cressida's words will whet Diomedes' desire by offering him a challenge but also implies that Cressida spoke the words for precisely this purpose. This is a classic situation of a woman depicted as saying the opposite of what she desires in the hopes of attaining it. Cressida's motivation is not that of the virginal daughter following her father's directives to enhance her value in the marriage market, but that of the mature woman teasing her suitor by playing upon the well-known predisposition of fighting men to respond to a challenge.

The male perspective on such gamesmanship is clearly seen in a passage from *The Two Gentlemen of Verona*. The Duke of Milan, a widower, has discovered that, contrary to his wishes, his daughter Silvia is about to elope with Valentine. The duke tricks Valentine into revealing his elaborate plot (which involves reaching Silvia's balcony with a rope ladder) by soliciting advice from Valentine on the unwritten rules of courtship. The duke pretends to have romantic interest in a woman who has rejected a gift he sent her. Valentine offers the duke the following advice:

> VALENT.:   A woman sometimes scorns what best contents her.
> Send her another; never give her o'er;
> For scorn at first makes after-love the more.
> If she do frown, 'tis not in hate of you.
> But rather to beget more love in you:
> If she do chide, 'tis not to have you gone;
> For why, the fools are mad, if left alone.
> Take no repulse, whatever she doth say;
> For 'get you gone,' she doth not mean 'away!'
>
> (3.1.93-101)

Valentine's advice goes beyond mere persistence. He recommends that the woman's words not be taken at face value but be given a contrary meaning. His justification for this recommendation is simple: women are "fools" who would be miserable if their own words were honored.

When Does "No" Mean "Yes"?

The step from playing hard to get to saying no and meaning yes is a short one. If women in the past were conditioned culturally to present as great a challenge as possible to their suitors, it became necessary for them sometimes to speak otherwise than their true feelings dictated. This necessity gradually became crystallized in the one-word response required when a man attempted verbally or physically to initiate intimate contact: women said no sometimes when they really meant yes. A man who discovered this dissemblance was put in the difficult position of having to guess the woman's true desires.

This unsatisfactory situation has become the focal point of controversy in recent years with the date rape controversy, in which a man has sometimes argued that, even though a woman said no, he thought that she really meant yes. Until recently, such legal arguments were often accepted by courts of law, and major law review articles from the 1950s and 1960s actually contributed to their acceptance. For example, a 1966 article in the *Stanford Law Review* stated, "Although a woman may desire sexual intercourse, it is customary for her to say, 'no, no, no' (although meaning 'yes, yes, yes') and to expect the male to be the aggressor.... It is always difficult in rape cases to determine whether the female really meant 'no'.... The problem of determining what the female 'really meant' is compounded when, in fact, the female had no clearly determined attitude – that is, her attitude was one of ambivalence."[41] A number of Shakespearean passages demonstrate the long history of a stereotype of women as not meaning what they say, if indeed they even know what they mean.

A woman's perspective on the question is presented in *The Two Gentlemen of Verona*. Julia is discussing the merits of her various suitors with her maidservant Lucetta, who produces a letter to Julia from Proteus. Julia in fact loves Proteus, but to hide her true feelings, she pretends to scorn the letter and refuses to read it. Lucetta leaves so Julia can think it over, and Julia chides Lucetta in a soliloquy for not having insisted that she read it:

> JULIA: And yet I would I had o'erlooked the letter:
> It were a shame to call her back again
> And pray her to a fault for which I chid her.
> What a fool is she, that knows I am a maid,
> And would not force the letter to my view!
> Since maids, in modesty, say "no" to that
> Which they would have the profferer construe "ay."
>
> (1.2.50-56)

Julia's vacillating and disingenuous conduct is enough to confuse anyone, yet she blames Lucetta for not having seized upon the stereotype of how maids are supposed to act and thus reversed the plain meaning of her words.

Shakespeare's poem *The Passionate Pilgrim* gives a male perspective. An older man is giving a younger man advice on how to court a woman. In one stanza he comments upon women's "wiles and guiles" as follows:

> The wiles and guiles that women work,
> Dissembled with an outward show,
> The tricks and toys that in them lurk,
> The cock that treads them shall not know.
>   Have you not heard it said full oft,
>   A woman's nay doth stand for nought?

(19.37-42)

That such an opinion of a woman's "nay" was widespread among men can also be seen in *Richard III*. Richard and Buckingham are plotting to win the throne for Richard. Buckingham gives Richard instructions about how to handle a public event at which Buckingham will urge a "reluctant" Richard to accept the crown. Buckingham advises Richard not to be easily won: "Play the maid's part, still answer nay, and take it" (3.7.50-51). This suggests that a woman's words may be disregarded and her true wishes ascertained by seeing whether she offers physical resistance to a man's initiatives.

"Utmost Resistance"

The traditional legal requirement that a woman demonstrate her "utmost resistance" in order to make out a claim of rape makes no sense from a number of perspectives. For one thing, most women are smaller and weaker than most men, thus rendering physical resistance in most cases futile. Indeed, one might posit a supposedly exaggerated example of a heavyweight boxing champion's raping a petite woman less than half his size, except that the case unfortunately would not be hypothetical.[42]

In *King John*, Philip is engaged in a dispute with his half-brother Robert Faulconbridge over their inheritance. Philip is the elder, but Robert claims that Philip was fathered by someone other than their presumed father, Sir Robert Faulconbridge. Philip finally confronts his mother, Lady Faulconbridge, on the question of his parentage. She reluctantly tells him the truth:

LADY F.: King Richard Coeur-de-Lion was thy father:
          By long and vehement suit I was seduced
          To make room for him in my husband's bed:
          Heaven lay not my transgression to my charge!
          Thou art the issue of my dear offence,

Which was so strongly urged past my defence.

(1.1.253-258)

The precise nature of Lady Faulconbridge's "defence" is not revealed. Whether verbal or physical, resistance to the sexual advances of a king must have seemed as difficult for a subject to make as resistance to Mike Tyson.

Another objection to the physical resistance requirement is that it obviously increases the woman's risk of bodily injury or even death. As one commentator put it, "[No other offense has] required victims to respond with physical resistance, and thus to risk intensifying their injuries in order to prove them."[43] The requirement of physical resistance puts the victim in the ridiculous position of having to choose between the risk of increased injury, possibly even death, and the risk that she will be unable to make out a legal claim of rape. In *The Rape of Lucrece,* the risks of resistance are even greater: the ordinary fear of death is compounded by the rapist's threat to leave his victim's body in circumstances that would compromise her honor:

> The precedent whereof in Lucrece view,
> Assail'd by night with circumstances strong
> Of present death, and shame that might ensue
> By that her death, to do her husband wrong:
> Such danger to resistance did belong,
>   That dying fear through all her body spread;
>   And who cannot abuse a body dead?

(1261-1267)

Although the requirement of utmost resistance (which reflects the literary theme of death before dishonor) has been replaced in most jurisdictions by a requirement of "reasonable resistance," the underlying question remains: why is physical resistance required at all? The answer to this question lies partially in the alleged unreliability of women's words, discussed above. Moreover, some feminist legal scholars see the requirement as a way of ensuring male access: a man may simply ignore a woman's words and proceed with impunity unless and until she literally fights him off.[44]

In *Cymbeline,* Posthumus has a bet with the unscrupulous Italian Iachimo that Iachimo will not be able to seduce his wife Imogen back in England. When Iachimo returns from England with a false report that he has won the wager, including information that appears to bear out his claim, Posthumus is devastated. In a soliloquy, he tries to assuage his anger and grief by imagining the circumstances of the seduction:

POST.:   Perchance he spoke not, but,
          Like a full-acorn'd boar, a German one,
          Cried "O!" and mounted; found no opposition
          But what he look'd for should oppose and she
          Should from encounter guard.

                                        (2.5.15-19)

Under Posthumus's imagined course of events, Iachimo did not rely on words at all but rather tested to see how much resistance resulted from his advances. The amount of resistance was no more than he expected, for Imogen simply tried to guard against "encounter," which likely meant penetration. In other words, she did not try to fight him off. He therefore decided to proceed. Under these circumstances, was Imogen seduced or was she raped? The obvious comfort her husband Posthumus takes in imagining this sequence of events leads one to conclude that he is assuming she was raped. However, her conduct might not have passed the utmost resistance test or even the reasonable resistance test imposed by courts today.

A final objection to the resistance requirement is that it is based on a male conception of how a reasonable victim would respond to a sexual attack. A male is expected to respond to aggression in the stereotypical manner of schoolboys fighting in the schoolyard; when a schoolboy is attacked, he hits or kicks back and has cuts and bruises to show for it. A woman's response is much more likely to be passive: she may be paralyzed with fear, and she very likely will cry. Susan Estrich, a feminist legal scholar who was herself a rape victim, has described the likely reaction of a woman who is raped by an abusive boyfriend: "A woman in such a position would not fight. She wouldn't fight; she might cry. Hers is the reaction of 'sissies' in playground fights.... Hers is, from my reading, the most common reaction of women to rape. It certainly was mine."[45]

The most detailed account of the reaction of a rape victim in the Canon is found in *The Rape of Lucrece*. The following two stanzas encapsulate the nature of Lucrece's response at the time of Tarquin's attack:

          Her pity-pleading eyes are sadly fixed
          In the remorseless wrinkles of his face;
          Her modest eloquence with sighs is mixed,
          Which to her oratory adds more grace.

> She puts the period often from his place;
>   And midst the sentence so her accent breaks,
>   That twice she doth begin ere once she speaks.
> . . . .
> For with the nightly linen that she wears
> He pens her piteous clamours in her head;
> Cooling his hot face in the chastest tears
> That ever modest eyes with sorrow shed.
> O, that prone lust should stain so pure a bed!
>   The spots whereof could weeping purify,
>   Her tears should drop on them perpetually.
>
> (561-567, 680-686)

Lucrece reacts in precisely the way that women critics say a typical rape victim will react, especially when she knows the assailant: with paralysis, pleading, and crying. This is quite a different response from the physical resistance to rape required by the male-dominated legal system.

The problems posed by dealing with concepts like force and resistance in a sexual context are obviously enormous. For the law simply to give credence and respect to a woman's stated wishes would be a lot simpler. If "no" were interpreted as meaning "no," a man who persisted in sexual advances after the woman has said no could be found legally culpable. In 1992, the New Jersey Supreme Court went even beyond this recommendation by interpreting that state's law of sexual assault to hold a man guilty in the absence of the use of force if he did not obtain the "affirmative and freely given permission" of the woman to the specific act of penetration. Thus in New Jersey a man may not argue that she did not say no; he must argue that she did say yes.[46]

Even such a commonsensical approach is not without its critics, however. Katie Roiphe, the author of a 1993 book on date rape, has criticized the notion of active consent as an example of political correctness gone awry: "This apparently practical, apparently clinical proscription cloaks retrograde assumptions about the way men and women experience sex. The idea that only an explicit yes means yes proposes that, like children, women have trouble communicating what they want.... Beyond its dubious premise about the limits of female communication, the idea of active consent bolsters stereotypes of men just out to 'get some,' and women who don't really want any."[47] One is led to question the capacity of the law, a blunt instrument at best, to devise a solution to this particular problem.

What Further Ordeals for the Victim?

Rape is generally said to be the most underreported felony in our society.[48] One of the probable reasons for this is the harsh treatment rape victims have often received after the crime itself. This treatment has sometimes been described as being as humiliating as the rape.[49] Following a police investigation in which the victim must repeatedly answer embarrassing questions from sometimes disbelieving police officers, her own sexual history may become public, and attempts may be made to humiliate her at the trial. The publicity that attends reporting the crime and prosecuting it in court sometimes results in the victim's loss of privacy and her stigmatization within the community. Her marital or romantic life may become damaged beyond repair. While some of these problems have been exacerbated by the mass media and public trials, still the seeds of their origin can be seen in the Canon.

Blame the Victim

The practice, if not the phraseology, of blaming the victim has been commonplace for a long time. Lucrece's mind dwells on this as she lies in bed after Tarquin has escaped:

> No man inveigh against the wither'd flower,
> But chide rough winter that the flower hath kill'd:
> Not that devour'd, but that which doth devour,
> Is worthy blame. O, let it not be hild
> Poor women's faults, that they are so fulfill'd
> > With men's abuses: those proud lords, to blame,
> > Make weak-made women tenants to their shame.
>
> (1254-1260)

Among the forms that blaming the victim may take are the charges that she "asked for it" by dressing or acting provocatively; she put herself at risk in a way that a prudent woman would not have; and she has a reputation for promiscuity. The Canon offers passages in which each of these strategies is used to place the blame on the victim.

As has already been discussed, Shakespeare created a scene with overtones of gang rape in *Troilus and Cressida* when he depicted the Greek soldiers taking turns kissing Cressida, who has been brought to the Greek camp in exchange for some prisoners. When she exits from the scene, Ulysses tells Nestor what he thinks of her in terms that almost say she asked for it:

ULYSSES: Fie, fie upon her!
There's language in her eye, her cheek, her lip,
Nay, her foot speaks; her wanton spirits look out
At every joint and motive of her body.
O, these encounterers, so glib of tongue,
That give accosting welcome ere it comes,
And wide unclasp the tables of their thoughts
To every ticklish reader! set them down
For sluttish spoils of opportunity
And daughters of the game.

(4.5.54-63)

In Ulysses' view, a woman who acts so provocatively to men in general is a slut and should be treated by the soldiers as fair game.

In the story of the rape of Dinah in Genesis, a woman is portrayed who might be accused of having recklessly put herself at risk. Dinah was the daughter of Jacob and Leah. The text says simply that she "went out to see the daughters of the land" (34.1). When a prince of the country, who was a Hivite, saw her, "he took her, and lay with her, and defiled her" (34.2). He thereupon developed a passion for her and asked his father to obtain her as his wife, even though there was no custom of intermarriage between the Hivites and the Israelites. The remainder of the story is about the elaborate plot of revenge visited upon the entire male Hivite population by Dinah's brothers.

Why did Dinah leave the protection of her own people and venture outside the Israelite settlement alone and unprotected? The text says only that she wanted to see the daughters of the land. This might have been a natural desire to satisfy her curiosity by seeking the companionship of other young women (she was apparently the only daughter in a household of sons). She may have been naive and unaware of the dangers presented for unaccompanied young women. More cynically, it might be argued that she intentionally disregarded the personal risk because she hoped to attract the attention of young men. All of this is speculation, for her motivation is simply not revealed.

Another woman who might have put herself at risk was Lavinia, the victim of the sadistic rape in *Titus Andronicus*. The woods in which Lavinia was attacked and mutilated are described in eerie terms both before and after the attack. Aaron, the evil Moor who first suggested the rape, describes the setting to Chiron and Demetrius as follows:

AARON: The forest walks are wide and spacious;
           And many unfrequented plots there are
           Fitted by kind for rape and villany:
           Single you thither then this dainty doe,
           And strike her home by force, if not by words:
           ·
           The emperor's court is like the house of Fame,
           The palace full of tongues, of eyes, and ears:
           The woods are ruthless, dreadful, deaf, and dull;
           There speak, and strike, brave boys, and take your turns;
           There serve your lusts, shadowed from heaven's eye,
           And revel in Lavinia's treasury.

                                        (2.1.114-118, 126-131)

To be sure, Lavinia had a good excuse to be in the woods (a hunting party), and she was accompanied by her husband Bassianus. However, the woods were known to be a dangerous place for both men and women, and Bassianus was murdered by the same assailants who raped Lavinia. Following the crimes, Lavinia's father, Titus, referred to the woods as "the ruthless, vast, and gloomy woods.... By nature made for murders and for rapes" (4.1.53, 58). Titus's words of remorse are hauntingly similar to words that have been spoken by victims from time immemorial: "O, had we never, never hunted there!" (4.1.56).

Yet another way victims are said to be blamed is by having their past sexual conduct questioned, as if the crime of rape is somehow less serious if the victim can be shown to have been a promiscuous woman or even a prostitute. Until recently, so much attention was paid in rape trials to the reputation of the victim that it was as if she, rather than the defendant, were on trial. As one feminist legal scholar put it, cross-examinations that were deemed relevant to the issue of consent "invited juries to believe that a woman who consented once would do so again, for anyone, anywhere, and anytime."[50] This approach distinguished rape from virtually every other crime; the law regards a murder as no less heinous because of the questionable character or low social standing of the victim.

The tendency to focus on the sexual reputation of the victim can be seen as early as the account of Dinah's rape in Genesis. When Jacob challenged his impetuous sons about the way they went about exacting vengeance on Shechem and the Hivites for the rape of their sister, the sons responded, "Should he deal with our sister as with an harlot?" (34.31). This implies that raping a harlot would have been a matter of course, and Dinah's brothers were only assuring that she not be treated as a harlot. Thus the focus seems to have been as much on the sexual reputation of the victim as on the guilt of the rapist.

In a similar but more subtle vein, Shakespeare puts special emphasis on the chastity of his two rape victims. In *The Rape of Lucrece,* Lucrece is introduced in the first stanza as "Collatine's fair love, Lucrece the chaste" (7), and her reputation for chastity is a primary theme of the poem. Similarly, in *Titus Andronicus,* Aaron says of Lavinia, "Lucrece was not more chaste/Than this Lavinia, Bassianus' love" (2.1.108-109). This emphasis on the victims' chastity seems intended to accentuate the horror of the rape, with an implied nexus to the guilt of the rapist. If in literature one exalts the victim to accentuate the rapist's guilt, in the courtroom one would conversely demean the victim to exonerate the accused. This is precisely what has happened in the traditional law of rape.

The legal system's tendency to focus on the sexual reputation of the victim has been a primary target of feminist criticism in recent years. As a result, significant reforms have been enacted to change this practice. These have not been without their critics, however. In a posthumously published work, Allan Bloom wrote, "It is an affront to raise the question of chastity as part of the criminality of rape. Whether it be a prostitute or Mother Teresa is unimportant, although not all juries have yet been persuaded of this. Rape is considered bad no longer because it assaults a weak and defenseless person's modesty, which is necessary to her exclusive attachment to the man she loves. Rape is now bad because it deprives women of power."[51]

Notwithstanding such objections, most jurisdictions have now enacted so-called rape shield statutes, which protect victims from questioning about their past sexual conduct. Shield statutes have even protected victims from questioning about their past sexual relationship with the alleged rapist himself. In *Michigan v. Lucas* (1991), the U.S. Supreme Court heard a challenge to such a statute as possibly violating the Sixth Amendment's guarantee of the rights to confront adverse witnesses and to present evidence. The Court observed that the statute in question was designed "to protect victims of rape from being exposed at trial to harassing or irrelevant questions concerning their past sexual behavior."[52] It concluded that the statute passed constitutional muster because it "represents a valid legislative determination that rape victims deserve heightened protection against surprise, harassment, and unnecessary invasions of privacy."[53] At last, the focus of rape trials can be on the guilt or innocence of the accused rather than on the victim.

The Stigma of Rape

Even after the initial trauma of a rape and the sometimes insensitive treatment accorded its victims by the criminal justice system, they face still further ordeals. Rape victims have long dreaded facing members of their community once word of the crime becomes public. This syndrome has often been referred to as the stigma of rape. It has a long history and is still prevalent. In earlier times, a different vocabulary was used to describe the syndrome: rather than "stigma" or "embarrassment," it might have been called "shame" or "disgrace." And yet the underlying meaning was the same then as it is now — the discomfort a rape victim experiences because of her realization that others' opinions of her may be affected by what has happened to her.

Shakespeare followed the Roman tradition that held that Lucretia (Lucrece) chose to kill herself rather than endure the shame of having been raped by Tarquin. Following the rape, Lucrece's thoughts turn immediately to how she will be able to face people in the light of what has happened:

> He thence departs a heavy convertite;
> She there remains a hopeless castaway;
> He in his speed looks for the morning light;
> She prays she never may behold the day,
> "For day," quoth she, "night's scapes doth open lay,
>   And my true eyes have never practised how
>   To cloak offences with a cunning brow.
>
> "They think not but that every eye can see
> The same disgrace which they themselves behold;
> And therefore would they still in darkness be,
> To have their unseen sin remain untold;
> For they their guilt with weeping will unfold,
>   And grave, like water that doth eat in steel,
>   Upon my cheeks what helpless shame I feel."
>
> (743-756)

Lucrece plaintively articulates her feelings of helpless shame to the group of nobles who will avenge the crime and then dramatically stabs herself, vowing that "no dame, hereafter living, /By my excuse shall claim excuse's giving" (1714-1715).

Lavinia likewise subscribes to the death before dishonor philosophy. Her attackers, however, have deprived her of the means of doing away with herself. Her father, Titus, thereupon takes matters into his own hands, likening himself to the Roman hero Virginius, who slew his daughter after she was raped. Titus asks the emperor Saturninus whether Virginius's action was appropriate. When Saturninus responds affirmatively, Titus asks the reason and is told:

SATURN.:   Because the girl should not survive her shame,
            And by her presence still renew his sorrows.

TITUS: A reason mighty, strong, and effectual;
            A pattern, precedent, and lively warrant,
            For me, most wretched, to perform the like.
            Die, die, Lavinia, and thy shame with thee;
            And, with thy shame, thy father's sorrow die!

                                                    (5.3.41-47)

Thus Titus was motivated by the need to end both Lavinia's shame and his own sorrow, and he achieved both objectives by a single act.

The principal ground on which the battle has been fought in recent years to eliminate the stigma of rape has been over whether or not the names of rape victims should be revealed by the media. Since the mid-1970s, two cases have been decided by the U.S. Supreme Court involving constitutional challenges to state statutes prohibiting the media from revealing the names of rape victims; in both cases, the Court held that the First Amendment's guarantee of freedom of the press was violated by the lower court's enforcement of the state statute under the circumstances of the case.[54] In one of those cases, *Cox Broadcasting Corp. v. Cohn* (1975), the rape victim did not survive, and it was her father who brought an action for damages, claiming that his own right to privacy had been invaded when a television station broadcast his daughter's name. (The question of the extent of the father's injury had not yet been determined by a Georgia court at the time of the appeal.) The Supreme Court held that the First Amendment's guarantee of freedom of the press precluded the state from making the broadcast the basis for civil liability because the information in the broadcast was obtained from public judicial records in connection with prosecution of the crime.

The opinions of representatives of the press, feminists, and victims have differed widely on whether the names of rape victims should be made public.[55] In the absence of a state statute (such as those involved in the two Supreme Court cases mentioned above), the question is a matter of journalistic ethics. The rape trial of William Kennedy Smith in Palm Beach, Florida, was a controversial case in point. Television broadcasts of the alleged victim superimposed a blue dot over her face and a beeping sound over her name whenever it was spoken. However, one major television network (NBC) and some major newspapers (including the *New York Times*) departed from their usual practice and identified the victim because of the celebrity of the case and the perceived unfairness of press coverage of questions concerning Smith's character without comparable attention to that of the victim.[56]

In the case of the Central Park jogger, on the other hand, the victim's identity was almost uniformly withheld (excepting only a few tabloids in the New York area). This unusual restraint on the part of the press, in a case that received massive national coverage, might be attributable to the extreme brutality of the crime and the importance of privacy for the victim's recovery. The fact that she was an investment banker who had attended elite schools might also have had some bearing on her treatment.[57]

Finally, some feminists have argued that withholding the names of rape victims, when names are released for all other major crimes, perpetuates the stigma of rape. To make a statement to this effect, one victim, Nancy Ziegenmeyer, went so far as to insist that the *Des Moines Register* tell her story with candor. When this action itself became a focus of controversy, she appeared on national television programs and wrote a book about her recovery.[58] Ziegenmeyer believes that public discussion can be good therapy both for individual victims and for a society that still stigmatizes rape; however, she underscores that the choice should be the victim's.[59]

The works of the Canon include all the major types of rapists recognized in the current scholarly literature. They also contain some portrayals of the reactions of rape victims drawn with sensitivity and accuracy, even by modern standards. The dilemmas and ordeals victims faced in bygone eras have been shown not to differ substantially from those that have become the focus of feminists' concern in recent years. The quandary over male-female communication and problems of blaming the victim, reflecting deeply entrenched sexist attitudes with which our society is still afflicted, can be shown to have originated from attitudes prevalent in these works. The patterns that have emerged from our new understanding of rape turn out to be patterns with a long history.

Obviously, some aspects of our contemporary problems could not have been envisioned by the authors of these texts. For example, DNA testing can now identify a rapist conclusively.[60] However, in spite of advances in some respects, the human dimension of certain problems remains as intractable as it ever was. For example, in cases where intercourse is admitted but the woman's consent is disputed, age-old problems are likely to persist.

Another example of change is the impact of AIDS, which has presented new questions of law and social policy. The possibility has been raised of equating rape and attempted murder in a way not before imagined. The AIDS epidemic has also had repercussions for the doctrine of consent in rape trials. In one recent case, a Texas grand jury refused to indict a man who said a woman had consented to sex because, as he was beginning what the prosecutors called a sexual assault, she requested that he wear a condom, and he agreed to do so. Following a public outcry, this decision was reversed by another grand jury, and the man was subsequently convicted.[61] The modern inversion of the classical literary theme death before dishonor is well demonstrated by such a case. The prevailing attitude in modern society is that any stigma that attaches to being raped is clearly preferable to death; therefore, a victim is likely to make whatever choices seem life-preserving and death-avoiding.

Unquestionably, much in the Canon's treatment of rape and rape victims is profoundly sexist and/or outdated, but there are also aspects of the Canon's treatment of this subject that reverberate closely with contemporary themes. Thus, for example, one can point to some sensitive aspects of Lucrece's reaction to being raped while recognizing the fundamental sexism and outdatedness of the death before dishonor philosophy that impels her to suicide at the end of the poem. What is important is that these works contain flashes of insight and characterization that are often astounding in their modernity as well as their artistry. This rich mixture of material, presenting many points of view, is well suited for teaching students about the realities they will face in a conflict-ridden world, while at the same time – as great literature – offering them an alluring respite from it.

Notes

1. Deborah L. Rhode. *Justice and Gender: Sex Discrimination and the Law* (Cambridge, Mass.: Harvard University Press, 1989), p. 244.

2. Susan Estrich, *Real Rape* (Cambridge, Mass.: Harvard University Press, 1987), p. 8.

3. The constitutional requirements set forth in *Furman v. Georgia*, 408 U.S. 238, 92 S. Ct. 2726, 33 L. Ed. 2d 346 (1972), led to a temporary suspension of executions in the United States and forced state legislatures to make a choice between amending their death penalty statutes to comply with the decision and abandoning the death penalty altogether.

4. *Coker v. Georgia*, 433 U.S. 584, 97 S. Ct. 2861, 58 L. Ed. 2d 207 (1977).

5. 433 U.S. at 587.

6. 433 U.S. at 597-598.

7. 433 U.S. at 603.

8. 433 U.S. at 611-612.

9. See Catharine A. MacKinnon, *Feminism Unmodified: Discourses on Life and Law* (Cambridge, Mass.: Harvard University Press, 1987), p. 87.

10. A. Nicholas Groth, director of Forensic Mental Health Associates, quoted in David Gelman, "The Mind of the Rapist," *Newsweek,* July 23, 1990, p. 47.

11. See generally chapter 3, "Men Who Rape: Psychodynamic and Sociocultural Evidence," in Linda B. Bourque, *Defining Rape* (Durham: Duke University Press, 1989).

12. Bourque, *Defining Rape,* p. 59.

13. Ibid., p. 16.

14. See, for example, MacKinnon, *Feminisim Unmodified,* pp. 86-87; Rhode, *Justice and Gender,* p. 250; and Bourque, *Defining Rape,* p. 16.

15. A. Nicholas Groth, *Men Who Rape: The Psychology of the Offender* (New York: Plenum Press, 1979), p. 5.

16. See editorial "The Castration Option," *New York Times,* March 10, 1992, p. A24.

17. Richard Seely, director of Minnesota's Intensive Treatment Program for Sexual Aggressiveness, quoted in Gelman, "The Mind of the Rapist," p. 47.

18. Susan Brownmiller, *Against Our Will: Men, Women, and Rape* (New York: Simon & Schuster, 1975), p. 380.

19. Cassandra Thomas, president of the National Coalition Against Sexual Assault, quoted in "The Castration Option," editorial in *New York Times,* March 10, 1992, p. A24.

20. Estrich, *Real Rape,* p. 82.

21. Groth, *Men Who Rape,* p. 13.

22. Raymond A. Knight, Ruth Rosenberg, and Beth Schneider, "Classification of Sexual Offenders: Perspectives, Methods, and Validation," in *Rape and Sexual Assault: A Research Handbook,* ed. Ann W. Burgess (New York: Garland, 1985), p. 253.

23. Ibid.

24. Groth, *Men Who Rape,* p. 116.

25. Brownmiller, *Against Our Will,* pp. 187 and 194.

26. Groth, *Men Who Rape,* p. 115.

27. The question (at 8.334-337) is made hypothetical by the use of the optative mood for the verb, in a future less vivid condition.

28. "The Tavern Rape: Cheers and No Help," *Newsweek,* March 21, 1983, p. 25.

29. Knight, Rosenberg, and Schneider, "Classification of Sexual Offenders," p. 253.

30. Ibid.

31. "Whether right or wrong, till I find the stream/To cool this heat, a charm to calm these fits/I am carried through Stygian waters, through the shades [i.e., through hell]."

32. Groth, *Men Who Rape,* p. 116.

33. "Not in My Town," *Newsweek,* June 1, 1987, p. 31; and "A Victim's Life Sentence," *People Weekly,* April 25, 1988, pp. 40-45.

34. Knight, Rosenberg, and Schneider, "Classification of Sexual Offenders," p. 253.

35. Translated by Robert Graves (London: Cassell, 1960). The sexual connotation of Graves's "personal discomfort" seems an appropriate translation in view of Nestor's appeal to a rudimentary sense of justice: Paris must be punished for having deprived Menelaus of his wife, and the Trojan men must be punished for having taken the Greek soldiers away from their wives for ten years. The obvious remedies are that Helen be restored to Menelaus and the Greek soldiers rape the Trojan women.

36. Robert G. Boling, *The Anchor Bible: Judges* (Garden City, N.Y.: Doubleday, 1982), p. 276.

37. "Going 'Wilding' in the City," *Newsweek,* May 8, 1989, p. 65.

38. Estrich, *Real Rape,* pp. 8-15.

39. Brownmiller, *Against Our Will,* pp. 19-20.

40. The stories are about Lot (who hosted two angels) and his two daughters at Genesis 19.1-11 and about the old man (who hosted the Levite and his concubine) and his daughter at Judges 19.22-30.

41. Roger B. Dworkin, "Resistance Standard in Rape Legislation, " *Stanford Law Review,* vol. 18, no. 4 (February 1966), p. 682. See sources cited by Susan Estrich, "Rape," *Yale Law Journal,* vol. 95, no. 6 (May 1986), pp. 1127-1129.

42. See Joyce Carol Oates, "Rape and the Boxing Ring," *Newsweek,* February 24, 1992, pp. 60-61.

43. Rhode, *Justice and Gender,* p. 247.

44. Estrich, *Real Rape,* p. 40.

45. Estrich, "Rape," p. 1111.

46. *State in Interest of M.T.S.,* 129 N.J. 422, 609 A. 2d 1266 (July 30, 1992).

47. Katie Roiphe, *The Morning After: Sex, Fear, and Feminism on Campus* (Boston: Little, Brown, 1993), pp. 62-63.

48. According to conservative estimates, up to eighty-four percent of rapes each year are never reported. See sources cited by the Majority Staff of the Senate Committee on the Judiciary, *The Response to Rape: Detours on the Road to Equal Justice* (Washington, D.C.: Senate Committee on the Judiciary, May, 1993), p. 27.

49. MacKinnon, *Feminism Unmodified,* p. 82. See also sources cited by Rhode, *Justice and Gender,* p. 248.

50. Rhode, *Justice and Gender,* p. 249.

51. Allan Bloom, *Love and Friendship* (New York: Simon & Schuster, 1993), p. 27.

52. *Michigan v. Lucas,* 111 S. Ct. 1743, 1745, 114 L. Ed. 2d 205 (1991).

53. 111 S. Ct. at 1746.

54. *Cox Broadcasting Corp. v. Cohn,* 420 U.S. 469, 95 S. Ct. 1029, 105 L. Ed. 2d 443 (1975), and *The Florida Star v. B.J.F.,* 491 U.S. 524, 109 S. Ct. 2603, 105 L. Ed. 2d 443 (1989).

55. See Barbara Kantrowitz, "Naming Names," *Newsweek,* April 29, 1991, pp. 26-32.

56. See David A. Kaplan, "Remove That Blue Dot," *Newsweek,* December 16, 1991, p. 26. While NBC reported the woman's name throughout the trial, the *New York Times* wavered, first printing her name (citing a belief that her identity had become well known) and then resuming the policy of withholding it because editors had come to believe that her privacy was being ef-

fectively shielded. The woman herself subsequently agreed to be interviewed on ABC. See Bill Carter, "Accuser in Rape Case Elects to Make Her Identity Public," *New York Times,* December 19, 1991 (L), p. B22.

57. See "The Jogger," editorial in *New York Times,* December 2, 1989, sec. 1, p. 26.

58. *Taking Back My Life* (New York: Summit Books, 1992).

59. Kantrowitz, "Naming Names," p. 31.

60. See Linda A. Fairstein, *Sexual Violence: Our War Against Rape* (New York: William Morrow, 1993), pp. 179-184.

61. "Man Is Convicted of Rape in Case Involving Condom," *New York Times,* May 14, 1993, p. A7.

3: Homophobia

THE WORD "HOMOPHOBIA" has only recently received wide currency, but the concept it embodies is of ancient lineage. In Western civilization, those who engage in homosexual practices have always been subjected to vilification and abuse. In recent years that sentiment has sometimes been said to be the last remaining "acceptable" prejudice, although in the 1990s its acceptability is beginning to wane. Increasingly, the media are bringing to public attention homophobic comments made by elected officials, in the same way that racial or ethnic slurs have been publicized in the past.[1]

"Homophobia" was originally a clinical term for a psychological disorder indicating an individual's obsession with homosexuality, caused by the repressed fear of latent homosexuality. Currently, the term has a more general meaning. It has been used primarily by supporters of gay rights, whose proffered definitions reflect their point of view. For example, the author of a book on the concept of homophobia defines it as "the irrational fear and hatred of those who love and sexually desire those of the same sex."[2] In a similar vein, the chairman of the American Psychiatric Association's committee on gay, lesbian, and bisexual issues has defined homophobia as "the irrational fear and hatred of homosexuals ... a psychological abnormality that interferes with the judgment and reliability of those affected."[3] A less sympathetic critic, calling the word a "favorite scatter-word of PC abuse," has opined, "Today it can be, and is, indiscriminately applied to anyone who shows the slightest reserve about this or that same-sexer, or disputes (however mildly) any claims of special entitlement (however extreme) made for them as a group or class."[4]

The public's increasing receptiveness to arguments favoring gay rights has resulted in a shift in the perspective of much of contemporary research. In the past, the approach of most scholars was to ask why gay people are different or what makes gay people the way they are. Now scholars are more likely to ask why society looks upon this difference as significant. Any pathology involved is increasingly likely to be viewed as that of society or of individual homophobes rather than of gay people. Recent scholars in the field have begun to ask why a difference in sexual preference is to be viewed as more significant than, say, the difference in manual preference between right-handers and left-handers or the difference in dietary preference between carnivores and vegetarians.[5]

The works of the Canon reveal the prevalence of homophobic attitudes in the various cultures they represent. Even in cultural contexts that indicate acceptance of homosexuality in elite social or artistic circles (as in Plato's Athens and Shakespeare's England), there is evidence of a popular backlash and pervasive anxiety over the morality of homosexual practices. If contemporary society continues to harbor deep-seated conflict about gay issues, one need look no further than the works of the Canon for a thorough exposition of that conflict's cultural roots.

Rationalizations

Explanations or excuses that may be superficially rational but are not the real reasons for something are rationalizations. Among the rationalizations often given for homophobic attitudes are that homosexuality is wrong because it is contrary to the word of God; homosexuality is wrong because it is contrary to nature; and homosexuality is wrong because it is contrary to social mores and/or public opinion. There are passages from the works of the Canon that depict each of these rationalizations.

Contrary to the Word of God

The most obvious example of a rationalization is one for which an elaborate logical explanation is not even attempted: that is, a simple appeal to divine authority on the assumption that the faithful will accept it unquestioningly. Organized opposition to gay rights in contemporary society has come in significant part from the religious right, including various fundamentalists and literalists who would interpret scripture as unequivocally forbidding homosexual practices. Especially notable among this group have been such high-profile televangelists as Jerry Falwell and Pat Robertson, who mobilized their followers into an antigay crusade during the 1992 general election.[6]

The Hebrew scriptures refer in six places to homosexual practices. Four of the six are simply references to sodomites as performing abominable acts contrary to the word of God.[7] (It has been argued that these four passages actually refer to cult prostitution, a practice of both men and women among neighboring tribes.[8]) In Leviticus, more specific proscriptions are attributed to the Lord as part of a lengthy list of laws spoken to Moses:

> Thou shalt not lie with mankind as with womankind: it is abomination.
>
> Neither shalt thou lie with any beast to defile thyself therewith: neither shall any woman stand before a beast to lie down thereto: it is confusion.
>
> Defile not ye yourselves in any of these things: for in all these the nations are defiled which I cast out before you:
>
> And the land is defiled: therefore I do visit the iniquity thereof upon it, and the land itself vomiteth out her inhabitants. (18.22-25)

Later in the same book, the Lord prescribes the penalty:

> If a man also lie with mankind, as he lieth with a woman, both of them have committed an abomination; they shall surely be put to death; their blood shall be upon them. (20.13)

This invocation of "the word of God" obviously poses a problem for those who regard the Bible as divinely inspired but wish to support gay rights. Their only recourse has been to point to the context in which these proscriptions appear. These passages from Leviticus are part of the Holiness Code covering a wide variety of religious practices, many of which are not observed in the modern world. For example, as a professor of Christian morals at Harvard has pointed out, the Code also prohibits eating raw meat, planting two different kinds of seed in the same field, and wearing clothing made from two different kinds of yarn.[9] If one takes the prohibition against homosexual acts seriously, consistency requires that one must also observe all of the Code's other dietary and hygienic strictures. This argument helps to put the passages from Leviticus into perspective, but it does not explain away the clear meaning of the words used. Homosexual acts are unequivocally prohibited, and divine authority is invoked as justification for the prohibition.

A passage from Plato's *Laws* demonstrates that both sides can use the same strategy. In book 1, three elderly men — an Athenian, a Spartan, and a Cretan — are discussing good and bad laws. The conversation turns to the custom in Sparta and Crete of men training in gymnasia, a practice that is said to lead to homosexuality, "a corruption of the pleasure of love." The Athenian then attempts to attach additional opprobrium to Cretan customs by referring to the story of Zeus and Ganymede, the handsome young cupbearer who was his favorite. The Athenian observes:

> And we all accuse the Cretans of concocting the story about Ganymede. Because it was the belief that they derived their laws from Zeus, they added on this story about Zeus in order that they might be following his example in enjoying this pleasure as well. (636c-d)

Thus invocation of divine authority was a practice known across cultures and used by both proponents and opponents of homosexual practices. When this kind of rationalization is relied upon, rational debate is foreclosed. That is why so many of those involved in the modern controversy over gay rights seem to have such uncompromising positions and do not appear to recognize their own homophobia for what it is.

Contrary to Nature

Another rationalization for homophobic attitudes is that homosexual practices are somehow contrary to nature. This terminology, although widely used, lends itself to so many different interpretations that it is impossible to point with certainty to any definite meaning. One scholar has noted, "The charge comes up now in ordinary discourse only against homosexuality. This social pattern suggests that the charge is highly idiosyncratic and has little, if any, explanatory force."[10] Another, following a lengthy exposition of alternative meanings, concluded, "The objection that homosexuality is 'unnatural' appears, in short, to be neither scientifically nor morally cogent and probably represents nothing more than a derogatory epithet of unusual emotional impact due to a confluence of historically sanctioned prejudices and ill-informed ideas about 'nature.'"[11]

It was Plato who first used the phrase "contrary to nature" with respect to homosexual practices. In the same part of the *Laws* discussed above, the Athenian is criticizing Sparta and Crete for the use of gymnasia. He observes:

> And, moreover, this institution, when of old standing, is thought to have corrupted the pleasures of love which are natural not to men only but also natural to beasts. For this your States are held primarily

responsible, and along with them all others that especially encourage the use of gymnasia. And whether one makes the observation in earnest or in jest, one certainly should not fail to observe that when male unites with female for procreation the pleasure experienced is held to be due to nature, but contrary to nature when male mates with male or female with female, and that those first guilty of such enormities were impelled by their slavery to pleasure. (636b-c)

In this context, it seems likely that the phrase "contrary to nature" means "unrelated to the process of reproduction."[12] The same argument could be used to denounce any sexual relations between male and female where contraceptives are used. Ironically, most opponents of gay rights would not argue for such a restrictive interpretation of what is "contrary to nature" in their own lives.

Another possible basis for the interpretation that homosexual practices are contrary to nature is the notion that people should not engage in such practices because animals do not. This argument is put forward by the Athenian in a later book of the *Laws:*

If we were to follow in nature's steps and enact that law which held good before the days of Laius, declaring that it is right to refrain from indulging in the same kind of intercourse with men and boys as with women, and adducing as evidence thereof the nature of wild beasts, and pointing out how male does not touch male for this purpose, since it is unnatural, – in all this we would probably be using an argument neither convincing nor in any way consonant with your States. (836c)

Some modern scholars have rejected this argument on the grounds that there are, in fact, examples from various species of sexual contact between members of the same sex.[13] More importantly, one might ask whether it is unnatural for people to shave facial hair or to write sonnets, neither of which animals do. As historian John Boswell has noted, the assumption that uniquely human behavior is unnatural "is fundamentally unsupportable in almost any context, biological or philosophical."[14]

Yet another possible interpretation of the "contrary to nature" argument is used by St. Paul in his letter to the Romans. Paul says that those who reject Christ have changed the natural or intended use of their bodies:

For this cause God gave them up unto vile affections: for even their women did change the natural use into that which is against nature:

And likewise also the men, leaving the natural use of the woman, burned in their lust one toward another; men with men working that which is unseemly, and receiving in themselves that recompence of their error which was meet. (1.26-27)

One problem with this argument is that many body parts have multiple functions. The mouth, for example, may be used for eating, for talking, for chewing gum, and for kissing, among other things. The difficulty is determining which of these disparate functions is the one proper function to the exclusion of all others (as unnatural).[15]

To define proper function, appeals are often made to the "design" or "order" of an organ, but this inevitably leads one back to the question of a designer or orderer, with all of its religious implications. The quest for God's plan as manifested in nature is a position historically identified with the Roman Catholic Church, and opposition to gay rights has come from such high Catholic officials as John Cardinal O'Connor, the archbishop of New York.[16]

Upon analysis, the rationalization that homosexuality is contrary to nature proves to be either meaningless or indistinguishable from the "contrary to the word of God" argument discussed above. The most important of the many possible meanings of this phrase are set forth clearly in passages from the Canon, which can provide an excellent basis for understanding how this rationalization has been used to condemn homosexuality for millenia.

Contrary to Public Opinion and/or Social Mores

A third rationalization for homophobia is that homosexual practices are wrong because they are "contrary to public opinion and/or social mores." This argument is entirely secular and does not depend on any particular religious presuppositions. It is circular and without logical foundation, holding that homosexuality should be condemned in the future because it has been condemned in the past. Legal philosopher Richard Mohr, having distinguished between morality that is merely "descriptive" and morality that is "prescriptive" or "normative" because it is in accord with certain principles of rationality and fairness, has observed, "One of our principles itself is that simply a lot of people's saying something is good, even over eons, does not make it so.

Our rejection of the long history of socially approved and state-enforced slavery is a good example of this principle at work."[17]

The rationalization that homosexual practices are somehow inherently immoral has been represented by such right-wing secular moralists as beauty pageant winner Anita Bryant and journalist Pat Buchanan. During the late 1970s, Bryant waged a national campaign against the threat that she claimed "militant homosexuality" posed to the nation's family values.[18] Following an outbreak of violence against gay marchers in the 1991 St. Patrick's Day parade in New York, Buchanan wrote in a column, "Prejudice simply means prejudgment. Not all prejudgments are rooted in ignorance; most are rooted in the inherited wisdom of the race. A visceral recoil from homosexuality is the natural reaction of a healthy society wishing to protect itself." [19]

The kind of homophobia demonstrated by these secular moralists may be found in what some might regard as an unlikely place in the Canon. The upper-class social stratum of fifth-century Athens, as depicted in the dialogues of Plato, is often regarded as highly tolerant of homosexual practices. While Plato's personal views on homosexuality, at least in his later years, may be more accurately gleaned from the passages of the Laws already cited, he does put into the mouths of his various dramatic characters eloquent defenses and depictions of the ancient Greek custom of pederasty. This custom entailed romantic and sexual liaisons between adolescent boys and adult males, who took responsibility for their charges' overall personal development.[20]

A careful reading of the dialogues reveals that there was not universal acceptance in fifth-century Athens of the practices that are sometimes exalted. There is significant evidence of a backlash of popular opinion against the institution of pederasty, and the adolescent boys who participated in pederastic relationships seem to have been subject to countervailing pressures from unspecified sources. It is said repeatedly that many people found such practices "shameful."

One example of this contention appears in the Symposium, which includes a number of speeches on the subject of love delivered at a drinking party. One of those speeches, that of Aristophanes, is sometimes cited today as the locus classicus for the view that homosexual orientation is genetically determined from birth and therefore should not be regarded as a moral failing.[21] Aristophanes offers a mythological explanation in which people are said to have originally been round creatures with four arms and four legs; when these creatures became too ambitious and sought to rival the gods, they were split down the middle. As a result, every person seeks to reunite with his or her other half, which may be of the same gender or of the opposite gender, depending upon whether the original creature was a male/female, a female/female, or a male/male. In the latter case, Aristophanes describes the situation as follows:

> Men who are sections of the male pursue the masculine, and so long as their boyhood lasts they show themselves to be slices of the male by making friends with men and delighting to lie with them and to be clasped in men's embraces; these are the finest boys and striplings, for they have the most manly nature. Some say they are shameless creatures, but falsely: for their behaviour is due not to shamelessness but to daring, manliness, and virility, since they are quick to welcome their like. (191e-192a)

The passage does not reveal who the "some" people are who spread this calumny or what the basis for their allegation is.

In the same dialogue, in a speech in which Pausanias alludes to a scandal surrounding the issue of pederasty, he draws a distinction between two goddesses whom he calls popular love and heavenly love. The former partakes of both male and female, while the latter is entirely male. Heavenly love leads men to wait until a boy becomes sufficiently mature so as not to be exploited. Popular love, on the other hand, leads men to do haphazard things and to abandon boys who are too young to protect themselves from abuse. Against this form of love, Pausanias says, a law should have been enacted:

> Good men, however, voluntarily make this law for themselves, and it is a rule which those "popular" lovers ought to be forced to obey, just as we force them, so far as we can, to refrain from loving our freeborn women. These are the persons responsible for the scandal which prompts some to say it is a shame to gratify one's lover: such are the cases they have in view, for they observe all their reckless and wrongful doings; and surely whatsoever is done in an orderly and lawful manner can never justly bring reproach. (181e-182a)

This passage offers the view that scandals resulting from homosexual affairs derived from the selfish and abusive conduct of the older lover toward the younger beloved, not from the homosexual acts themselves. (The same reasoning might usefully be applied to heterosexual affairs, then or now.)

As a result of the prevalence of scandal, no doubt youths were sub-ject to conflicts and pulls in different directions over whether to enter into homosexual relationships with older men. Thus, in the *Phaedrus*, when a speech of Lysias is read concerning the preferability of submit-ting to a nonlover rather than to a lover, one of the reasons given is that a nonlover is likely to be much more discreet about the nature of the relationship:

> Now if you are afraid of public opinion, and fear that if people find out your love affair you will be disgraced, consider that lovers, believing that others would be as envious of them as they are of oth-ers, are likely to be excited by possession and in their pride to show everybody that they have not toiled in vain; but the non-lovers, since they have control of their feelings, are likely to choose what is really best, rather than to court the opinion of mankind. (231e-232a)

This passage reveals how much was at stake in the adolescent's choice of a lover. If he chose wrongly, not only was he apt to be mistreated, but he would also be likely to face public disgrace when the affair be-came known. Unscrupulous older men seem to have derived self-esteem from "scoring" as often as possible with handsome youths, which provided motivation for them to make their successes known. Given this set of circumstances, there is no wonder that a tinge of scandal came to surround the entire institution of pederasty. Similarly today, public opinion against gays tends to focus on abuses that might exist (for example, at gay bars or in gay bathhouses) rather than on re-sponsible, long-term relationships.

Gay Bashing

Given the prevalence of homophobic attitudes just described, one would expect to find manifestations of "gay bashing" of one kind or another in the works of the Canon. In fact, many of the contemporary manifestations of homophobia may be detected in these works, includ-ing associating homosexuality with morally offensive conduct of other kinds, stereotyping how gay people look and act, subjecting them to ridicule and prurient curiosity, and depicting them as in conflict with close family members because of their sexual practices.

Guilt by Association

One age-old method of raising questions about the morality of any conduct is to associate it with other conduct commonly believed to be immoral. Thus homosexuality has come to be associated in some people's minds with a variety of undesirable practices (promiscuity, pedophilia, and – because of AIDS – drug use), none of which bears any necessary relationship to it.

Two passages in the Hebrew scriptures are often cited as demonstrating the Lord's opposition to sodomy. In the story of Sodom and Gomorrah at Genesis 19.1-25, Lot offers hospitality to the angels visiting Sodom. When a gang of local men surrounds Lot's house and demands to be given the visitors "in order that we might know [that is, have intercourse with] them," Lot refuses and offers his own two virgin daughters instead. Before the matter is resolved, the Lord's anger at the gang members' conduct results in their being struck blind and eventually in the destruction of the city.

A similar story is told at Judges 19.1-30. A Levite and his concubine are staying with an old man from Gibeah who has offered them shelter in his house. When a gang of ruffians demands that the Levite be given to them for the same purpose, the old man offers them his own virgin daughter and the concubine instead. The concubine is accepted, and she is gang-raped and killed by the ruffians. In both of these stories, it is clear that the homosexual aspects of the gangs' crimes are incidental to the plot. Rape and violence are more important factors, as is the violation of the sacred custom of hospitality, which most scholars believe to be the main point of the stories.[22]

Through his skill in the art of denunciation, St. Paul created guilt by association. In his first letter to the Corinthians, he lists those who will not inherit the kingdom of God as follows:

> Know ye not that the unrighteous shall not inherit the kingdom of God? Be not deceived: neither fornicators, nor idolaters, nor adulterers nor effeminate, nor abusers of themselves with mankind,
>
> Nor thieves, nor covetous, nor drunkards, nor revilers, nor extortioners, shall inherit the kingdom of God. (6.9-10)

A similar listing is found in his first letter to Timothy:

> Knowing this, that the law is not made for a righteous man, but for the lawless and disobedient, for the ungodly and for sinners, for

unholy and profane, for murderers of fathers and murderers of mothers, for manslayers,

For whoremongers, for them that defile themselves with mankind, for menstealers, for liars, for perjured persons, and if there be any other thing that is contrary to sound doctrine. (1.9-10)

Moderate theologians who wish to support gay rights have attempted to explain away these passages as an expression of St. Paul's objection to the secular sensuality that prevailed in Greco-Roman culture.[23] If his opposition was to secular sensuality (both homosexual and heterosexual), surely Paul was skilled enough with words to have made that meaning clear. In fact, the plain meaning of the words quoted above is that Paul opposes homosexual acts. These are listed along with other practices that are commonly considered immoral, creating associational links in the minds of Paul's readers.

Pedophilia is an offense often identified with homosexuality. Fear of pedophilia has long been a reason for society's general reluctance to allow gay men to occupy such sensitive positions as teachers, coaches, and Boy Scout leaders, in which they will have the opportunity to "prey upon" young, impressionable boys. Because of the Greek custom of pederasty, this perceived danger was not unknown to Plato, and he openly discusses it. For example, in the *Symposium,* when Pausanias distinguishes between the two goddesses heavenly love and popular love, he says that heavenly love, with its affinity for the male, is preferable:

Even in the passion for boys you may note the way of those who are under the single incitement of this Love: they love boys only when they begin to acquire some mind – a growth associated with that of down on their chins. For I conceive that those who begin to love them at this age are prepared to be always with them and share all with them as long as life shall last: they will not take advantage of a boy's green thoughtlessness to deceive him and make a mock of him by running straight off to another. Against this love of boys a law should have been enacted, to prevent the sad waste of attentions paid to an object so uncertain: for who can tell where a boy will end at last, vicious or virtuous in body and soul? (181d-e)

Even in cases of heavenly love, where the lover's conduct is appropriate and beneficial to the boy, a passage from the *Republic* advises the use of discretion. Socrates says to his interlocutor:

"Thus, then, as it seems, you will lay down the law in the city that we are founding, that the lover may kiss and pass the time with and touch the beloved as a father would a son, for honourable ends, if he persuade him. But otherwise he must so associate with the objects of his care that there should never be any suspicion of anything further, on penalty of being stigmatized for want of taste and true musical culture." (403b-c)

A contemporary example of fear of pedophilia and stigmatization for want of taste was reported at an elite New England prep school. In 1992, Larry L. Bateman, chairman of the drama department at Phillips Exeter Academy, was accused of having seduced boys and made pornographic videos of them. Mr. Bateman denied the charges, but critics pointed to factors in his past – such as his authorship of a play about male teachers who seduced students into homosexual acts – as having given the school ample notice of his dangerous tendencies. An editorial in a conservative magazine stated, "Few people, so far, openly endorse pedophilia. But Mr. Bateman's career suggests that plenty of progressive-minded people have been winking at it, or at least have refrained from suspecting it, lest they be accused of 'homophobia.'"[24]

The pattern that emerges from these passages demonstrating guilt by association is similar to the pattern that emerged concerning rationalizations: it is difficult to extract from people with homophobic attitudes exactly what their moral objection to homosexuality is. Homosexuality has been condemned by association with such separate, distinguishable behaviors as rape, violence, promiscuity, and pedophilia. While most people would agree that these latter forms of behavior are morally objectionable, they are not necessarily related to the homosexual practices of consenting adults.

Stereotypes

Another manifestation of homophobic attitudes is the perpetuation of stereotypes of how gay people look and act. Because of the larger number and higher visibility of gay men compared to lesbians, the Canon has more passages containing stereotypes of such men. The principal such stereotype is that gay men are effeminate, seeking to look and act as much like women as possible. This generalization has been contested by many recent scholars on various grounds.

John Boswell takes issue with the stereotype on empirical grounds, saying that it is "almost certainly the result of antipathy to homosexuality rather than empirical observation." He adds, "Atypical conformity to gender expectations appears in fact to be randomly distributed in most populations, completely independent of sexual preference; but if even a very small percentage of gay women are more masculine or a very few gay men more feminine than their nongay counterparts, they will corroborate the stereotype in the mind of a public predisposed to believe it and usually possessed of no large sampling as a control."[25] Certainly the public has not been disabused of this notion through awareness of such highly publicized exceptions as a handsome actor with leading-man sex appeal (Rock Hudson[26]) and a former director of the F.B.I. known for his tough-guy image (J. Edgar Hoover[27]).

Another scholar, Richard Mohr, has looked at this stereotype from the perspective of the social purpose it serves: "Stereotypes ... are social constructions that perform central functions in maintaining society's conception of itself. On this understanding, it is easy to see that the anti-gay stereotypes surrounding gender identification are chiefly means of reinforcing still powerful gender roles in society. If, as this stereotype presumes (and condemns), one is free to choose one's social roles independently of gender, many guiding social divisions, both domestic and commercial, might be threatened.... The accusations 'fag' and 'dyke' exist in significant part to keep women in their place and to prevent men from breaking ranks and ceding away theirs."[28]

Implicit in this analysis of gender roles is the assumption that an accusation of femininity made against a man is a reproach. This point is brought out by Plato in a passage in the *Laws* where the Athenian is lecturing the Spartan and the Cretan concerning how homosexuality should be treated by the laws of an ideal state. He says that the true test for any laws should be which ones tend toward virtue and which ones do not. He raises the question whether a system of legalized homosexuality would tend to promote virtue among the citizens:

> Will it engender in the soul of him who is seduced a courageous character, or in the soul of the seducer the quality of temperance? Nobody would ever believe this; on the contrary, as all men will blame the cowardice of the man who always yields to pleasures and is never able to hold out against them, will they not likewise reproach that man who plays the woman's part with the resemblance he bears to his model? Is there any man, then, who will ordain by law a practice like that? Not one, I should say, if he has a notion of what true law is. (836d-e)

What resemblance the man who plays "the woman's part" might bear to "his model" is spelled out in more detail in other dialogues. In the *Phaedrus,* Socrates is delivering a speech favoring the nonlover over the lover as a potential sponsor for a youth. Socrates describes the kind of situation presented when a youth becomes involved with an unscrupulous lover who does not have the youth's best interests at heart. Such a lover may have an ingrained need to feel superior to the youth and will therefore seek to thwart his development:

> He will plainly court a beloved who is effeminate, not virile, not brought up in the pure sunshine, but in mingled shade, unused to manly toils and the sweat of exertion, but accustomed to a delicate and unmanly mode of life, adorned with a bright complexion of artificial origin, since he has none by nature, and in general living a life such as all this indicates, which it is certainly not worth while to describe further. (239c-d)

Socrates' point is that the nonlover, not having the ego needs of the lover, would be more likely to encourage his beloved to develop in a masculine direction. However, Socrates was not naive when it came to the relative numbers of those who met his ideals and those who did not; thus his description of the unhealthy situation might well be taken as a stereotype of what was, in fact, quite common.

Effeminacy is often attributed to men who have strong intellectual or artistic interests, sometimes leading to questioning of their sexual orientation. In the *Gorgias,* Callicles is discussing the role that the study of philosophy should play in one's education. He says that he considers such study entirely appropriate for a young man of liberal mind. However, it should not be carried too far:

> But when I see an elderly man still going on with philosophy and not getting rid of it, that is the gentleman, Socrates, whom I think in need of a whipping. For as I said just now, this person, however well endowed he may be, is bound to become unmanly through shunning the centres and marts of the city, in which, as the poet said, "men get them note and glory"; he must cower down and spend the rest of his days whispering in a corner with three or four lads, and never utter anything free or high or spirited. (485d)

This stereotype is not unlike the one that many businessmen (who frequent "the centres and marts of the city") hold of academics. It also resembles the stereotype evoked by former vice-president Spiro Agnew when he referred to some of his critics as "effete intellectual snobs." [29]

In the *Iliad,* Patroclus was Achilles' dear friend who wore his armor into battle while Achilles sulked in his tent over a personal affront that had wounded his pride. It was Achilles' grief over the death of his friend that impelled him back into battle and resulted in the Greek victory over the Trojans in the ten-year war. While Homer portrays Patroclus as gentle and loving, there is no indication that he was sexually involved with Achilles; to the contrary, Homer says at 9.663-668 that he and Achilles slept with their respective concubines at opposite ends of their tent. Nevertheless, later tradition seized upon Patroclus's gentle nature and the intensity of his friendship with Achilles to infer that Patroclus was the passive partner in such a relationship, and Shakespeare built upon this tradition in his portrayal of Patroclus in *Troilus and Cressida*.

Thersites was the ideal character for Shakespeare to use to direct homophobic recriminations against Patroclus. Another character whom Shakespeare borrowed from Homer, Thersites was portrayed in the *Iliad* as a common soldier of disgusting appearance who was accustomed to spewing forth bitter torrents of abuse against his superiors (at 2.212-277). In *Troilus and Cressida,* Shakespeare has Thersites confront Patroclus about his sexual practices:

THERS.: Prithee, be silent, boy; I profit not by thy talk: thou art thought to be Achilles' male varlet.

PATR.: Male varlet, you rogue! what's that?

THERS.: Why, his masculine whore.... No! why art thou then exasperate, thou idle immaterial skein of sleave-silk, thou green sercenet flap for a sore eye, thou tassel of a prodigal's purse, thou? Ah, how the poor world is pestered with such waterflies, diminutives of nature!

(5.1.16-20, 34-39)

While the precise meaning of all of Thersites' images may elude us, nevertheless the stereotype he evokes is one of femininity: diminutive stature, luxurious clothing, and a tendency to flit about. Invocation of this stereotype is not consistent with what Homer says about Patroclus's prowess as a fierce warrior.

Another example of the stereotype of femininity may be found in Shakespeare's sonnets. It is well-known that some of the sonnets were written to a male love-interest of the poet. Sonnet 20 is explicit about the female qualities of this unknown man:

A woman's face with Nature's own hand painted
Hast thou, the master-mistress of my passion;

A woman's gentle heart, but not acquainted
With shifting change, as is false women's fashion;
. . . .
And for a woman wert thou first created;
Till Nature, as she wrought thee, fell a-doting,
And by addition me of thee defeated,
By adding one thing to my purpose nothing.

(1-4, 9-12)

Thus the poet explicitly describes his male love-interest as female in every important respect but one: nature added one anatomical feature that did not serve the poet's purposes.

Ridicule and Curiosity

Other forms homophobia frequently takes are ridiculing gay people and expressing curiosity about their sexual practices. Noting the various epithets that are sometimes used for gays ("queens, fairies, limp-wrists, nellies"), one scholar has observed, "These stereotypes of mismatched or fraudulent genders provide the materials through which gays and lesbians become the butts of ethnic-like jokes. These stereotypes and jokes, though derisive, basically view gays and lesbians as ridiculous."[30]

Many people trace their first awareness of homosexuality to schoolyard exchanges with other children, and peer pressure to express homophobic opinions often develops within this context. This syndrome is of ancient lineage and can be detected in a number of passages in the Canon. For example, in the *Phaedrus,* Socrates says that a beloved will naturally be friendly toward a lover who serves him, "although he may at some earlier time have been prejudiced by his schoolfellows or others, who said that it was a disgrace to yield to a lover" (255a). And in the *Symposium,* Pausanias describes some of the pressures that exist in Athens against homosexuality: "... and when they observe a boy to be guilty of such a thing his playmates and fellows reproach him, while his reproachers are not in their turn withheld or upbraided by their elders as speaking amiss" (183d).

The element of humor seems irrepressibly linked with conversations that allude to homosexuality. In the *Laws,* the Athenian is discussing the use of gymnasia in Sparta and Crete, and he admits that his comments on this subject might or might not be taken seriously:

And whether one makes the observation in earnest or in jest, one certainly should not fail to observe that when male unites with female for procreation the pleasure experienced is held to be due to nature, but contrary to nature when male mates with male or female with female. (636c)

Clearly homosexuality was a subject about which there was jesting in Plato's Athens. Similarly, in Shakespeare, one finds Hamlet able to joke with his schoolfellows Rosencrantz and Guildenstern about his own predilections, even at the end of a lugubrious speech:

HAMLET: What a piece of work is a man! how noble in reason! how in-finite in faculty! in form and moving how express and admi-rable! in action how like an angel! in apprehension how like a god! the beauty of the world! the paragon of animals! And yet, to me, what is this quintessence of dust? man delights not me: no, nor woman neither, though by your smiling you seem to say so.

ROSEN.:   My lord, there was no such stuff in my thoughts.

HAMLET: Why did ye laugh then, when I said "man delights not me"?

ROSEN.:   To think, my lord, if you delight not in man, what lenten en-tertainment the players shall receive from you.

(2.2.315-330)

Akin to the humor that homosexuality sometimes elicits is curiosity about actual homosexual practices. This kind of curiosity is apparent in *Troilus and Cressida* when the Trojan beauty Cressida is handed over to the Greeks in exchange for some prisoners. Cressida is heartily greeted by the Greek leaders, each of whom kisses her in turn. When it is Pa-troclus's turn, Cressida makes allusion to his sexual practices, which earlier scenes have brought into question:

CRESSIDA: In kissing, do you render or receive?

PATR.:   Both take and give.

CRESSIDA: I'll make my match to live,
The kiss you take is better than you give;
Therefore no kiss.

(4.5.36-39)

Cressida's aversion to kissing Patroclus because of these doubts is a homophobic reaction not unlike that encountered today, when it is not unusual to hear homosexual practices described as disgusting. Such abuse, which homosexuals have endured for millenia, is amply depicted in the works of the Canon.

Reaction of Family Members

Another, and possibly the most painful, form of bashing that gay people often endure is rejection by their immediate family members. A frequent theme in gay literature is the difficulty children have in telling their parents about their sexual orientation.[31] Especially in the case of a gay man, the father sometimes takes his son's revelation as an indication of failure in the son's upbringing or, worse, somehow a reflection on the father's virility.

A poignant depiction of a father's anger over his son's questionable relationship with a male friend is found in the account of David and Jonathan in I Samuel. The two young men are best friends and appear to be sexually involved. (Later, after Jonathan is killed in battle, David laments at II Samuel 1.26, "I am distressed for thee, my brother Jonathan: very pleasant hast thou been unto me: thy love to me was wonderful, passing the love of women.") When Jonathan's father Saul plots to kill David for political reasons, Jonathan is instrumental in helping David escape. He tries to explain David's absence from a ritual feast by telling his father that David has gone to Bethlehem for a family gathering. Saul, however, does not accept this explanation:

> Then Saul's anger was kindled against Jonathan, and he said unto him, Thou son of the perverse rebellious woman, do not I know that thou hast chosen the son of Jesse [David] to thine own confusion, and unto the confusion of thy mother's nakedness? (20.30)

One wonders how many distraught fathers of gay or bisexual men have sought solace in the thought that surely the blame (whether genetic or environmental) must lie with their wives, not with them.

Equally problematic is the gay or bisexual man's relationship with his wife, which is likely to be strained if not destroyed when she becomes aware of his sexual practices outside the marriage. David's relationship with his wife Michal is troubled, and in II Samuel she sarcastically denounces his dancing and his immoral conduct before the handmaids:

> Then David returned to bless his household. And Michal the daughter of Saul came out to meet David, and said, How glorious was the king of Israel to day, who uncovered himself to day in the

eyes of the handmaids of his servants, as one of the vain fellows shamelessly uncovereth himself!

And David said unto Michal, *It was* before the Lord, which chose me before thy father, and before all his house, to appoint me ruler over the people of the Lord, over Israel: therefore will I play before the Lord.

And I will yet be more vile than thus, and will be base in mine own sight: and of the maidservants which thou hast spoken of, of them shall I be had in honor.

Therefore Michal the daughter of Saul had no child unto the day of her death. (6.20-23)

David's threat to be even more vile than his wife has already witnessed and to be base in his own sight is a virtual manifesto of sexual freedom. As king, David was in a uniquely privileged position for this kind of self-expression, and it apparently did not impair his effectiveness as Israel's leader.

Current Points of Controversy

Modern society has inherited the deep-seated conflict about homosexuality that the works of the Canon so clearly demonstrate. Given the egalitarian tenor of our own age and the rapid social progress that has been made in removing the barriers of discrimination against other minorities, the gay rights movement might have been predicted. There are several battlefields in the current conflict; primary among them are the quest for equal treatment, the drive for acceptance of gays in the military, the demand for legal recognition of gay marriages, and the desire for teaching about alternative lifestyles in the schools. Each of these can be linked to relevant passages from the Canon.

The Quest for Equal Treatment

Our society's ambivalence about homosexuality is demonstrated by the fact that many states still have laws on the books making sexual practices such as sodomy a crime, while at the same time nondiscrimination codes are being amended to add sexual orientation to the list of personal characteristics that may not be the basis for discrimination. This apparent inconsistency might be justified by pointing out that the criminal laws apply to specific sex acts, while the nondiscrimination laws apply more generally to sexual orientation. However, if sexual orientation is a personal characteristic for which one should not be penalized in obtaining employment or access to public accommodations, why should there be a state interest in prohibiting one from engaging in private, consensual acts that are the ordinary outlet for sexual expression by similarly oriented adults? In fact, the criminal laws and the nondiscrimination laws reflect contrasting attitudes toward homosexuality, both of which persist in our society today.

As one might expect on a matter of intense social conflict, the U.S. Supreme Court has been called upon to serve as the ultimate arbiter on homosexuality in America. The principal case to reach the Court in recent years was *Bowers v. Hardwick* (1986), in which the constitutionality of the Georgia statute criminalizing consensual sodomy was challenged on the grounds that the statute violates the substantive due process requirement of the Fourteenth Amendment.[32] The challengers argued that there is a fundamental right for adults to engage in consensual sexual relations in the privacy of their own home without state interference. The statute was upheld in a 5 to 4 decision, in which moralistic and libertarian principles came into direct conflict. An ambivalent and anguished Justice Lewis Powell cast the deciding vote, and both sides rendered vehement opinions.[33]

In the majority opinion, Justice Byron White rejected arguments that would have extended to acts of consensual sodomy the same constitutional protection as is accorded other fundamental rights in family matters, such as marriage and procreation. His justification was simple: "Proscriptions against that conduct have ancient roots. Sodomy was a criminal offense at common law and was forbidden by the laws of the original 13 States when they ratified the Bill of Rights."[34] Similarly, Chief Justice Warren Burger wrote in a concurring opinion, "Decisions of individuals relating to homosexual conduct have been subject to state intervention throughout the history of Western civilization. Condemnation of those practices is firmly rooted in Judaeo-Christian moral and ethical standards.... To hold that the act of homosexual sodomy is somehow protected as a fundamental right would be to cast aside millenia of moral teaching."[35]

Starkly contrasting with the moralistic approach of the majority was the libertarian approach of the minority. In his dissenting opinion Justice Harry Blackmun wrote, "The fact that individuals define themselves in a significant way through their intimate sexual relationships with others suggests, in a Nation as diverse as ours, that there may be

many 'right' ways of conducting those relationships, and that much of
the richness of a relationship will come from the freedom an individual
has to *choose* the form and nature of these intensely personal bonds. In a
variety of circumstances we have recognized that a necessary corollary
of giving individuals freedom to choose how to conduct their lives is
acceptance of the fact that different individuals will make different
choices."[36] Blackmun also seized upon the other side's references to
Judaeo-Christian values as an inappropriate justification for secular legislation, which must be advanced by the state as serving purposes other
than conformity with religious doctrine.[37] Moreover, when the religious basis for the decision is removed, the majority's opinion can be
seen to be based on circular reasoning: evidence of past prejudice is
used to justify its continuance.[38]

Interesting parallels can be drawn between the opinions of the two
sides in the *Bowers* case, on the one hand, and passages from two dialogues of Plato, on the other. The libertarian approach may be found
in the *Symposium,* which dates from Plato's middle years. This dialogue
contains several speeches on the subject of love delivered by various
dramatic characters at a drinking party. (Since Plato was obviously depicting the variety of viewpoints that prevailed in Athens at the time, it
would be misleading to attribute any of these opinions to him.)
Pausanias delivers a speech in which he examines the political motivation for the suppression of pederasty:

> But in Ionia and many other regions where they live under for-
> eign sway, it is counted a disgrace. Foreigners hold this thing, and all
> training in philosophy and sports, to be disgraceful, because of their
> despotic government; since, I presume, it is not to the interest of their
> princes to have lofty notions engendered in their subjects, or any
> strong friendships and communions; all of which Love is pre-
> eminently apt to create.... Thus where it was held a disgrace to gratify
> one's lover, the tradition is due to the evil ways of those who made
> such a law — that is, to the encroachments of the rulers and to the
> cowardice of the ruled. (182b-d)

Pausanias goes on to contrast such a despotic regime with the libertarian practices of Athens, where a lover is given "a free hand for performing such admirable acts as may win him praise" but not for acts
that will bring reproach (182e). Pausanias idealizes Athens as the state
where the proper balance between individual freedom and the common good has been struck, and the emphasis on individual freedom

clearly encompasses sexual matters. The key consideration is not the nature of the acts that are performed but whether they are done in a base or a noble fashion.

A more moralistic approach is presented in the *Laws,* which Plato wrote in his later years. Criticizing other states for having laws that allow homosexual practices, the Athenian refers to an ancient law against "indulging in the same kind of intercourse with men and boys as with women" (836c). That law was justified by an appeal to nature that he admits would not be convincing in his own day. He argues that the proper test for any law should be whether or not it promotes virtue:

> Moreover, that object which, as we affirm, the lawgiver ought always to have in view does not agree with these practices. For the enquiry we always make is this – which of the proposed laws tends toward virtue and which not. Come then, suppose we grant that this practice is now legalized, and that it is noble and in no way ignoble, how far would it promote virtue? Will it engender in the soul of him who is seduced a courageous character, or in the soul of the seducer the quality of temperance? Nobody would ever believe this.... (836d)

The Greek concept of "virtue" is used here to supply the moral standard for which the Supreme Court in the *Bowers* case had to rely on the Judaeo-Christian tradition. In both instances, however, individual freedom of choice is subsumed to a "greater good" at the hands of the moral majority.

The battle over issues of decriminalization and nondiscrimination continues. While sodomy statutes are still on the books in many states, they are largely unenforced. The movement to amend nondiscrimination laws to include sexual orientation has continued, but not without a backlash. In the November 1992 general election, an initiative was approved in Colorado that amended the state constitution to prohibit the addition of sexual orientation to any state or city nondiscrimination code. In July 1993, however, a state district judge ruled the measure, known as Amendment 2, unconstitutional because it violates the equal protection clause of the Fourteenth Amendment of the U.S. Constitution.[39] Further litigation may be expected.

Gays in the Military

One of the most difficult and intransigent issues President Clinton faced in the early days of his presidency was the conflict over lifting the ban on gays in the United States military. Having made a campaign pledge to issue an executive order removing the ban, Clinton was apparently unprepared for the degree of resistance he would encounter from both the military and Congress. Following a national uproar over the issue, the administration was forced to accept a compromise proposal: "Don't ask, don't tell." This policy ended the military's practices of asking recruits about their sexual orientation and ferreting out gays already in the ranks but prohibits homosexual members from disclosing their status and provides for the discharge of those who engage in homosexual conduct.[40]

The late Randy Shilts, author of a 1993 book on the experience of gays in the military, wrote, "The military's policies have had a sinister effect on the entire nation: Such policies make it known to everyone serving in the military that lesbians and gay men are dangerous to the well-being of other Americans; that they are undeserving of even the most basic civil rights. Such policies also create an ambience in which discrimination, harassment, and even violence against lesbians and gays is tolerated and to some degree encouraged."[41] Opponents of gays in the military respond by denying that the issue is one of civil rights at all. Rather, they say, it is an issue of national defense. As United States Army Major Melissa Wells-Petry, author of a 1993 book defending the ban on gays in the military, put it, "Social reformation is neither the province nor the mission of America's fighting force.... Indeed, as General MacArthur poignantly observed, the military has a single, fixed, determined, inviolable mission − 'it is to win our wars.'" [emphasis in original].[42]

The principal argument put forward by Major Wells-Petry is that the only consideration in establishing the standards for eligibility to serve in the military should be whether or not a given standard would make for a better (that is, more combat-ready) military. She concludes that admitting homosexuals could not possibly contribute to meeting this objective.[43] It is interesting that some passages in the dialogues of Plato accept her premise concerning the need for combat readiness but at the same time argue against her on whether having homosexual couples in the fighting force contributes to meeting that objective. The arguments made by Plato's characters are based on the special motivation that romantically linked men would have to be courageous in battle.[44] In the *Symposium,* Phaedrus declares that love is a boon to achievement among fighting men:

And such men as these, when fighting side by side, one might almost consider able to make even a little band victorious over all the world. For a man in love would surely choose to have all the rest of the host rather than his favourite see him forsaking his station or flinging away his arms; sooner than this, he would prefer to die many deaths: while, as for leaving his favourite in the lurch, or not succouring him in his peril, no man is such a craven that Love's own influence cannot inspire him with a valour that makes him equal to the bravest born. (178e-179a)

Plato makes another point about motivation for valor in the *Republic,* where Glaucon is describing to Socrates the award that the law should provide to the valorous soldier who has distinguished himself in battle. Glaucon says that the hero should be given adulation and kisses; then he says,

And I add to the law the provision that during that campaign none whom he wishes to kiss be allowed to refuse, so that if one is in love with anyone, male or female, he may be the more eager to win the prize. (468b-c)

These passages indicate that, at least according to one point of view prevalent in Plato's time, more emphasis ought to be placed on how to motivate the troops to fight bravely and less on gender considerations in the choice of a lover.

Even in the culture of Plato's dialogues, however, there was an undercurrent of anxiety about how effectively some passive partners might be able to serve in battle. In the *Phaedrus,* Socrates is praising the nonlover as a better sponsor for a youth than a lover, whose jealousy and need to feel superior will lead him to deprive the youth of appropriate physical training. As a result, the youth will grow up to be effeminate, delicate, and unmanly. Socrates concludes:

We can sum it all up briefly and pass on. A person with such a body, in war and in all important crises, gives courage to his enemies, and fills his friends, and even his lovers themselves, with fear. (239d)

It is important to realize that Socrates is arguing here not that all passive partners should be barred from the military but rather that they should have active partners who will have their best interests at heart and not be threatened by their physical and intellectual development.

Another argument of today's opponents of gays in the military is that the close quarters and lack of personal privacy in sleeping and bathing facilities would lead to problems if gays were intermixed with other troops. Special attention has been devoted to the cramped space and communal living arrangements on submarines and aircraft carriers, where closeness is measured in inches. Much the same argument must have been on the mind of the Athenian in the *Laws* when he criticized the Spartan and Cretan practice of using gymnasia for training because it gave rise to homosexuality:

> So these common meals, for example, and these gymnasia, while they are at present beneficial to the States in many other respects, yet in the event of civil strife they prove dangerous; and, moreover, this institution, when of old standing is thought to have corrupted the pleasures of love which are natural not to men only but also natural to beasts. (636b)

The Greek practice of men training naked in the gymnasia might have elicited fears similar to those expressed by contemporary soldiers who worry about roving eyes in the showers.[45]

Yet another way the argument against gays in the military is expressed is in terms of the adverse effect on "morale and discipline." These words are actually euphemisms for the strong prevalence of homophobic attitudes among the troops and the threat of disruption resulting from the unwanted presence of gays. One clinical psychologist has argued compellingly that fear of latent homosexuality is the real reason for this potential for violence, which is almost always directed against gay men rather than women: "This no doubt reflects military demographics, but it also reflects the manner in which the hatred of male homosexuality is founded on fears of femininity. The equation is simple: male homosexuality equals femininity, which produces fear, which produces aggression. More specifically, hatred of gay men is based on fear of the self, not of an alien other."[46]

The dynamics of this fear and hatred were not unknown to Shakespeare, who has Patroclus in *Troilus and Cressida* lament the ill feelings against an effeminate man in time of war. Patroclus confides to his close friend Achilles that the troops hold him personally responsible for Achilles' refusal to fight:

PATR.:   To this effect, Achilles, have I moved you:
            A woman impudent and mannish grown
            Is not more loathed than an effeminate man
            In time of action. I stand condemned for this;
            They think my little stomach to the war

> And your great love to me restrains you thus:
> Sweet, rouse yourself; and the weak wanton Cupid
> Shall from your neck unloose his amorous fold,
> And, like a dew-drop from the lion's mane,
> Be shook to air.

(3.3.216-225)

Of course, Achilles' refusal to fight has nothing to do with his love for Patroclus. The ultimate irony is that Achilles' stubbornness eventually results in the death of Patroclus, who foolishly enters the battle clad in Achilles' armor.

The potential of the presence of gays to cause disruption within military ranks must be balanced against the demand for equal treatment. In our constitutional system, it is the role of the courts, and ultimately of the U.S. Supreme Court, to fashion an appropriate balance of conflicting interests if the other branches of government are unwilling or unable to do so. So far, the courts have deferred to the judgment of the military on this question, although the volume of cases raising constitutional questions has increased dramatically over the past decade.

In 1992 the Supreme Court declined the government's request that it review an appeals court decision in a case challenging the ban on gays as violating the equal protection clause of the Fifth Amendment.[47] In that case, the appeals court required the government to employ a higher than normal level of scrutiny ("an active rational basis test") to its justification for the ban. Of importance was the court's direction that the military's ban could not be justified by the prejudice of other soldiers against homosexuals; to hold otherwise, it said, would be to give legal effect to private biases.[48] By refusing to hear the case, the Supreme Court did not necessarily endorse the interpretation of the appeals court; more likely, it was attempting to leave the matter to the political processes at work in the other two branches of government.

While anxieties and fears about homosexuality have been prevalent among fighting men throughout the ages, they seem to have been exacerbated in contemporary culture by the ongoing revolution in gender roles and the great uncertainty concerning gender-related behavior among young people today. A military culture is highly dependent upon "going by the rules," and yet — where matters of gender are concerned — nobody seems to know exactly what the rules are anymore. As Randy Shilts wrote, "For generations, after all, the military has been an institution that has promised to do one thing, if nothing else, and that is to take a boy and make him a man. The military's gay policy crisis in the past decade reflects the turmoil of a nation thrust into conflict over our society's changing definition of manhood."[49]

Gay Marriages

Unhappy marriages for gay and bisexual people seem to have been prevalent in both Hebrew and Greek societies. As has been discussed, King David's marriage to Michal was troubled in part because she disapproved of his various sexual practices outside the marriage. In the *Symposium*, Plato has Aristophanes give a mythological explanation for the fact that some people are attracted to members of the opposite sex and some to members of their own. Concerning men who were originally united to other men and who are always seeking their original "other half," Aristophanes concludes:

> So when they come to man's estate they are boy-lovers, and have no natural interest in wiving and getting children, but only do these things under stress of custom; they are quite contented to live together unwedded all their days. (192a-b)

Eliminating "the stress of custom" has become one of the primary objectives of the contemporary gay rights movement. However, gay people are no longer contented "to live together unwedded all their days," as pressure has increased for legal recognition of same-sex marriages. A 1993 decision by the Supreme Court of Hawaii, interpreting that state's constitutional prohibition against discrimination on the basis of sex, may pave the way for legal recognition of same-sex marriages there. Hawaii would be the first state to take this significant step.[50]

Teaching about Gays in the Schools

Any emotionally charged issue about which there is intense social conflict will eventually emerge as an issue for the public schools. This has happened with respect to organized prayer, the distribution of condoms, and even access to guns. It was inevitable that the question of homosexuality would also surface in the schools, and the principal battleground on that front so far has been the use of certain curricular materials designed to teach children about "alternative lifestyles" such as those of families in which the parents are gay men or lesbians.

The power of early childhood education to influence cultural values and alter social patterns has been recognized since ancient times. In his later years, Plato was particularly concerned about the development of social institutions that would preserve Athenian culture by the proper upbringing of the young. In the *Laws,* he uses education about incest as an example of how to maintain widespread agreement about a law that is effective in the tricky area of sexual relations. The Athenian observes that nobody ever even considers violating the law against acts of incest. He then suggests to the Spartan Megillus the reason this is so:

ATHENIAN: And does not the reason lie in this, that nobody speaks of them otherwise, but every one of us, from the day of his birth, hears this opinion expressed always and everywhere, not only in comic speech, but often also in serious tragedy....

MEGILLUS: Thus much at least you are quite right in saying – that public opinion has a surprising influence, when there is no attempt by anybody ever to breathe a word that contradicts the law.

(838c-d)

The Athenian then suggests that an effective way to combat homosexuality (as well as other undesired sexual practices) would be through comparable mastery of public opinion against it. Megillus is politely skeptical that this could ever come about.

Similar skepticism would be in order for the prospect that any consensus might emerge in our educational system today. The American public is deeply divided over the issue of homosexuality. A March 1993 *New York Times* poll showed just how deep that division is: when asked whether homosexual relations between consenting adults should be legal, only forty-six percent of those polled said yes; when asked whether homosexuality should be considered an acceptable alternative lifestyle, only thirty-six percent said yes; and fifty-five percent said that they would object to having a homosexual as a child's elementary school teacher.[51]

In light of these poll results, it should have come as no surprise when controversy erupted over introduction of the Rainbow Curriculum in the New York City public schools. This curriculum, which included education about gay and lesbian families as an acceptable alternative lifestyle, contributed to Schools Chancellor Joseph A. Fernandez's departure in 1993.[52] Even among the usually liberal voters of Oregon, there was significant support for an unsuccessful initiative in the 1992 general election that would have required the state's educational institutions to treat homosexuality as "abnormal, wrong, unnatural, and perverse" and as constituting behavior "to be discouraged and avoided."[53] Clearly the war for mastery of public opinion on how homosexuality should be treated in the public schools is far from over.

The works of the Canon reveal how pervasive homophobia has been in Western civilization. Homophobic attitudes have been present even in societies as enlightened as Plato's Athens (where pederasty was an accepted practice among the upper class) and Elizabethan England (where a noted poet did not hesitate to reveal his bisexuality). Manifestations of homophobia — in the form of stereotypes, harassment, and criminalization — have persisted for millenia.

Those who look to the Canon to bolster their belief that homosexuality is immoral will be unsettled to find that there is profound questioning of this assumption and that mere rationalizations are revealed to be just that. On the other hand, those who look to the Canon for a sense of unencumbered enlightenment or freedom from the chains of unfounded prejudice will also be disappointed. Throughout these works, there is a pervasive undercurrent of homophobic bias, and the same fears and anxieties have attended this issue as have attended any departure from the sexual practices of the majority.

As the pace of social change in recent years has quickened, many people have been unable to handle the resulting uncertainty, especially where gender roles are concerned. There has been what Randy Shilts termed "an upheaval in the sexual psyche of this nation" as society has attempted to redefine what it means to be a man and what it means to be a woman in today's world.[54] Polls continue to show that American society is deeply divided over homosexuality, a subject that has been called "as fiery as abortion yet imbued with more primal fears and deep social and religious constraints," resulting in "the rhetorical equivalent of the fog of battle."[55] The works of the Canon are especially valuable for teaching about this subject: not only are they the texts that uniquely document the "deep social and religious constraints" concerning homosexuality, but they also provide a rich basis for gaining an understanding of homophobia, the kinds of justifications that are offered for it, and the discomfiting forms it takes in everyday life.

Notes

1. See, for example, D. Drummond Ayres, Jr., "An Uproar over Comments by Republicans in Virginia," *New York Times,* March 19, 1993, p. A8.

2. Suzanne Pharr, *Homophobia: A Weapon of Sexism* (Inverness, Calif.: Chardon Press, 1988), p. 1.

3. Richard A. Isay, "Removing the Stigma," letter to the editor, *New York Times,* September 2, 1992, p. A18.

4. Robert Hughes, *Culture of Complaint: The Fraying of America* (New York: Oxford University Press, 1993), p. 19.

5. John Boswell uses the example of manual preference in *Christianity, Social Tolerance, and Homosexuality* (Chicago: University of Chicago Press, 1980), p. 59. David M. Halperin uses the example of dietary preference in *One Hundred Years of Homosexuality* (New York: Routledge, 1990), pp. 26-27.

6. See Bill Turque, "Gays under Fire," *Newsweek,* September 14, 1992, pp. 34-40.

7. The four references are Deuteronomy 23.17, I Kings 14.24, I Kings 22.46, and II Kings 23.7.

8. See, for example, David F. Greenberg, *The Construction of Homosexuality* (Chicago: University of Chicago Press, 1988), pp. 136-141. Greenberg concludes, "It cannot be stressed too strongly that none of the campaigns against cult prostitution was directed at homosexuality in the population at large" (141).

9. Peter J. Gomes, "Homophobic? Re-Read Your Bible," *New York Times,* August 17, 1992, p. A19.

10. Richard D. Mohr, *Gays/Justice: A Study of Ethics, Society, and Law* (New York: Columbia University Press, 1988), p. 34.

11. Boswell, *Christianity, Social Tolerance, and Homosexuality,* p. 15.

12. The Greek phrase used by Plato is *para phusin,* the primary meaning of which is "unrelated to the process of reproduction." See the discussion at Boswell, *Christianity, Social Tolerance, and Homosexuality,* pp. 13-14, n. 22.

13. R. H. Denniston, "Ambisexuality in Animals," in *Homosexual Behavior: A Modern Reappraisal,* ed. Judd Marmor (New York: Basic Books, 1980), pp. 25-40.

14. Boswell, *Christianity, Social Tolerance, and Homosexuality,* p. 12.

15. Mohr, *Gays/Justice,* pp. 35-36.

16. See Sam Roberts, "Cardinal Reflects on Role as a Moral Lightning Rod," *New York Times,* June 2, 1993, pp. A1 and B12.

17. Mohr, *Gays/Justice,* p. 32.

18. See generally her book *The Anita Bryant Story: The Survival of Our Nation's Families and the Threat of Militant Homosexuality* (Old Tappan, N.J.: Revell, 1977).

19. Quoted in editorial "The Other Minority," *New Republic,* March 30, 1992, p. 7.

20. See Kenneth J. Dover, *Greek Homosexuality* (Cambridge, Mass.: Harvard University Press, 1989), pp. 153-170.

21. Recent scholarship on Greek homosexuality has maintained that our modern categories of the heterosexual and the homosexual have no precise equivalent in classical antiquity. Such scholars as Michel Foucalt and David Halperin have argued that the crucial distinction for males was that between the active and passive roles in intercourse; so long as a male took the active role, the gender of the partner was unimportant. See Martha C. Nussbaum, "The Softness of Reason: A Classical Case for Gay Studies," *New Republic,* July 13, 1992, p. 35.

22. See, for example, Greenberg, *The Construction of Homosexuality,* pp.135-136.

23. Gomes, "Homophobic? Re-Read Your Bible," p. A19.

24. "Man Trouble," editorial in *National Review,* August 31, 1992, p. 18.

25. Boswell, *Christianity, Social Tolerance, and Homosexuality,* p. 24.

26. Rock Hudson and Sara Davidson, *Rock Hudson: His Story* (New York: William Morrow, 1986), pp. 12-13.

27. Anthony Summers, *Official and Confidential: The Secret Life of J. Edgar Hoover* (New York: G. P. Putnam's Sons, 1993), p. 12.

28. Mohr, *Gays/Justice,* p. 24.

29. This frequently quoted phrase came from an October 1969 speech in which Agnew castigated "an effete corps of impudent snobs who characterize themselves as intellectuals." Theo Lippman, Jr., *Spiro Agnew's America* (New York: Norton, 1972), p. 189.

30. Mohr, *Gays/Justice,* pp. 22-23.

31. For an insightful discussion of how homophobia develops in families, creating conflict in gay children, see Marshall Kirk and Hunter Madsen, *After the Ball: How America Will Conquer Its Hatred and Fear of Gays in the '90's* (New York: Doubleday, 1989), pp. 121-129.

32. *Bowers v. Hardwick,* 478 U.S. 186, 106 S. Ct. 2841, 92 L. Ed. 2d 140 (1986).

33. Justice Powell disclosed his continuing ambivalence about his vote in *Bowers* in a 1990 speech at New York University Law School. The private papers of the late Justice Thurgood Marshall, to which the public has recently gained access, contain further revelations about Powell's anguish and the complex "poker-playing strategies" of Court members in this case. Neil A. Lewis, "In Marshall Papers, Rare Glimpse at Court," *New York Times,* May 25, 1993, pp. A1 and A8.

34. 478 U.S. at 192.

35. 478 U.S. at 196-197.

36. 478 U.S. at 205-206.

37. 478 U.S. at 211.

38. See Deborah L. Rhode, *Justice and Gender: Sex Discrimination and the Law* (Cambridge, Mass.: Harvard University Press, 1989), pp. 144-145.

39. Dirk Johnson, "Colorado Ban on Gay Rights Laws Is Ruled Unconstitutional," *New York Times,* December 15, 1993, p. A11.

40. See "Text of Pentagon's New Policy Guidelines on Homosexuals in the Military," *New York Times,* July 20, 1993, p. A12.

41. Randy Shilts, *Conduct Unbecoming: Gays and Lesbians in the U.S. Military* (New York: St. Martin's Press, 1993), p. 4.

42. Melissa Wells-Petry, *Exclusion: Homosexuals and the Right to Serve* (Washington, D.C.: Regnery Gateway, 1993), pp. 189-190.

43. Ibid., pp. 187-188.

44. For a discussion of the Spartan and Theban traditions of pairs of lovers in the military, see Berkeley classics professor David Cohen's op-ed piece "Notes on a Grecian Yearn," *New York Times,* March 31, 1993, p. A13.

45. Plato describes the Greek practice of exercising naked in the *Republic* at 452a-d.

46. Ken Corbett, "Between Fear and Fantasy," *New York Times,* February 3, 1993, p. A15.

47. *Cheney v. Pruitt,* 963 F. 2d 1160 (9th Cir. 1991), *cert. denied* 113 S. Ct. 655, 121 L. Ed. 2d 581 (1992).

48. 963 F. 2d at 1165.

49. Shilts, *Conduct Unbecoming,* pp. 5-6.

50. *Baehr v. Lewin,* 852 P. 2d 44 (Hawaii, May 5, 1993). See Jane Gross, "After a Ruling, Hawaii Weighs Gay Marriages," *New York Times,* April 25, 1994, pp. A1 and C12.

51. The *New York Times*/CBS News Poll, reported in "How the Public Views Gay Issues," *New York Times,* March 5, 1993, p. A11.

52. See Tony Hiss, "The End of the Rainbow," *New Yorker,* April 12, 1993, pp. 43-54.

53. Timothy Egan, "Oregon Measure Asks State to Repress Homosexuality," *New York Times,* August 16, 1992, pp. 1 and 17.

54. Shilts, *Conduct Unbecoming,* p. 6.

55. Catherine S. Manegold, "The Odd Place of Homosexuality in the Military," *New York Times,* April 18, 1993, sec. 4, p. 1.

4: Abortion

A S DIVIDED AS American society is over homosexuality, the controversies that have been spawned by the gay rights movement pale
in comparison to those surrounding abortion. The topic of abortion
has engendered irresolvable differences over what has proved to be an
intractable issue, and the fabric of American society has been rent by
the escalating and even violent passions felt by both sides in the conflict. In spite of the massive amount of media attention given to abortion and the best efforts of many who have attempted to find a
common ground between the so-called pro-life and pro-choice camps,
no resolution to this bitter struggle is in sight.

One of the reasons for the intensity of the debate over abortion is
that it is really over more wide-ranging concerns in our society than
simply the termination of unwanted pregnancies. This particular issue
has become the lightning rod for a broader struggle between differing
outlooks on many of life's most fundamental concerns. As ethicist Daniel Callahan put it, "For both the prochoice modernizers and the prolife
traditionalists, abortion serves as a perfect symbol for such pervasive
issues as the roles and rights of the sexes, the family, the relationship
between law and morality, the nature and malleability of social reality,
and the place of reason and choice in human life."[1] Kristin Luker, a
feminist scholar who has written on abortion as a social issue, concurs:
"At issue is an attitude not only about a single issue – abortion – but
about an entire view of the world. On almost every relevant dimension
of life, prolife and prochoice values are internally coherent, vigorously
defended, and mutually antagonistic."[2]

Inability to come to terms with the moral dimension of abortion is a
peculiarly American and comparatively recent phenomenon.[3] In its
landmark 1973 decision on abortion, the U.S. Supreme Court traced
the history of abortion in the West and found that, while the practice
has been known to exist since ancient times, only in the modern era
has it been considered a serious moral or legal offense.[4] Thus, while
there is much in the Canon that deals with the human aspects of unwanted pregnancies and the options available to those involved, the

question of whether abortion is right or wrong tends not to be addressed directly. Of possibly greater importance, however, is the fact that the works of the Canon uniquely articulate the cultural values by reference to which society must grapple with the problem in modern terms. This chapter will demonstrate that the cultural values on which both pro-choice and pro-life advocates rely have an early and full exposition in the works of the Canon. First, some background concerning the constitutional basis for the abortion debate is in order.

The Constitutional Basis for *Roe v. Wade*

The Supreme Court had some notion of what it was getting into when, in the 1973 case *Roe v. Wade,* it declared that a woman has a fundamental constitutional right to terminate her pregnancy. Justice Harry Blackmun began his opinion for the 7 to 2 majority as follows: "We forthwith acknowledge our awareness of the sensitive and emotional nature of the abortion controversy, of the vigorous opposing views, even among physicians, and of the deep and seemingly absolute convictions that the subject inspires."[5] However, it is unlikely that the Court could have foreseen that the blockading of abortion clinics and the murder of a physician who performed abortions would result from its groundbreaking decision.[6]

The facts of the case were unexceptional. The plaintiff was a young waitress and single mother ("Jane Roe") who was pregnant again and unable to procure a safe, legal abortion because of the restrictive laws in Texas, which allowed the procedure only when it was medically necessary to save the mother's life. Roe's attorney, a young woman only five years out of law school, had experienced the terror of an illegal Mexican abortion in 1967 and therefore made up in personal commitment for what she lacked in legal experience.[7] The class action suit was pressed to the highest court in the land at a time when both the nation's political climate and the Court's ideological makeup were receptive. The result was what one noted legal scholar has called "undoubtedly the best known case the United States Supreme Court has ever decided," surpassing even such famous cases as *Dred Scott v. Sandford* (1857) and *Brown v. Board of Education* (1954).[8]

The Court's sweeping holding in *Roe v. Wade* invalidated the existing abortion statutes in 49 of the 50 states.[9] The essence of the holding was that a woman has a fundamental constitutional right to terminate her pregnancy during its early stages without state interference. The basis for this constitutional right was found in the notion of personal liberty embodied in the Fourteenth Amendment's due process clause ("nor shall any State deprive any person of life, liberty, or property, without due process of law"). The guarantee against deprivation of liberty was held to include the right to privacy which a long line of cases had found within the penumbra of the specific rights enumerated in the Bill of Rights. Citing several such cases involving marriage, procreation, contraception, family relationships, and child rearing, the Court concluded, "This right of privacy ... is broad enough to encompass a woman's decision whether or not to terminate her pregnancy."[10]

This right of privacy was held to be not absolute, however, and the Court concluded that it must be weighed against any compelling state interests in regulation. In the Court's view, there is no state interest sufficiently compelling to overcome the woman's privacy right during the first trimester of her pregnancy. During this time, decisions about abortion may be made by a woman and her physician without state interference. The state's interest in protecting maternal health becomes compelling after the first trimester, at the point at which mortality rates from abortion exceed mortality rates from childbirth. Thus the state may enact regulations intended to protect maternal health after the first trimester. Only after the second trimester is there a compelling state interest in protecting fetal life, beginning at the point at which the fetus is capable of surviving outside the womb. Thus after the second trimester a state may prohibit abortion altogether.[11]

Roe v. Wade's trimester framework was a bold venture into "judicial rulemaking," and it became the subject of widespread criticism from many different perspectives. Some critics predictably lamented the Court's intrusion into territory rightfully occupied by other branches of government. Others claimed that the trimester approach would prove unwieldy and unworkable. Still others predicted technological advances that would render the precise trimester system obsolete in a short time.[12] In spite of these criticisms, the trimester system worked reasonably well for almost twenty years, and newly-published evidence indicates that it did, in fact, comport with scientific advances in neonatology.[13]

When the Court announced its most recent major abortion decision in June 1992, there was widespread speculation that *Roe v. Wade* might not survive in the tribunal's new ideological climate. The decision in

Planned Parenthood v. Casey demonstrated how fractured the Court continues to be over the entire set of issues surrounding abortion. There was no majority opinion in the case. A plurality opinion written by Justice Sandra Day O'Connor, who was joined by Justices Anthony Kennedy and David Souter, stated that "the essential holding of *Roe v. Wade* should be retained and once again reaffirmed." The opinion retraced the line of privacy cases cited in *Roe* and concluded, "We have no doubt as to the correctness of those decisions. They support the reasoning in *Roe* relating to the woman's liberty because they involve personal decisions concerning not only the meaning of procreation but also human responsibility and respect for it."[14]

The trimester system did not fare as well. The three justices of the plurality rejected the trimester approach of *Roe* as "elaborate" and "rigid," favoring instead a new standard: state regulation of abortions at any time prior to fetal viability would be allowed so long as such regulation does not constitute an "undue burden" on a woman's right to an abortion.[15] In a separate opinion, Justice Blackmun, the original author of *Roe v. Wade,* praised the plurality for what he called "an act of personal courage and constitutional principle" but argued that "the factual premises of the trimester framework have not been undermined, and the *Roe* framework is far more administrable, and far less manipulable, than the 'undue burden' standard adopted by the joint opinion."[16]

The *Casey* decision showed the Court to be more divided about the issue of abortion than in any previous case. The 5 to 4 decision to reaffirm a woman's constitutional right to terminate her pregnancy was by the slimmest of margins, and Justice Blackmun wrote ominously of future prospects: "I fear for the darkness as four Justices anxiously await the single vote necessary to extinguish the light.... I am 83 years old. I cannot remain on this Court forever, and when I do step down, the confirmation process for my successor well may focus on the issue before us today. That, I regret, may be exactly where the choice between the two worlds will be made."[17]

Blackmun's pessimism in June 1992 proved unwarranted in view of the outcome of the presidential election the following November. With the retirement of conservative Justice Byron White and the selection of Ruth Bader Ginsburg as his successor, a woman's right to choose seems secure for the immediate future. Still, Justice Blackmun's comment about the role of abortion in the confirmation process is apt. In spite of Ginsburg's strong reputation as an advocate for women's rights, following her nomination the media devoted considerable attention to comments she had made in the past questioning *Roe's* reliance on the right of privacy as the basis for a woman's constitutional right to terminate her pregnancy.[18] In raising this question, Ginsburg joined many other legal scholars, including many feminists, who believe that a woman's right to choose might logically have been grounded in the equal protection clause of the Fourteenth Amendment.[19]

Because of the new standard announced in the splintered decision in *Casey* and the changing makeup of the Court, many more years of thrashing through the legal and moral uncertainties surrounding abortion are likely. It is inevitable that attention will continue to be focused on the two major points for which *Roe v. Wade* will be remembered: that the constitutional right to privacy encompasses a woman's right to terminate her pregnancy and that this right must be balanced against state interests in protecting fetal life, depending upon the stage of pregnancy. Both of these doctrines have cultural roots that are just beneath the surface in the works of the Canon.

Privacy Considerations in the Canon

While the legal protection afforded to privacy is a relatively new development in American constitutional law, the concept of privacy — whether or not it is articulated in a coherent way — has been an omnipresent aspect of human experience. Basic questions about how much of one's life to share, and with whom, have been common to people of all eras. The notion that there are some aspects of life that should be shielded from public view and/or protected from outside interference is fundamental to the very concept of a civilized people. Especially with respect to the areas delineated by the Supreme Court in *Roe v. Wade* (marriage, procreation, contraception, family relationships, and the raising of children), Western culture has generally recognized the need for some degree of personal autonomy, and governmental authorities have intruded into these areas at their peril. Certain passages from the works of the Canon demonstrate sensitivity to the need for privacy in the formation of families through marriage and procreation (private choices), in sexual relations (private acts), and in domestic surroundings (private space).

Private Choices

Ever since the emergence of Western civilization from hazy archaic eras, restrictions on choice in marriage and sexual relations have often been depicted as an affront to human sensibilities and therefore insufferable. Given American society's emphasis on the family unit as the primary transmitter of cultural values, it is not surprising that some of the most important cases establishing the constitutional right to privacy have dealt with marriage and procreation. Among the cases cited by the Supreme Court in *Roe* was a 1967 decision in which a Virginia statute forbidding interracial marriage was declared unconstitutional. In that case Chief Justice Earl Warren wrote, "The freedom to marry has long been recognized as one of the vital personal rights essential to the orderly pursuit of happiness by free men. Marriage is one of the basic civil rights of man, fundamental to our very existence and survival."[20]

The private and intimate nature of decisions concerning marriage and procreation can be seen in the examples of two young women who have reached marriageable age. In the *Odyssey,* Nausicaa is the daughter of King Alcinous of Phaeacia, the remote island on whose shores Odysseus has washed up after his raft was destroyed in a storm. Nausicaa will be crucial to Odysseus's rescue, and to summon her to the shore where Odysseus lies half dead, Athena devises a scheme. She appears to the sleeping Nausicaa in the form of one of her girlfriends and chastises her for having neglected to wash the apparel that will eventually be needed for her wedding. Athena reminds her that attendance to such things will likely result in good reports about her in the community, and she already has suitors among the noblest youths in the land. When Nausicaa awakens, she marvels at the dream she has had and hurries to tell her parents. However, when she gets her father's ear, she is unable to reveal what has transpired. Instead, she asks for permission to use a mule-driven wagon to transport the routine family laundry to the seashore. Homer then observes:

> So she spoke, for she was ashamed to name gladsome [possibly "fruitful"] marriage to her father; but he understood all, and answered, saying: "Neither the mules do I begrudge thee, my child, nor aught beside." (6.66-68)

Any parent of an adolescent child will immediately recognize Nausicaa's reluctance to divulge further information to her parents. Details about romantic interests and potential mates often fall strictly within a teenager's zone of privacy.

While Nausicaa's privacy relates to the general subject of her readiness for marriage, *Romeo and Juliet* portrays a young woman who has already selected her future mate but encounters an insurmountable obstacle to her choice in the ancient feud between their respective families (an obstacle that must have seemed tantamount to the obstacle of race in Virginia before 1967). Her father, Lord Capulet, insists that she marry a man of his choosing, and Juliet resists having his choice forced upon her. Lord Capulet flies into a rage at his daughter's ingratitude for his efforts on her behalf and threatens to disown her:

> CAPULET: And then to have a wretched puling fool,
> A whining mammet, in her fortune's tender,
> To answer "I'll not wed; I cannot love,
> I am too young: I pray you pardon me."
> But, and you will not wed, I'll pardon you:
> Graze where you will, you shall not house with me.
> . . . .

> JULIET: Is there no pity sitting in the clouds,
> That sees into the bottom of my grief?
> O, sweet my mother, cast me not away!
> Delay this marriage for a month, a week;
> Or, if you do not, make the bridal bed
> In that dim monument where Tybalt lies.

(3.5.185-190, 198-203)

Juliet is unable to tell her father the real reason she rejects his choice: her romantic involvement with a young man of the rival Montague family. (Given her intention to elope with Romeo, her claim that she is too young to marry is clearly a false pretense.) Juliet's predicament has long symbolized the tragedy that ensues when the freedom to choose one's mate is denied.

A woman at a different stage of life is portrayed in the *Odyssey*. Odysseus's wife Penelope has awaited news of her husband for the ten years of the Trojan War and an additional ten as he has struggled to return home. Her fellow citizens of Ithaca have gradually given up hope that he might still be alive, and fierce competition has arisen among a group known as the suitors, who vie for Penelope's hand in marriage. Odysseus's household is obviously one of great substance, and the suitors have become increasingly brazen in their riotous behavior as they daily consume everything in sight. Penelope has repeatedly put off the suitors' demands that she select one of them as her new husband, and she has even resorted to her famous scheme of weaving by day and unweaving by night to delay having to make a decision as promised upon completion of the shroud.

In an assembly of Ithacan citizens, Telemachus, the young son of Odysseus and Penelope, confronts the suitors about their unprincipled behavior. Antinous answers him angrily, placing the blame directly on Penelope:

> Send away thy mother, and command her to wed whomsoever her father bids, and whoso is pleasing to her. But if she shall continue long time to vex the sons of the Achaeans, mindful in her heart of this, that Athene has endowed her above other women with knowledge of fair handiwork and an understanding heart, and wiles.... Yet this at least she devised not aright. For so long shall men devour thy livelihood and thy possessions, even as long as she shall keep the counsel which the gods now put in her heart. Great fame she brings on herself, but on thee regret for thy much substance. For us, we will go neither to our lands nor elsewhither, until she marries that one of the Achaeans whom she will. (2.113-117, 122-128)

Penelope's reason for keeping her thoughts private ("the counsel which the gods put in her heart") is obvious: she clings to hope that Odysseus is still alive and will return home. Because this possibility is preferable to any of the offers she has had, Penelope refuses to relent and insists upon her freedom *not* to marry.

All of these passages demonstrate the intensely personal sense of privacy that pervades people's thoughts and feelings about their prospects for marriage and future family life. In two instances (Nausicaa and Juliet), young women are seen just emerging from childhood, with its subjugation to the total control of their fathers. As they enter upon their own adult lives, among the first matters in which they expect self-determination are marriage and procreation. In the third instance (Penelope), a middle-aged woman is seen using desperate measures to preserve her freedom of choice in the face of pressures from all sides.

If these women's expectation of self-determination can be seen as legitimate within the microcosm of their individual family situations, a fortiori these are matters in which the state has no proper role in a free society. Thus it is entirely logical that the Supreme Court accorded marriage and procreation constitutional protection under the rubric of the right to privacy in its earliest stages. As is the case with all such basic human concerns, the expectation of privacy in these matters is evident in the works of the Canon.

Private Acts

Sexual relations are, to many people's minds, the quintessentially private form of human conduct. This widely held perception was perhaps responsible for the fact that a case involving sexual relations is often said to have spawned the line of privacy cases which led to *Roe v. Wade*. In that 1965 case, a Connecticut statute forbidding the use of contraceptives was held unconstitutionally to intrude upon the right of marital privacy. In a frequently quoted passage, Justice William O. Douglas wrote, "Would we allow the police to search the sacred precincts of marital bedrooms for telltale signs of the use of contraceptives? The very idea is repulsive to the notions of privacy surrounding the marriage relationship."[21]

The notion that marital relations should be conducted in private has strong cultural roots. In Genesis, this lesson is conveyed in a very practical way. Acting on instructions from the Lord, Isaac and his wife Rebekah settle in the land of Gerar. When the men of Gerar ask Isaac about the fair woman who accompanies him, he tells them that she is his sister rather than his wife. His motivation for lying is unclear; he claims that it is to prevent harm to himself because of the jealousy that Rebekah's beauty would arouse. In any event, the truth eventually becomes apparent:

> And it came to pass, when he had been there a long time, that Abimelech king of the Philistines looked out at a window, and saw, and, behold, Isaac was sporting with Rebekah his wife.
> And Abimelech called Isaac, and said, Behold, of a surety she *is* thy wife: and how saidst thou, She is my sister? And Isaac said unto him, Because I said, Lest I die for her. (26.8-9)

Whatever Isaac's real motivation, his lack of discretion in "sporting with" his wife outdoors within public view was not smart. His reckless conduct gave away the secret which he had tried to keep even at the cost of lying to his neighbors.

A passage in the *Iliad* involves trickery of a different sort. Zeus, the father of the gods, has promised to allow the Trojans temporarily to prevail against the Greeks in the Trojan War. His wife Hera and his brother Poseidon both support the Greeks. Hera is plotting to distract

Zeus's attention from the battlefield to give Poseidon an opportunity to influence the outcome of the battle without interference from his more powerful brother. She decides to make use of Zeus's well-known sexual appetite and, with the help of Sleep, keep him away from the scene of action. When Hera arrives at the highest peak of Mt. Olympus, Zeus greets her and is overcome by passion. He proposes that they make love on the spot:[22]

> Hera's answer was as sly as before: "Revered Son of Cronus, what a shocking idea! Do you actually mean us to make love up here, in full sight of Olympus? Suppose some god were to play spy, and tell the other Immortals all he had seen? I should not have the face to go home after that; it certainly would give me a pardonable grievance against you. But if I must humour you in this inconvenient fashion, pray escort me to your Olympian bedchamber, with its stout doors hinged to pillars, built by our son Hephaestus. We can be private there." (14.329-340)

Zeus does not quibble with Hera's concern for privacy, but rather uses his divine powers to allay her qualms:

> "No, no, Hera," replied Zeus. "You need not fear that any god or man will witness our marital sport! I shall spread an immense golden cloud over you, which the brightest eye in existence, the Sun's, would fail to pierce." (14.341-345)

This done, Hera has no further grounds to insist that they go elsewhere, so her plot is carried out atop the highest peak of Mt. Olympus, near Zeus's throne.

A different motivation for privacy is presented when a couple is involved in an illicit affair. Under such circumstances, the great outdoors might seem to provide a locale suitable for avoiding detection. However, an unsecured environment poses its own risks, as was discovered by two characters in *Titus Andronicus*. Tamora, the captive queen of the Goths, has married the Roman emperor Saturninus. Nevertheless, she continues her affair with Aaron the Moor, whom she meets in the woods for a tryst during a hunting party. When Saturninus's younger brother Bassianus and his wife Lavinia happen upon the scene, Tamora complains bitterly of this intrusion into her privacy. She calls Bassianus a "saucy controller of our private steps" and an "unmannerly intruder" (2.3.60, 65). In response, Lavinia notes that the real reason Tamora is berating Bassianus for sauciness is that she has been "intercepted in [her] sport" (2.3.80). Bassianus then serves notice of his intention to tell his brother what he has seen. This passage demonstrates that claims to a right of privacy in sexual acts are not necessarily dependent on the legitimacy of those acts; rather, claimants seem to invoke a natural or inherent right to privacy that they believe everyone should automatically recognize and respect.

As a philosopher, Plato is more apt to theorize abstractly than to dramatize concretely. Therefore, he seeks to provide reasons for maintaining privacy in sexual matters. In the *Hippias Major,* Socrates and Hippias are discussing the relationship between the pleasant, on the one hand, and the good or beautiful, on the other. Socrates says that many ordinary activities, such as eating and drinking, cannot be denied to be pleasant, and he questions whether one must therefore deny them any possibility of also being beautiful. Then he adds as a comic afterthought, "and as to the act of sexual love, we should all, no doubt, contend that it is most pleasant, but that one must, if he perform it, do it so that no one else shall see, because it is most repulsive to see" (299a).

A more considered discussion of the same question may be found in the *Laws,* where Plato – ever the social engineer – has the Athenian suggest a rationale for the state to encourage privacy in sexual matters. He says that it is a worthy state objective to make sex "a less tyrannical mistress":

> This would come about if indulgence in sexual intercourse were devoid of shamelessness; for if, owing to shame, people indulged in it but seldom, in consequence of this rare indulgence they would find it a less tyrannical mistress. Let them, therefore, regard privacy in such actions – yet not the entire avoidance of such actions – as honourable – sanctioned both by custom and by unwritten law; and want of privacy as dishonourable. (841a-b)

Thus Plato's view is one of the sources of the strong Western tradition that privacy in sexual relations is best for all concerned.

Because abortion is related to the process of reproduction and reproduction usually follows sex, it is logical that the Supreme Court would find its own precedents concerning marital privacy and the use of contraceptives a source of legal authority for the abortion question. In so doing, it drew upon a strong cultural tradition emphasizing the need for privacy in sexual matters, one that is well represented in the works of the Canon.

Private Space

As used in common parlance, the concept of privacy includes a clearly territorial or spatial component. Most people seem to have a homing instinct for a physical location to which they may retreat and in which they feel shielded from the world's demands and intrusions. Among the privacy cases cited by the Supreme Court in *Roe v. Wade* was a 1969 case in which the conviction of a Georgia man for having obscene material in his bedroom was reversed because the Georgia obscenity statute as applied had violated the First Amendment. In that case, Justice Thurgood Marshall wrote, "Whatever may be the justifications for other statutes regulating obscenity, we do not think they reach into the privacy of one's own home. If the First Amendment means anything, it means that a State has no business telling a man, sitting alone in his own house, what books he may read or what films he may watch."[23] As has already been discussed, four years earlier Justice Douglas wrote of "the sacred precincts of marital bedrooms."[24] Obviously the bedroom has a special claim to protection as a sort of sanctum sanctorum.

In II Kings, the kings of Syria and Israel are at war. Elisha the prophet is an adviser to the king of Israel and has been able to give him much helpful advice. When the king of Israel seems repeatedly to have inside information about Syria's military strategy, the king of Syria fears that there is a spy in his camp:

> Therefore the heart of the king of Syria was sore troubled for this thing; and he called his servants, and said unto them, Will ye not shew me which of us is for the king of Israel?
> And one of his servants said, None, my lord, O king: but Elisha, the prophet that is in Israel, telleth the king of Israel the words that thou speakest in thy bedchamber. (6.11-12)

The point of the story is that Elisha's prophetic powers, not spies, are the source of the information that is reaching the king of Israel. What is noteworthy in this context, however, is that words spoken in a bedchamber are used as the best example of communications that should be strictly private.

Another instance of the bedroom viewed as private space is found in *Cymbeline*. Posthumus, a banished Englishman, goes to Rome, where he makes elaborate boasts to a group of men about his wife Imogen's beauty, chastity, and fidelity to him. Iachimo, an unscrupulous Italian, makes a wager with Posthumus that he can seduce Imogen back in England. When Imogen rejects Iachimo and he seems about to lose the wager, he hides in her bedroom in a trunk, from which he intends to emerge after she goes to sleep. He plans to make observations that he will use to support his false claim that he succeeded in seducing her:

IMOGEN: Sleep hath seized me wholly.
        To your protection I commend me, gods.
        From fairies and the tempters of the night
        Guard me, beseech ye.
                       Sleeps. Iachimo comes from the trunk.

IACHIMO: The crickets sing, and man's o'erlabour'd sense
        Repairs itself by rest.
       . . . .
                       But my design,
        To note the chamber: I will write all down:
        Such and such pictures; there the window; such
        The adornment of her bed; the arras, figures,
        Why, such and such; and the contents o' the story.
        Ah, but some natural notes about her body,
        Above ten thousand meaner moveables
        Would testify, to enrich mine inventory.
        O sleep, thou ape of death, lie dull upon her!
        And be her sense but as a monument,
        Thus in a chapel lying!

                                  (2.2.7-12, 23-33)

Iachimo has violated Imogen's privacy if not her honor, and the image of him standing motionless over her bed as she sleeps is deeply disturbing. The desire for privacy and a sense of security as one sleeps reflects a basic human need.

The bedroom is the place where people are sometimes disrobed, where they at times engage in their most intimate activities, and where more often than not they are totally vulnerable in their repose. Thus, even though there is no legal distinction between one type of room and another in a private home, the bedroom was the logical place for the Supreme Court to focus upon in giving the right to privacy a spatial dimension. In so doing, the Court was able to use the cultural predisposition to regard the bedroom as the most private of places, a predisposition that is evident in the works of the Canon.

The Stages of Pregnancy

A second major innovation for which *Roe v. Wade* is known is that a woman's right to terminate her pregnancy must be balanced against state interests in protecting fetal life, depending upon the stage of pregnancy. The key elements of the *Roe* framework are division of the pregnancy span into three roughly equal trimesters and use of the concept of viability (ability to survive outside the womb) as the point after which the state may regulate for the purpose of protecting fetal life. Although the Court seemed to abandon the trimester framework in 1992, use of the concept of viability continues. While one cannot expect literary works of the past to have been written with the sophistication of modern medicine in delineating the stages of fetal development, nevertheless many fundamental points were clearly grasped by those who produced these texts.

Prior to Viability

In *Love's Labour's Lost,* Costard the clown has been a letter carrier between Armado, a Spaniard known as a braggart, and his girlfriend Jaquenetta, a common country girl. During the rehearsal for a pageant in which Armado will play Hector and Costard will play Pompey, Costard reveals that Jaquenetta is pregnant by Armado. (It is unclear how Costard knows this, for apparently it is news to Armado.) The revelation takes place in a jocular exchange begun when Costard interrupts Armado's lines:

ARMADO: This Hector far surmounted Hannibal, –

COSTARD: The party is gone, fellow Hector, she is gone; she is two months on her way.

ARMADO: What meanest thou?

COSTARD: Faith, unless you play the honest Troyan, the poor wench is cast away: she's quick [pregnant]; the child brags in her belly already: 'tis yours.

(5.2.677-683)

Costard's apparent motive for claiming that the two-month-old fetus ("the child") already "brags in her belly" is to support his allegation that Armado is definitely the father. This statement is made for dramatic effect, and it is unlikely that it indicates a considered view on anyone's part that a fetus of this age already possesses the personality traits of its parents.

Movement of the fetus within the womb has long been the first unmistakable evidence of life within. In *All's Well That Ends Well,* a riddle alludes to the pregnancy of Helena, a character who is falsely rumored to be dead, by pointing to the fetus's activity: "Dead though she be, she feels her young one kick:/So there's my riddle: one that's dead is quick" (5.3.303-304). It might be instructive to note the words Shakespeare uses to describe the fetus in this and the previous passages: "the child" and "her young one." This use of language comports with the pro-life movement's insistence on referring to zygotes, embryos, and fetuses alike as unborn children.

Fetal movement more vigorous than a kick is reported in Luke. That book opens with the story of the births of John the Baptist and Jesus. An angel appears to the virgin Mary and tells her of the forthcoming birth of Jesus. The angel also tells Mary that her cousin Elisabeth, who was thought to be barren, is in her sixth month of pregnancy and will bear a son. After the angel has departed, Mary rushes to the hill country to visit Elisabeth. When Mary enters Elisabeth's house, she calls out to greet her:

> And it came to pass, that, when Elisabeth heard the salutation of Mary, the babe leaped in her womb; and Elisabeth was filled with the Holy Ghost:
> And she spoke out with a loud voice, and said, Blessed art thou among women, and blessed is the fruit of thy womb.
> And whence is this to me, that the mother of the Lord should come to me?
> For, lo, as soon as the voice of thy salutation sounded in mine ears, the babe leaped in my womb for joy. (1.41-44)

The notion of a six-month-old fetus "leaping for joy" might be difficult to explain were it not presented within a context of two unusual pregnancies, one of a virgin and the other of a barren woman "well stricken in years." Obviously Luke has taken a common physiological fact — the tendency of a six-month-old fetus to move, sometimes vigorously — and given it a religious interpretation. As the angel reminded Mary a few lines before, "with God nothing shall be impossible" (1.37).

After Viability

As was discussed above, the point at which the fetus becomes viable, or capable of living outside the womb, was crucial to both the 1973 *Roe* decision and the 1992 *Casey* decision. Legally, this is the point after which the state may impose regulations to protect fetal life, including the outright prohibition of abortion. The notion of a minimum age for viability is evident in a number of passages in the Canon.

At the beginning of *King John,* two sons of the late Sir Robert Faulconbridge are arguing their respective cases for inheritance rights before King John. The younger son, his father's namesake, was recognized as legitimate, while the elder son, known as Philip the Bastard, was rejected by his father as illegitimate. On his deathbed, Sir Robert based his contention about Philip's parentage on the timing of his conception. The younger son puts it as follows to King John:

> ROBERT: Large lengths of seas and shores
> Between my father and my mother lay,
> As I have heard my father speak himself,
> When this same lusty gentleman was got.
> Upon his death-bed he by will bequeath'd
> His lands to me, and took it on his death
> That this my mother's son was none of his;
> And if he were, he came into the world
> Full fourteen weeks before the course of time.
>
> (1.1.105-113)

The normal human gestation period is two-hundred sixty-six days, or thirty-eight weeks. If Philip needed to be fourteen weeks premature to be legitimate, that means that he should have been born after a gestation period of only twenty-four weeks. That would put him — with almost eerie accuracy — right on the cusp of viability. Two scientists recently wrote on this point, "Up to twenty-four weeks, the probability of survival is either zero or extremely low. From that point on, however, it rises dramatically, reaching quite high levels by twenty-six weeks."[25] (Of course, these figures are to some extent affected by the availability of modern medical technology; however, they are also affected by physiological factors, especially lung development, that are not affected by such technology.[26])

The most famous survivor of premature birth in Shakespeare is the villainous king in *Richard III*. Richard is one of the most dazzlingly evil characters in Western literature, and Shakespeare links his deranged personality to his deformed body (a hunched back). In addition, various grotesque abnormalities attended his premature birth, such as the presence of visible teeth. At the beginning of the play. Richard describes himself in the following terms:

RICHARD: I, that am rudely stamped, and want love's majesty
            To strut before a wanton ambling nymph;
            I, that am curtail'd of this fair proportion,
            Cheated of feature by dissembling nature,
            Deform'd, unfinish'd, sent before my time
            Into this breathing world, scarce half made up,
            And that so lamely and unfashionable
            That dogs bark at me as I halt by them.

                                                    (1.1.16-23)

It is uncertain exactly how many weeks premature Richard's birth was. His statement that he was "scarce half made up" could be taken in terms of either the gestation period or birth weight. If the former was the intended meaning, that would mean that he was born after a gestation period of only nineteen or twenty weeks. It is highly unlikely, even under modern conditions, that a fetus this young could survive.[27] However, Shakespeare clearly intended to portray Richard as having been a freak of nature at birth. It is interesting that, in the same line, Richard refers to being sent into "this breathing world"; this reference to lung development identifies one of the principal barriers to survivability at such a young age.

Richard's murderous behavior evokes the hatred of many in the play, and in the passionate outbursts of those who rail against him, the circumstances of his birth figure prominently. For example, Queen Margaret, who hates Richard as the murderer of her husband and son, calls him "Thou elvish-mark'd, abortive, rooting hog!/Thou that wast seal'd in thy nativity/The slave of nature and the son of hell!" (1.3.228-230). Lady Anne, whose husband was murdered by Richard, delivers the following curse on him:

ANNE: If ever he have child, abortive be it,
            Prodigious, and untimely brought to light,
            Whose ugly and unnatural aspect
            May fright the hopeful mother at the view;
            And that be heir to his unhappiness!

                                                    (1.2.21-25)

Obviously she is wishing for Richard a perpetuation of the legacy of his own suffering. Having premature offspring with abnormalities sufficient to disturb others but not to cause death is a horrible curse. (The great irony of the passage is that Lady Anne will eventually marry Richard, and thus the curse will devolve upon her.)

Premature birth also plays a prominent part in *Macbeth*. Macbeth has killed Duncan, and he now places a lot of stock in that part of the witches' prophecy that said that "none of woman born/Shall harm Macbeth" (4.1.80-81). Near the end of the play, he is confronted on the battlefield by Macduff, who has joined forces with Duncan's son and the king of England. As fighting portends, Macduff makes a dramatic revelation:

MACDUFF: Despair thy charm;
          And let the angel whom thou still hast served
          Tell thee, Macduff was from his mother's womb
          Untimely ripp'd.

                                                  (5.8.13-16)

This apparent reference to delivery by Caesarian section demonstrates awareness that a fetus becomes viable and may be removed from the womb under some circumstances. As used here, "untimely" seems to mean before natural childbirth, not before viability.

These passages taken together indicate a general awareness of the concept of viability and of the time after which viability exists. More specifically, gestation is understood to be a gradual process without clear lines of demarcation between stages of development. There is comprehension that a fetus is capable of living outside the womb in the later stages of pregnancy. There seems to be intuitive understanding of the need for the lungs to have developed sufficiently for the newborn to breathe on its own. And there is awareness of the complications and abnormalities that can result from the premature birth of an incompletely developed fetus. All these understandings provide a suitable conceptual framework for consideration of the possibility – and the morality – of abortion.

Status of the Fetus

The legal and philosophical literature on abortion has long groped to find an appropriate characterization of the status of the fetus and its relationship to the woman who carries it. This matter has never been satisfactorily resolved. Feminist legal scholar Catharine MacKinnon has written, "Sometimes there are no adequate analogies. As it is, the fetus has no concept of its own, but must be like something men have or are: a body part to the Left, a person to the Right. Nowhere in law is the fetus a fetus."[28] In his 1992 book on abortion, Roger Rosenblatt makes a similar point: "In a way, the fetus itself is an entity of uncertainty and as such reflects the ambiguities as well as the sanctity of the life it represents."[29]

An examination of the works of the Canon provides a wide variety of images and characterizations of the fetus, some viewing it as dependent life clearly within the control of the mother and others viewing it as independent human life merely awaiting its turn. Unavoidably, each side of the abortion debate tends to seize upon those characterizations that support its position.

Dependent Life

Arguments favoring a woman's right to bodily self-determination are strongly based in the liberal political tradition. A woman's right to control her own body cannot be denied within this tradition, and yet this begs the question of what is her relationship to the fetus within her. Assuming that the fetus is dependent upon the woman and that its interests are subordinate to hers, several possible analogies are presented: the fetus as property interest, the fetus as body part, and the fetus as parasite or boarder.

Property Interest

In Exodus, the Lord is giving Moses on Mount Sinai the various commandments and judgments that Moses is to convey to his people. One judgment covers a situation in which men who are fighting strike a woman hard enough to cause a miscarriage, but the woman is not otherwise injured:

> If men strive, and hurt a woman with child, so that her fruit depart from her, and yet no mischief follow: he shall be surely punished, according as the woman's husband will lay upon him; and he shall pay as the judges determine. (21.22)

A different rule applies, however, if the woman is killed or seriously injured:

> And if any mischief follow, then thou shalt give life for life,
> Eye for eye, tooth for tooth, hand for hand, foot for foot,

> Burning for burning, wound for wound, stripe for stripe.
>
> (21.23-25)

If a fetus were considered a person with fully protected rights, the penalty for causing its destruction would be death for the party responsible. Because the loss of the fetus could be compensated for by payment of money, with its worth assessed by its potential parent, Judaic law appears to have regarded the fetus as a property interest of the parent.[30]

In *A Midsummer Night's Dream,* Oberon and Titania, king and queen of the fairies, are arguing over possession of a young Indian boy whom they both want. The queen is vigorously arguing her case: the boy's mother was a voteress of her order with whom she had a special friendship. Often they sat on the seashore, watching the ships sail by:

> TITANIA: When we have laughed to see the sails conceive
> And grow big-bellied with the wanton wind;
> Which she, with pretty and with swimming gait
> Following, — her womb then rich with my young squire, —
> Would imitate, and sail upon the land,
> To fetch me trifles, and return again,
> As from a voyage, rich with merchandise.
>
> (2.1.128-134)

The image of the voteress's womb "rich with my young squire," even as she playfully imitated a ship returning from a voyage "rich with merchandise," is vivid. It is difficult to assess the meaning of equating the unborn squire with merchandise, however, in view of the fact that the word appears in a metaphor in which the mother herself is compared with a ship, also a piece of property. In addition, the passage appears in a context in which the fairies are arguing over possession of the squire even after he has become a boy. When people are viewed as property, the usefulness of the analogy of the fetus as property evaporates.

Body Part

A second analogy that has often been used is that of the fetus as a body part of the mother. Catharine MacKinnon has observed, "Considering the fetus a body part has been the closest the law has come to recognizing fetal reality and protecting women at the same time. Since men have body parts over which they have sovereignty, deeming the fetus to be 'like that' has seemed the way to give women

sovereignty over what is done to their bodies, in which the fetus inevitably resides."[31] Of course, the principal problem with this analogy is
that the fetus does not perform any bodily function necessary to the
woman; rather, it may even dangerously tax her other bodily systems
without consequent advantage to her.

Pericles contains both language explicitly using the body parts imagery and striking evidence of the temporariness of that imagery when
the mother dies in childbirth. As Pericles and his pregnant wife Thaisa
are returning by ship to Pericles' home city of Tyre, a violent storm
strikes. The nurse Lychorida enters with a newborn infant and tells
Pericles that Thaisa has died in childbirth. Lychorida hands the infant
to Pericles and laments:

> LYCHOR.:   Here is a thing too young for such a place,
> Who, if it had conceit, would die, as I
> Am like to do: take in your arms this piece
> Of your dead queen.
>
> PERICLES: How, how, Lychorida!
>
> LYCHOR.:   Patience, good sir; do not assist the storm.
> Here's all that is left living of your queen,
> A little daughter: for the sake of it,
> Be manly, and take comfort.
>
> (3.1.15-22)

Even if the fetus is considered a body part of the mother, one
would assume that this relationship would cease at the moment of
birth. Thus the nurse in this passage must have meant to refer to the
infant as "what was, until moments ago, a piece of your [now] dead
queen." This meaning comes through in a later passage, where, after
many years, Pericles meets his long-lost daughter Marina in Ephesus,
where she is serving as a priestess in a convent. When Pericles seeks to
confirm her identity by asking her mother's name, Marina responds,
"Thaisa was my mother, who did end/ The minute I began" (5.1.213-
214). The fetus must cease being a body part upon separation from the
mother's body, and this view is in keeping with the interpretation, held
by many in classical antiquity, that human life begins with the first
breath.[32]

Parasite or Boarder

The feminist scholar Rosalind Petchesky has observed, "Feminists
writing on abortion usually have not claimed that a pregnant woman

'owns' the fetus or that it is part of her body. On the contrary feminists have generally characterized an unwanted pregnancy as a kind of bodily 'invasion.'"[33] This invasion has usually been analyzed in terms of the demands the fetus makes on the body in which it resides. Its principal demand is for nourishment: but for the continual provision of food and oxygen through the woman's bloodstream, the fetus would not survive.

In the *Laws,* the Athenian is holding forth about the virtues of exercise for a body's good health. He observes that when bodies receive the most food, they consequently require the most exercise. Clinias mischievously asks whether that means prescribing the most exercise for newborn babies. The Athenian responds, "Nay, even earlier than that, – we shall prescribe it for those nourished inside the bodies of their mothers" (789a). When Clinias asks incredulously whether he is speaking of unborn babes, he responds that that is indeed what he means. (The explanation that follows emphasizes that all bodies benefit, as by a tonic, from shaking and motion.)

A mother's viewpoint on her relationship to the fetus is given in *III Henry VI.* Henry, a weak king, has been compelled by his rival to the throne, the Duke of York, to agree to cede the throne to York and his progeny, but only after Henry is dead. Queen Margaret is furious with her husband for disinheriting their son. She says that the king's action was contrary to nature for a father and that he could not have done it if he had had a mother's physical relation to the child:

> Q. MAR.:   Hath he deserved to lose his birthright thus?
> Hadst thou but loved him half so well as I,
> Or felt that pain which I did for him once,
> Or nourish'd him as I did with my blood,
> Thou wouldst have left thy dearest heart-blood there,
> Rather than have made that savage duke thine heir
> And disinherited thine only son.
>
> (1.1.219-225)

In the queen's view, maternal bonds are created by the utter dependence of the fetus on the mother. In spite of such bonds, however, the imagery of helpless dependence tends to favor a woman's right to choose whether to allow such an "invader" to use her body.

In a celebrated article first published in 1971, philosopher Judith Jarvis Thomson used the example of a woman who wakes up one morning to discover that, during the night and without her permission, she has been attached by tubes to a famous violinist with a kidney disorder. If the tubes are detached, he cannot survive. He will need to continue using the woman's circulatory system for only about nine months. The article discusses the nature of her duty, if any, to remain attached to the violinist until he can survive on his own.[34]

Thomson's example makes explicit not only that the violinist is a "person" but that he is a valuable person with many contributions yet to make to society. Even granted this assumption, Thomson shows that the woman's duty to sustain the violinist under the circumstances is highly questionable.[35] While her example involves cleansing impurities from the blood, the analysis would be similar for providing nourishment. The fetus may be viewed as a parasite or as an uninvited boarder, but in either case the question presented is whether a woman has a duty to allow the use of her body to supply nourishment.

Independent Life

All of the passages in the preceding section presented images of the fetus as dependent life whose interests are likely to be subordinated to those of the woman in whose body it resides. In this section, images are presented of the fetus as essentially independent life faced with the temporary inconvenience of having to inhabit someone else's body. The specific images presented are the fetus as prisoner and, more generally, the fetus as divinely-created human being.

Prisoner

The notion that a fetus is somehow being incarcerated and compelled to inhabit another's body against its will is prevalent in those passages that refer to it as a prisoner. This helps to offset the image of an uninvited boarder or invader who imposes upon a woman; certainly it was not the fetus's choice to be put in the predicament it is in. This image also preserves the sense of temporariness in the situation: in due course, the fetus will necessarily be freed from its confinement.

In *Titus Andronicus,* Aaron the Moor is the illicit lover of Tamora the Goth, who has married the Roman emperor Saturninus. Aaron is talking to Tamora's two grown sons about the infant Tamora has recently borne him:

AARON: He is your brother, lords, sensibly fed
               Of that self-blood that first gave life to you,
               And from that womb where you imprison'd were

He is enfranchised and come to light.

(4.2.122-125)

When the fetus is viewed as a prisoner, the womb must be viewed as a prison. This inanimate imagery is used in the impersonal description of the place where Tamora's sons' lives began: Aaron describes the womb as their former prison rather than as a part of their mother's body.

Along similar lines, in *The Winter's Tale,* King Leontes of Sicily has imprisoned his wife Queen Hermione because he believes that her pregnancy is by another man. Paulina goes to the prison to visit Hermione and learns that she has just given birth to a daughter. Paulina persuades the jailer to allow her to take the infant out of the prison to show it to the king and convince him that it is his. Her argument to the jailer draws an analogy between the infant's escape from the prison of the womb and its escape from an actual prison:

GAOLER: Madam, if't please the queen to send the babe,
                I know not what I shall incur to pass it,
                Having no warrant.

PAULINA: You need not fear it, sir:
                This child was prisoner to the womb and is
                By law and process of great Nature thence
                Freed and enfranchised.

(2.2.56-61)

In both of the above cases, questions have been raised about the legitimacy of the children who are described as having been "enfranchised" by their release from the prison of the womb. In view of the inferior legal status accorded bastards in Shakespeare's time, there is a touch of irony in this description of the infants' new biological status: they may have been freed, but into a society apt to keep them in shackles because of their parentage.

Divinely-Created Human Being

A final characterization of the fetus's status is different from the others in that, rather than drawing an analogy between its status and that of some other entity, it simply states a religious conclusion – namely that the fetus is a full-fledged member of the human race, created in the image of God and embodying a uniquely precious human spirit. Like all basically religious tenets, such a characterization defies rational proof. Its acceptance or rejection is a matter of individual predilection and belief.

In *Twelfth Night,* Sebastian and Viola are twins who were separated in a shipwreck, each presuming the other dead. At the end of the play, when the two are reunited, Viola says that Sebastian must be the spirit of her dead bother:

VIOLA: Such a Sebastian was my brother too,
              So went he suited to his watery tomb:
              If spirits can assume both form and suit
              You come to fright us.

SEBASTIAN: A spirit I am indeed;
              But am in that dimension grossly clad
              Which from the womb I did participate.

                                              (5.1.240-245)

Sebastian's characterization of himself as a spirit clad in the form of a human body from the womb represents a fundamentally religious perspective on "ensoulment" of the fetus.[36]

The Hebrew scriptures contain many passages intended to demonstrate the Judaic belief in the eternal omniscience of God. One of the ways the scriptures demonstrate that belief is by statements to the effect that God knew an individual before he was born or even before he was conceived. Thus in Jeremiah the Lord says to the prophet Jeremiah, "Before I formed thee in the belly, I knew thee; and before thou camest forth out of the womb I sanctified thee, and I ordained thee a prophet unto the nations"(1.5). In a similar vein, the psalmist of Psalm 139 describes God's role in creating him:

> For thou hast possessed my reins: thou hast covered me in my mother's womb.
>
> I will praise thee; for I am fearfully and wonderfully made: marvellous are thy works; and that my soul knoweth right well.
>
> My substance was not hid from thee, when I was made in secret, and curiously wrought in the lowest parts of the earth.
>
> Thine eyes did see my substance, yet being unperfect; and in thy book all my members were written, which in continuance were fashioned, when as yet there was none of them. (13-16)

"In thy book all my members were written" has sometimes been taken as a reference to the unique genetic code that is present in each human being from the time of conception. This code is often used as the basis for the argument that every unborn human being – whether zygote, embryo, or fetus – is a unique person endowed by its creator with a right to life.[37]

Unwanted Pregnancies: What To Do?

Methods of birth control have been known and practiced since ancient times.[38] In discussing the ideal state of the *Republic,* Plato has Socrates envision people "not begetting offspring beyond their means lest they fall into poverty or war" (372c). Later, in the *Laws,* he has the Athenian propose that the size of the ideal state be limited to a set number of households: "There are many contrivances possible: where the fertility is great, there are methods of inhibition" (740d). In keeping with the reticence of classical authors about sexual matters, the specific methods of inhibition are not enumerated.

Regardless of the availability of birth control, unwanted pregnancies have always been a fact of life. Whether because of age or marital status, because of the size of an existing family, or because of their economic or psychological incapacity to care for a child, women have always been faced with pregnancies they would rather not have had. When an unwanted pregnancy occurs, what is needed is a realistic assessment of the practical alternatives available to the pregnant woman. While such alternatives are not explicitly weighed anywhere in the Canon, references are made in passing to some of the options that were available in the cultures represented by these works: "putting the mother away," inducing miscarriage, infanticide, abandoning the newborn, and secret adoption.

"Put the Mother Away"

In past eras, the first thought that might occur to a man who had impregnated a woman not his wife would be to remove her from the scene before her pregnancy began to show and questions were raised. This strategy was most likely to be used when the woman involved was of low social class and thus easy to relocate. The prevalence of this strategy may be discerned from the passage in *Love's Labour's Lost* previously cited, in which Costard the clown tells Armado of his rustic girlfriend's pregnancy and says, "Faith, unless you play the honest Troyan, the poor wench is cast away" (5.2.681-682).

The strategy of quietly removing the mother from public view was also pursued for humane purposes. This can be seen in the story of the virgin birth in Matthew:

> Now the birth of Jesus Christ was on this wise: When as his mother Mary was espoused to Joseph, before they came together, she was found with child of the Holy Ghost.
>
> Then Joseph her husband, being a just man, and not willing to make her a public example, was minded to put her away privily. (1.18-19)

One can only speculate what this putting away might have entailed. Presumably it would have involved relocating Mary to another community and fabricating a story to explain how she came to be pregnant. Clearly Joseph saw this as doing her a favor, lest she have to endure the public scandal that would ensue.

Peremptory treatment is accorded a woman at a more advanced stage of pregnancy in *Measure for Measure*. Having impregnated his girlfriend Juliet, Claudio has been sentenced to die for violating the law against fornication. Even as the acting minister of justice, Lord Angelo, is rejecting his appeal, Juliet suffers her first contractions nearby. The provost asks what should be done with her, and Angelo replies, "Dispose of her/To some more fitter place, and that with speed" (2.2.16-17). With the father of her child about to be executed, Juliet is in dire straits. Her predicament is recognized by Angelo, who makes a rare compassionate gesture: "See you the fornicatress be removed:/Let her have needful, but not lavish, means;/There shall be order for't" (2.2.23-25).

Induce Miscarriage or Kill the Fetus

A second option for those confronted with an unwanted pregnancy was to terminate it by artificial means, whether by inducing miscarriage with drugs or by destroying the fetus through violent intervention. Both types of abortion have been known and practiced since ancient times.[39]

In the *Theaetetus,* Socrates digresses from the thread of the argument to describe his role as an intellectual midwife. His mother had been a real midwife, and Socrates often uses the metaphor of physical labor and delivery to describe what he does. In describing the occupational skills of midwives, he makes the following observation:

> And furthermore, the midwives, by means of drugs and incanta-
> tions, are able to arouse the pangs of labour and, if they wish, to
> make them milder, and to cause those to bear who have difficulty in
> bearing; and they cause miscarriages if they think them desirable.
> (149d)

Socrates does not reveal under what circumstances the midwives might
have considered miscarriages desirable. The fact that the matter was
left to the midwives' discretion is strong evidence that abortion was not
considered murder, a crime of the severest gravity to the Greeks, as it
is to modern society. The use of drugs for this purpose calls to mind
current controversies over availability in the United States of RU486,
the French-made "abortion pill."[40]

The *Republic* contains an allusion to the practical difficulties that
could sometimes be encountered in effecting an abortion. Socrates has
been discussing the laws concerning procreation that would be instituted in the ideal state. The right to bring forth a child would be restricted to men and women in their prime. Those beyond the lawful
age for procreation would be allowed sexual freedom, but the state
would warn them against producing offspring:

> First admonishing them preferably not even to bring to light any-
> thing whatever thus conceived, but if they are unable to prevent a
> birth to dispose of it on the understanding that we cannot rear such
> an offspring. (461c)

Why people might have been unable to prevent a birth is unclear. Perhaps the drugs used by midwives, like RU486, were effective only in
the early stages of pregnancy. Perhaps their availability was limited.
Whatever the reason, what is endorsed here is clearly a policy of state-
sanctioned abortion or infanticide. Interestingly, the Supreme Court in
Roe v. Wade cited this passage, along with one from Aristotle's *Politics,* as
authority for its statement that "Most Greek thinkers ... commended
abortion, at least prior to viability."[41]

A reference to the possibility of feticide is also found in *Richard III.*
The women who have suffered grievous losses at the hands of King
Richard are finally ganging up to heap reproaches and vilification upon
him. Together they lie in wait and block his train as it tries to pass.
When the king asks who is intercepting his expedition, his mother, the
Duchess of York, is the first to speak:

DUCHESS: O, she that might have intercepted thee,
By strangling thee in her accursed womb,
From all the slaughters, wretch, that thou hast done!

(4.4.137-139)

It is unlikely that abortions were thought to have been effected by strangling fetuses still in the womb. The use of the word "intercepted" might indicate that the reference is to the time when the fetus is coming through the birth canal and is thus first vulnerable to strangling.

Infanticide

Infanticide was practiced widely and without apparent moral compunction in the ancient world, and it is difficult for modern sensibilities to adjust to such a different value system. The practice of "exposing" unwanted infants, whether or not they were defective, was commonplace in Greek and Roman cultures; they were simply left in outdoor locations where, vulnerable to the elements and animal predators, they would certainly die if they were not rescued by divine or human intervention.[42] Societies that readily accepted such infanticide could hardly be expected to object to abortion.

In the *Republic,* Socrates proposes a process of "selective breeding" for humans in his ideal state. Only the offspring of those who excel will be raised. The offspring of others will be relegated to a dim but unspecified fate:

> The offspring of the good, I suppose, they will take to the pen or creche, to certain nurses who live apart in a quarter of the city, but the offspring of the inferior, and any of those of the other sort who are born defective, they will properly dispose of in secret, so that no one will know what has become of them. (460c)

It is noteworthy that, here again, the pervasive notion of secrecy, or privacy, is an important factor in making decisions about procreation.

While Western nations do not condone selective infanticide based on the qualities of the parents, they have confronted serious questions about how to handle defective infants. It is generally known in medical circles that some physicians withhold life-preserving treatment and thus quietly allow severely handicapped infants with no prospect of a meaningful existence to die.[43] Even such decisions, which constitute a passive form of infanticide, have caused public outcries, as in the celebrated 1983 case known as Baby Jane Doe. In that case, right-to-life proponents sought and temporarily won court orders requiring a hospital in Stony Brook, New York, to perform surgery on a severely handicapped infant, contrary to the wishes of its parents.[44]

Active forms of infanticide seem to have been far rarer in the West, and the antiabortion movement has used the image of "killing babies" to shock its audiences out of what it sees as their complacency. In the works of the Canon, the act of killing an infant has been used to demonstrate an especially horrifying capacity for evil. Such demented characters as Medea and Richard III might have killed young children, but killing an infant is somehow even more chilling. Shakespeare uses this perception in his portrayal of two of his most thoroughly evil female characters. In Macbeth, Lady Macbeth is egging her husband on to carry out their plan to murder Duncan. When he hesitates, she questions his manhood and says that he does not have even the resolve that she, a woman, has:

LADY MACBETH: I have given suck, and know
How tender 'tis to love the babe that milks me:
I would, while it was smiling in my face,
Have pluck'd my nipple from his boneless gums,
And dash'd his brains out, had I so sworn as you
Have done to this.

(1.7.54-59)

In *Titus Andronicus*, as noted earlier, Tamora continues her illicit affair with Aaron the Moor even after her marriage to the Roman emperor Saturninus. When she gives birth to an infant, its dark skin reveals unmistakably that it is the child of Aaron rather than of Saturninus. Tamora therefore gives the infant to her two grown sons, Chiron and Demetrius, to be slain:

CHIRON: It shall not live.

AARON: It shall not die.

NURSE: Aaron, it must; the mother wills it so.

AARON: What, must it, nurse? Then let no man but I do execution on my flesh and blood.

(4.2.80-84)

When Aaron's ploy to get hold of the infant fails, he is forced to draw his sword:

AARON: Now, by the burning tapers of the sky,
              That shone so brightly when this boy was got,
              He dies upon my scimitar's sharp point
              That touches this my first-born son and heir!

                                                      (4.2.89-92)

This passage reveals dramatically the right that a father might assert to participate in the decision whether his child is to live or die. Fathers have made such claims in modern disputes over a woman's right to terminate her pregnancy; to date, these claims have generally failed.[45]

Abandonment or Secret Adoption

There is a thin line between infanticide through exposure and abandoning an infant with the hope that it will be rescued and raised by someone else. Some mothers may have chosen to interpret their actions as the latter, even in cases in which the likelihood of rescue was slim. Having the child raised through secret adoption, if this could be arranged, must have been an attractive alternative, although support payments would likely have been expected.

One indication of whether a mother leaves an infant with the expectation that it will die or the hope that it will live is the physical condition in which it is found. Every urban newspaper carries occasional stories about a newborn infant's being discovered – sometimes alive, sometimes dead – in a trash can or dumpster.[46] In such cases, the infant might not have been washed after birth and might even still have the umbilical cord attached. According to the book of Ezekiel, this was the condition in which Israel was cast out and left to die until the Lord passed by and took pity on it:

> And as for thy nativity, in the day thou wast born thy navel was not cut, neither wast thou washed in water to supple thee; thou wast not salted at all, nor swaddled at all.
>
> None eye pitied thee, to do any of these unto thee, to have compassion upon thee; but thou wast cast out in the open field, to the loathing of thy person, in the day that thou wast born.
>
> And when I passed by thee, and saw thee polluted in thine own blood, I said unto thee when thou wast in thy blood, Live; yea, I said unto thee when thou wast in thy blood, Live. (16.4-6)

This may be contrasted with the situation in which an infant is abandoned with the mother's clear intent that it be adopted and raised by someone else. At Exodus 2.1-9, the parents of Moses have hidden him for his first three months of his life because of the Pharaoh's edict that the male babies of the Hebrews be killed. When his mother can no longer hide him, she makes him an ark of bulrushes and daubs it with slime and pitch to keep the water out. She then sets him adrift in the reeds by the river's shore, in a location where he is sure to be found by the Egyptian royalty who frequent that area.

In *The Winter's Tale,* an infant has been abandoned to the elements in an ambiguous way. King Leontes of Sicily believes that the infant daughter his wife Queen Hermione has delivered is not his. Vowing that he will not "rear another's issue" (2.3.192-193), he directs Antigonus, a lord at his court, to dispose of the infant:

LEONTES: We enjoin thee,
           As thou art liege-man to us, that thou carry
           This female bastard hence and that thou bear it
           To some remote and desert place quite out
           Of our dominions, and that there thou leave it,
           Without more mercy, to its own protection
           And favor of the climate.
           . . . .
           Where chance may nurse or end it. Take it up.

ANTIGONUS: I swear to do this, though a present death
           Had been more merciful. Come on, poor babe:
           Some powerful spirit instruct the kites and ravens
           To be thy nurses! Wolves and bears, they say,
           Casting their savageness aside have done
           Like offices of pity.

                                            (2.3.173-179, 183-189)

A shepherd finds the infant wrapped in a luxurious blanket that contains gold and deduces that it is the child of a noblewoman, possibly the product of an illicit union. He therefore decides to raise it as his own. The ambiguity of the circumstances in which the infant was left probably results from the fact that the mother is not involved at all but rather two men, one harsh (King Leontes) and the other pitying (Antigonus).

As has already been shown, in *Titus Andronicus* there is disagreement between the two parents over the fate of their illegitimate child. The empress Tamora wants the dark-skinned infant killed to destroy the evidence of her adulterous affair with Aaron the Moor. He, on the other hand, is intent on enabling the infant, his only child and heir, to

survive. The obvious solution to this problem is for the infant to be secretly adopted and raised by a family elsewhere. As fortune would
have it, Aaron knows of a countryman living nearby whose wife has
just given birth to a fair-skinned infant. Through bribery and promises
that the couple's own son will be raised as a future ruler, Aaron arranges an exchange, and his problem seems for the moment to be
solved (at 4.2.151-180).

These passages demonstrate that women have had a variety of options available for dealing with unwanted pregnancies through the
ages. Which option they pursued seems to have been more a matter of
circumstance and exigency than of morality. There is no clear evidence
in the works of the Canon that abortion was regarded as murder or
even as a heinous offense. The question of whether a fetus or newborn
should survive has been largely determined by the practicalities of each
situation. Such decisions seem to have been shrouded by that cloak of
privacy that prevents us from seeing into many of the intimate details
of people's lives in bygone eras.

Abortion: A Question of Religious Values?

If opposition to abortion is not based on a strong cultural tradition,
and if a woman's right to terminate her pregnancy has not been consis-
tently denounced within the Western tradition as a legal or moral offense, why has such virulent opposition to the practice arisen in
American society over the past century, especially since the *Roe v. Wade*
decision in 1973? The answer to that question seems to lie partly in the
rise of religious fundamentalism, which has made the abortion issue its
own. Pro-life proponents usually base their arguments against abortion
on certain religious or spiritual presuppositions about the nature and
value of human life that can be neither proven nor refuted. Pro-choice
proponents, on the other hand, more often base their arguments on the
practicalities of life in today's world, with all its complications and difficulties. This difference in approach is largely a matter of personal religious orientation and belief, in which the state has no role to play in the
American constitutional system.

Among the disputed points in the abortion debate that seem to be
based on religious or spiritual presuppositions are whether the innocence of the fetus is relevant to a woman's right to choose; whether being born is always and necessarily a good thing; and whether all

human life, without exception, is sacred. Each of these arguments, which reflect a fundamental outlook upon life, springs from an over-arching interpretation of the meaning of human existence. The works of the Canon, which are at the core of the Western humanistic tradi-tion, have provided the framework within which Western thought has considered such questions.

Innocence of the Fetus

Characterization of a fetus as innocent is most easily understood in contexts in which the innocence of the fetus is contrasted with the guilt of its mother. This type of situation is crystallized when the mother is sentenced to die because of her crimes, and the death of the guilty mother will necessarily result in the death of the innocent fetus. This is precisely the situation presented in *I Henry VI,* where Joan la Pucelle (Joan of Arc) has been captured by the English army and sentenced to be burned at the stake. Joan tries to avoid execution by feigning preg-nancy:

> JOAN: Will nothing turn your unrelenting hearts?
> Then, Joan, discover thine infirmity,
> That warranteth by law to be thy privilege.
> I am with child, ye bloody homicides;
> Murder not then the fruit within my womb,
> Although ye hale me to a violent death.
>
> (5.4.59-64)

Joan obviously has reason to believe that the authorities might be reluc-tant to take any action against her that will result in the destruction of the innocent "fruit within [her] womb."

In the works of the Canon, references to the innocence of an un-born or newborn child sometimes relate to the circumstances of its conception. Because unwanted pregnancies were often the result of il-licit affairs, inevitably offspring from such unions were stigmatized by society and sometimes even by the parents themselves. For example, in *II Henry IV,* Prince Hal is teasing his friend Poins about his relatively low social standing. He accuses Poins of having fathered children out of wedlock, among other things, and adds, "and God knows, whether those that bawl out the ruins of thy linen shall inherit his kingdom: but the midwives say the children are not in the fault; whereupon the world increases, and kindreds are mightily strengthened" (2.2.26-30).

An infant's innocence of the circumstances of its conception is a theme in *The Winter's Tale*, when Queen Hermione delivers a baby girl whose paternity is in question. Her husband, King Leontes, has alleged that the child is not his and has imprisoned his wife as punishment for her alleged infidelity. Paulina visits the prison and is told by Emilia that the queen has given birth to a daughter:

EMILIA: A daughter, and a goodly babe,
Lusty and like to live: the queen receives
Much comfort in 't; says, "My poor prisoner,
I am innocent as you."

(2.2.26-29)

In this case, the mother relies on the infant's presumed innocence as a standard of comparison for herself. Even as the infant has committed no crime, so is she innocent of the charge of adultery.

The circumstances of conception come to the fore in one important aspect of the modern abortion debate. Arguments against abortion based on the innocence of the fetus encounter the greatest difficulty in cases involving rape and incest. Only the most hard-line opponents of abortion refuse to allow an exception for such cases, even though the fetus conceived through rape or incest is certainly as innocent as any other fetus.

But the circumstances of conception are not what antiabortion activists have in mind when they describe what goes on in abortion clinics as "the slaughter of innocents." They have in mind a much more general notion that, because the fetus has not yet taken any action that might be considered morally culpable, it remains innocent and thus entitled not to be killed. This is an overly simplistic approach to a complicated question, however. Philosopher James Rachels has offered a closer analysis of the concept of innocence. According to Rachels, the legal concept of innocence is essentially a negative notion. A person's innocence consists in his *not* having done certain things for which he would forfeit certain rights, in this context things for which he would forfeit his right not to be killed. If a person is innocent, then certain kinds of justifications for killing him (for example, that he is a murderer or an enemy in time of war) cannot be used. He concludes, "The fact of innocence rules out these justifications of killing – but that is all it does. *It does not rule out other possible justifications.*" [emphasis in original].[47] This is why the argument concerning the innocence of the fetus in a legal sense is largely irrelevant to the abortion debate; certainly none of the arguments favoring a woman's right to terminate her pregnancy is based upon the concept of punishing the fetus for its misdeeds.

If the innocence of the fetus in a legal sense is irrelevant to the abortion debate, then the word "innocence" must be used in a religious sense, meaning that a fetus has not yet committed any sins in this world. In that case, the argument means nothing more than that the fetus is unborn. Such a religious meaning is alluded to in the writings of St. Paul. In his letter to the Romans, Paul is recounting the history of the children of Israel. He tells the story of Isaac and Rebecca and the birth of their twin sons Esau and Jacob:

> And not only this; but when Rebecca also had conceived by one, even by our father Isaac;
> (For the children being not yet born, neither having done any good or evil, that the purpose of God according to election might stand, not of works, but of him that calleth;)
> It was said unto her, The elder shall serve the younger.
> As it is written, Jacob have I loved, but Esau have I hated. (9.10-13)

Paul's point here is that the preference for Jacob over Esau was not based on which son had performed good works but rather was the fulfillment of God's own purpose. However, his allusion to the fact that the unborn children had not yet "done any good or evil" indicates the real basis of the "innocence of the fetus" argument, which is clearly religious in nature.

Is Being Born a Positive Thing?

Another implicit assumption made by opponents of abortion is that being born is always and necessarily a positive thing. A television commercial widely used by the pro-life movement asserts, "After all, everyone deserves a chance to be born." Such a basic affirmation of life is at the root of religious faith, and arguments can be made that it constitutes a "healthy" outlook on life. Still, the question remains of whether every-one must subscribe to that outlook as a matter of law. Ethicist Sidney Callahan captures well the religious underpinnings of this outlook: "The prolife belief in benevolence and the response of gratitude contribute to the view that life is good. Life is a precious gift and is better, far better, than the absence of life. There is an ultimate bias in favor of life, fruitfulness, abundance, and procreation that influences where a person begins any discussion of issues such as abortion."48

Perhaps ironically, the most profound questioning of the religious assumption that being born is always a good thing may be found in the Hebrew scriptures. For example, Job in his misery repeatedly wishes that he had been either stillborn or miscarried:

> Why died I not from the womb? why did I not give up the ghost when I came out of the belly?...
> Or as an hidden untimely birth I had not been; as infants which never saw light.
> There the wicked cease from troubling; and there the weary be at rest. (3.11, 16-17)

> Wherefore then hast thou brought me forth out of the womb? Oh that I had given up the ghost, and no eye had seen me!
> I should have been as though I had not been; I should have been carried from the womb to the grave. (10.18-19)

Similarly, the prophet Jeremiah despairs when he is put in the stocks and curses the man who long ago announced to his father that a male child had been born:

> Because he slew me not from the womb; or that my mother might have been my grave, and her womb to be always great with me.
> Wherefore came I forth out of the womb to see labour and sorrow, that my days should be consumed with shame? (20.17-18)

One might wonder why these expressions of regret are directed at being born rather than at being conceived. At no time do the writers of these passages direct recriminations against their parents for having conceived them, perhaps because of the seriousness that was accorded the commandment to honor one's parents.

Both Job and Jeremiah eventually overcome their despair and refind their purpose in life through their faith in the Lord. To the believer, their subsequent reaffirmation of life is of far greater importance than their temporary despair. However, the attitudes that they voice during their dark intervals cannot be overlooked as one human response to the trials and tribulations of life.

A more extended description of the experience of being miscarried is found in Ecclesiastes. The preacher is denouncing the vanity of life, and he offers an example of a kind of life that is less valuable than "an untimely birth":

> If a man beget an hundred children, and live many years, so that the days of his years be many, and his soul be not filled with good, and also that he have no burial; I say, that an untimely birth is better than he.
>
> For he cometh in with vanity, and departeth in darkness, and his name shall be covered with darkness.
>
> Moreover he hath not seen the sun, nor known any thing: this hath more rest than the other. (6.3-5)

In all of these passages, the death of a fetus is regarded as a neutral event, a passing into nothingness devoid of both joys and sorrows. For those who choose abortion as preferable to bearing an unwanted child, such a fate may not seem all that bad. As was stated at the beginning of this section, much depends on a person's psychological makeup and fundamental outlook on life. There will always be some who, with King Lear, believe that "When we are born, we cry that we are come/To this great stage of fools" (4.6.186-187). For such persons to be denied the right to terminate a pregnancy because of others' belief that being born is always a positive thing would appear to violate the fundamental meaning of freedom of religion.

Is All Human Life Sacred?

Some opponents of abortion base their argument on what they see as the innate, intrinsic value of human life, which they say derives from its sacred character. The very word "sacred" has strong religious connotations for most people, at a minimum evoking a notion of the mysterious and inexplicable. In an important 1993 book, legal theorist Ronald Dworkin has argued that the idea of the sacred may be interpreted in a secular as well as a conventionally religious way. He points to the horror one feels at the willful destruction of any human life and offers the explanation that the life of a single human organism, regardless of its form or shape, commands respect and protection because of the complex creative investment it represents and because of our wonder at the processes that created it.[49]

Dworkin denies that his analysis is necessarily theistic.[50] Nevertheless, clear articulation of a point of view very much akin to the one he offers is found primarily within a theistic context, as in the Hebrew scriptures. For example, in Isaiah, there is a description of the Lord's role in the creation of a human being:

> Thus saith the Lord, thy redeemer, and he that formed thee from the womb, I am the Lord that maketh all things; that stretcheth forth the heavens alone; that spreadeth abroad the earth by myself. (44.24)

And, in Ecclesiastes, the preacher reminds man of his ignorance of such matters:

> As thou knowest not what is the way of the spirit, nor how the bones do grow in the womb of her that is with child: even so thou knowest not the works of God who maketh all. (11.5)

Dworkin concludes that our disagreements over abortion are "at bottom spiritual," but he maintains that recognition of that fact should help to bring us together because Americans as a people have grown used to the idea that real community is possible across deep religious divisions.[51] Recognition of the basically religious or spiritual nature of the abortion debate has led some legal scholars to raise the possibility of an argument for individual choice based on the guarantee of freedom of religion under the First Amendment. This possibility has been discussed in legal circles for some time without eliciting much enthusiasm.[52] However, it was revived by Justice John Paul Stevens in his separate opinion in a 1989 abortion case and may be explored further as the national trauma over abortion continues and the possibility of consensus seems remote.[53]

When the Supreme Court relied upon a series of cases defining a constitutional right to privacy to find that a woman has a right to terminate her pregnancy, it looked to cases involving marriage and procreation, the use of contraceptives, and bedroom possession of obscene materials. None of the cases on which the Court relied presented a situation closely analogous to abortion. The tenuousness of the connection rendered the holding in *Roe v. Wade* less than secure, and in the two decades since *Roe* was decided, it has been subjected to repeated attacks in the courts and in the streets. Alternative grounds for a woman's right to choose have been suggested, including the right to equal protection of the laws under the Fourteenth Amendment and the right to freedom of religion under the First Amendment. As the makeup of the Court changes and the ideological climate of the country shifts, further evolution of the law concerning abortion may be expected.

Many of the questions routinely raised in the abortion debate are based upon religious or spiritual presuppositions. Such questions as whether the innocence of the fetus is relevant to a woman's right to choose, whether being born is always and necessarily a good thing, and whether all human life without exception is sacred must be answered in the context of a comprehensive philosophy of the meaning of human existence. The works of the Canon, which are at the core of the Western humanistic tradition, have provided the framework within which Western thought has considered fundamental questions of this nature. As a consequence, these works are well suited for exploration of the topic of abortion. Through them, students are exposed to the cultural resources they will need to understand and grapple with the complex legal, medical, and social aspects of abortion. In the final analysis, however, they must develop their own responses to these questions, because definitive answers are neither given nor implied.

No current issue of public policy calls more urgently than does abortion for the exercise of the qualities of mind and traits of character that a liberal education engenders, such as the ability to think critically, a willingness to tolerate the views of others, and recognition of the separate realms of reason and faith. Our society's handling of the abortion question has degenerated to a point where blockading of private property, lethal violence against medical personnel, and efforts by government to censor communications between physician and patient seem all too routine, and rational discourse has been largely foreclosed. There is a need for those who are familiar with the cultural background of abortion to reframe public discussion of the issues and to reinstitute a climate of reasoned debate about the legal and social alternatives.

Almost everyone does agree on one point, that abortion is an undesirable means of meeting the need for population control and the desire for reproductive choice. With scientific advances in the options for contraception and improved education concerning their use, the possibility of reducing, if not eliminating, the demand for abortions exists. An appreciation of the long history and moral complexities of the subject, gained through exposure to the works of the Canon, would aid the next generation in finding a more acceptable solution to the age-old problem of unwanted pregnancies.

Notes

1. Daniel Callahan, "The Abortion Debate: Is Progress Possible?" in *Abortion: Understanding Differences,* ed. Sidney Callahan and Daniel Callahan (New York: Plenum Press, 1984), p. 319.

2. Kristin Luker, "Abortion and the Meaning of Life," in *Abortion: Understanding Differences,* ed. Sidney Callahan and Daniel Callahan, p. 31.

3. Roger Rosenblatt, *Life Itself: Abortion in the American Mind* (New York: Random House, 1992), pp. 53 and 100.

4. *Roe v. Wade.* 410 U.S. 113 at 129-141, 93 S. Ct. 705, 35 L. Ed. 2d 147 (1973). Justice Blackmun wrote, "It perhaps is not generally appreciated that the restrictive criminal abortion laws in effect in a majority of States today are of relatively recent vintage. Those laws ... are not of ancient or even of common-law origin. Instead, they derive from statutory changes effected, for the most part, in the latter half of the 19th century" (at 129).

5. 410 U.S. at 116.

6. See Larry Rohter, "Battle over Protests at Abortion Clinics Shifts to High Court," *New York Times,* April 28, 1994, pp. A1 and A8; and Eloise Salholz, "The Death of Dr. Gunn: A Physician Becomes a Casualty of the Abortion Wars," *Newsweek,* March 22, 1993, p. 34.

7. Sarah Weddington, *A Question of Choice* (New York: G. P. Putnam's Sons, 1992), pp. 52 and 11-14.

8. Ronald Dworkin, *Life's Dominion: An Argument about Abortion, Euthanasia, and Individual Freedom* (New York: Alfred A. Knopf, 1993), p. 102.

9. Laurence H. Tribe, *Abortion: The Clash of Absolutes* (New York: Norton, 1992), p. 13.

10. 410 U.S. at 153.

11. 410 U.S. at 162-164.

12. See Deborah L. Rhode, *Justice and Gender: Sex Discrimination and the Law* (Cambridge, Mass.: Harvard University Press, 1989), pp. 209-210.

13. Harold J. Morowitz and James S. Trefil, *The Facts of Life: Science and the Abortion Controversy* (New York: Oxford University Press, 1992), pp. 159-160. The conclusions reached by Morowitz and Trefil were summarized in an op-ed piece entitled "Roe v. Wade Passes a Lab Test," *New York Times,* November 25, 1992, p. A21.

14. *Planned Parenthood v. Casey,* 112 S. Ct. 2791, 120 L. Ed. 2d 674, at 694 and 699 (1992).

15. 120 L. Ed. 2d at 711-713.

16. 120 L. Ed. 2d at 749.

17. 120 L. Ed. 2d at 745 and 758.

18. Linda Greenhouse, "On Privacy and Equality: Judge Ginsburg Still Voices Strong Doubts on Winning Strategy Behind Roe v. Wade," *New York Times,* June 16, 1993, pp. A1 and A11.

19. See, for example, Catharine A. MacKinnon, *Feminism Unmodified: Discourses on Life and Law* (Cambridge, Mass.: Harvard University Press, 1987), pp. 96-102, and "Reflections on Sex Equality under Law, *Yale Law Journal,* vol. 100, no. 5 (March 1991), pp. 1308-1324; Deborah L. Rhode, *Justice and Gender: Sex Discrimination and the Law* (Cambridge, Mass.: Harvard University Press, 1989), p. 213; and Tribe, *Abortion,* p. 105.

20. *Loving v. Virginia,* 388 U.S. 1, at 12, 87 S. Ct. 1817, 18 L. Ed. 2d 1010 (1967).

21. *Griswold v. Connecticut,* 381 U.S. 479, at 485-486, 85 S. Ct. 1678, 14 L. Ed. 2d 510 (1965).

22. Translated by Robert Graves (London: Cassell, 1960).

23. *Stanley v. Georgia,* 394 U.S. 557, at 565, 89 S. Ct. 1243, 22 L. Ed. 2d 542 (1969).

24. See text at note 21 above.

25. Morowitz and Trefils, *The Facts of Life,* pp. 133-134.

26. Ibid., pp. 136-138.

27. Ibid., pp. 143-145.

28. Catharine A. MacKinnon, "Reflections on Sex Equality under Law," *Yale Law Journal,* vol. 100, no. 5 (March 1991), p. 1314.

29. Rosenblatt, *Life Itself,* p. 71.

30. See the discussion at Rosenblatt, *Life Itself,* p. 61.

31. MacKinnon, "Reflections on Sex Equality under Law," p. 1314.

32. Both Plato's successors in the Academy and the Roman Stoics held the view that human life began with the first breath. See Rosenblatt, *Life Itself,* pp. 59 and 63.

33. Rosalind P. Petchesky, *Abortion and Woman's Choice: The State, Sexuality, and Reproductive Freedom* (New York: Longman, 1984), p. 7.

34. Judith Jarvis Thomson, "A Defense of Abortion," *Philosophy & Public Affairs,* vol. 1, no. 1 (1971), pp. 47-66. More than twenty years after its publication, Thomson's article is still regularly discussed in the scholarly literature on abortion. See Tribe, *Abortion,* pp. 129-130; Dworkin, *Life's Dominion,* p. 54; and MacKinnon, "Reflections on Sex Equality under Law," pp. 1314-1315.

35. Thomson, "A Defense of Abortion," p. 56.

36. For a discussion of the relation between ensoulment and abortion, see Dworkin, *Life's Dominion*, pp. 40-48.

37. See Morowitz and Trefils, *The Facts of Life*, pp. 44-49.

38. John M. Riddle, *Contraception and Abortion from the Ancient World to the Renaissance* (Cambridge, Mass.: Harvard University Press, 1992), pp. 1-7; and Paul Carrick, *Medical Ethics in Antiquity: Philosophical Perspectives on Abortion and Euthanasia* (Dordrecht: D. Reidel, 1985), pp. 104-107.

39. Riddle, *Contraception and Abortion*, pp. 7-10; and Carrick, *Medical Ethics in Antiquity*, p. 107.

40. See Jill Smolowe, "The Abortion Pill: New, Improved, and Ready for Battle," *Time*, June 14, 1993, pp. 48-54.

41. 410 U.S. at 131.

42. Riddle, *Contraception and Abortion*, pp. 10-14; and Carrick, *Medical Ethics in Antiquity*, pp. 107-108.

43. Rachels, *The End of Life*, pp. 30-32.

44. See Richard Sherlock, *Preserving Life: Public Policy and the Life Not Worth Living* (Chicago: Loyola University Press, 1987), pp. 1-7; and James Rachels, *The End of Life: Euthanasia and Morality* (Oxford: Oxford University Press, 1986), pp. 60-62.

45. Tribe, *Abortion*, pp. 198-199.

46. Ari L. Goldman, "Girl, 17, Accused of Killing Baby She Secretly Delivered," *New York Times*, June 3, 1993, p. A16.

47. Rachels, *The End of Life*, p. 71.

48. Sidney Callahan, "Value Choices in Abortion," in *Abortion: Understanding Differences*, ed. Sidney Callahan and Daniel Callahan, p. 294.

49. Dworkin, *Life's Dominion*, p. 84.

50. Ibid., p. 25.

51. Ibid., p. 101.

52. See generally Peter S. Wenz, *Abortion Rights as Religious Freedom* (Philadelphia: Temple University Press, 1992). This argument is endorsed by Dworkin (*Life's Dominion*, p. 166) and was once held by Tribe (*Abortion*, p. 116, note 3).

53. *Webster v. Reproductive Health Services*, 492 U.S. 490, at 566-567, 109 S. Ct. 3040, 106 L. Ed. 2d 410 (1989).

5: The Right to Die

DEATH IS AT the same time the most universal aspect of human experience and the most forbidden to dwell upon. People have always contemplated when and how they will die, and the works of the Canon reflect this basic human preoccupation. Concerns about the quality of life and the terms on which life is or is not worth living abound in the Canon. Although these concerns have been prevalent from the beginning of Western civilization, recent developments in medical technology to keep people alive by artificial means have brought a heightened public awareness of questions concerning the timing and manner of death.[1]

As these questions have begun to be discussed openly in various public forums and in the media, they have become increasingly politicized. One journalist, noting that many religious leaders and specialists in medical ethics see the approach of a "critical juncture" in our attitudes toward dying, has written, "Many on both sides believe that the nation is embarking on a struggle as protracted, as emotional and as ethically unyielding as the battle over abortion."[2] The two sides on the right-to-die issue replicate closely the two sides on the abortion issue, as is apparent from the similarity in jargon, pitting those who are "pro-life" against those who are "pro-choice." One author, having described the polarities as "the ultimate value of human life in a deadly conflict with the right of control and autonomy," has observed, "As in the struggle for reproductive choice, two such strong values collide with one another that each side bypasses the critical issue of the other. It is a conflict of value hierarchies and core belief systems where, not surprisingly, resolution and compromise are seemingly impossible."[3]

This clash of value systems can be seen in the public response to the publication in 1991 of *Final Exit,* a practical guide to "self-deliverance" and assisted suicide, written by the founder and executive director of the National Hemlock Society.[4] Reaction to the book, which became a national best-seller, tended to be either virulently condemning or highly complimentary. An example of the former response was that of Leon Kass, who called the book "evil" and said that it should never have been written: "This is not the usual and notorious evil of malicious intent or violent manner; this is humanitarian evil, evil with a smile: well-meaning, gentle, and rational — especially rational. For this reason it is both harder to recognize as evil and harder to combat."[5] The viewpoint of the late Isaac Asimov could not be more contrary: "No decent human being would allow an animal to suffer without putting it out of its misery. It is only to human beings that human beings are so cruel as to allow them to live on in pain, in hopelessness, in living death, without moving a muscle to help them. It is against such attitudes that this book fights."[6]

For many, the right-to-die movement is symbolized by Dr. Jack Kevorkian, a maverick Michigan pathologist who has waged a tireless campaign for legalization of physician-assisted suicide. Kevorkian's methods, involving videotaped interviews with his patients and use of a homemade "suicide machine," have been denounced even by many supporters of his cause. His one-person crusade drew massive publicity with each successive suicide (at this writing he has assisted in twenty), leading Michigan authorities to prosecute him in the spring of 1994 for violation of a statute prohibiting assisted suicide.[7] In a quieter fashion, numerous grassroots efforts to secure a right to physician-assisted suicide have been under way. Initiatives to this effect have been put on the ballot in several states, although none has yet succeeded.[8] In addition, in many locales right-to-die societies have held seminars and workshops to instruct the terminally ill (especially AIDS patients) on the practicalities of suicide.[9]

A Constitutional Right to Die

The question of whether an individual has a legal right to terminate unwanted medical treatment came to the forefront of the public's attention in 1976 in the highly publicized case of Karen Ann Quinlan.[10] In that case, the parents of a young woman who was in a persistent vegetative state with no hope of recovery sought legal authorization for removal of the respirator that was preserving their daughter's biological existence. The New Jersey Supreme Court held that she had a privacy right under the federal and state constitutions to refuse unwanted medical treatments, and that this right included the withdrawal of life support systems already in place. The New Jersey attorney general subsequently sought review by the U.S. Supreme Court, which refused to hear the case.[11] When Karen was removed from the respirator, however, contrary to everyone's expectation she did not stop breathing. Because her parents were unwilling to have nutrition and hydration stopped, she continued in a comatose state for nine more years before she died in 1985.[12]

It was not until 1990 that the U.S. Supreme Court decided its first case addressing the issue of whether individuals have a constitutional right to die. In *Cruzan v. Director, Missouri Dept. of Health,* the parents of another young woman in a persistent vegetative state sought permission to remove life support systems, this time the tubes that were providing nutrition and hydration to their comatose daughter.[13] In a splintered 5 to 4 decision, the Court found that there is a constitutional right to refuse unwanted medical treatment, apparently including life-saving nutrition and hydration.[14] However, this right, which was said to be a liberty interest protected by the due process clause of the Fourteenth Amendment, must be balanced against legitimate state interests, including a state interest in the general protection of human life. As a result, the Court upheld Missouri's strict standard concerning the necessary proof of what Nancy Cruzan's wishes would have been, and because no reliable evidence was presented, Missouri's decision not to allow withdrawal of artificial nutrition and hydration tubes was affirmed.

Five separate opinions were filed by the nine justices in the *Cruzan* case, presenting a mosaic whose complexity and bitterness rivals that of some recent abortion rulings. In a scathing opinion concurring in the result, Justice Scalia wrote, "I would have preferred that we announce, clearly and promptly, that the federal courts have no business in this field; that American law has always accorded the State the power to prevent, by force if necessary, suicide — including suicide by refusing to take appropriate measures necessary to preserve one's life; that the point at which life becomes 'worthless,' and the point at which the means necessary to preserve it become 'extraordinary' or 'inappropriate,' are neither set forth in the Constitution nor known to the nine Justices of this Court any better than they are known to nine people picked at random from the Kansas City telephone directory."[15]

In equally passionate terms, Justices William J. Brennan and John Paul Stevens dissented in separate opinions. Justice Brennan wrote, "Dying is personal. And it is profound. For many, the thought of an ignoble end, steeped in decay, is abhorrent. A quiet, proud death, bodily integrity intact, is a matter of extreme consequence.... Yet Missouri and this Court have displaced Nancy's own assessment of the processes associated with dying. They have discarded evidence of her will, ignored her values, and deprived her of the right to a decision as closely approximating her own choice as humanly possible. They have done so disingenuously in her name, and openly in Missouri's own."[16] Justice Stevens wrote, "However commendable may be the State's interest in human life, it cannot pursue that interest by appropriating Nancy Cruzan's life as a symbol for its own purposes.... A State that seeks to demonstrate its commitment to life may do so by aiding those who are actively struggling for life and health."[17]

With the tragic case of Nancy Cruzan, clearly the battle lines were drawn. In late 1990, Nancy's parents were finally able to convince the Missouri courts, through previously unpresented evidence, that their daughter had in fact expressed a desire not to continue living in a vegetative state. When removal of the tubes providing nutrition and hydration was authorized, the right-to-life movement denounced what it called "the frenzy to kill Nancy Cruzan," and twenty-five protesters were blocked and arrested as they tried to get into her hospital room to reconnect the tubes.[18] Several of the nurses who had cared for her protested and wept out of sympathy for her, leading Ronald Dworkin to observe, "We cannot understand the public debate over euthanasia unless we make sense of these attitudes."[19]

There are a number of ironies surrounding these legal developments. For example, it is ironic that the first cases to consider whether there is a constitutional right to die have involved persons in a persistent vegetative state; the legal debate has centered upon the values of liberty, choice, autonomy, and self-determination – none of which can have any meaning for a comatose person. Another irony is that, under the current state of the law, one can choose to die a lingering death by refusing to eat, by refusing life-saving treatments, or even by being disconnected from life support systems already in place; however, one cannot choose to die by a quick and painless injection of a lethal drug, which a personal physician could easily provide.[20] And the U.S. Supreme Court has still not addressed the important question of whether a conscious and functioning person has a constitutional right simply to commit suicide, alone or assisted.

A Rational Choice?

As public debate over the right to die has evolved, considerable attention has been focused on such distinctions as that between meaningful life and mere biological existence and on such questions as whether life is worth living in certain debilitated conditions. Opponents of the right to die often use so-called slippery slope arguments, alleging that, because of the potential for widespread euthanasia of society's weakest and most vulnerable members, it is dangerous for such questions even to be raised. Proponents of the right to die counter that appropriate safeguards against this danger can be devised and that it would be irrational not to discuss these questions as the cost of prolonging mere biological existence escalates.

The works of the Canon reveal that questions of this nature have been raised and explored for millenia and that the deepest ruminations about the value of life and the meaning of death are at the core of the Western humanistic tradition. Reflections on these themes are illustrated in the contexts of incurable illness, bodily impairment, mental anguish, and old age.

Incurable Illness

Although the societies of the past were not acquainted with what is now called a persistent vegetative state, they were well acquainted with the ravages of incurable disease and the prolonged period of pain and suffering that often preceded death. It was in this context that questions were most often raised about whether life in such a terminal condition is worth living. Plato addresses this issue directly and unequivocally in the *Crito*. Socrates is conversing with Crito on the general subject of whose opinion (that of the general public versus that of the acknowledged expert) ought to be followed in various fields of endeavor. As was his custom, Socrates is asking Crito leading questions in anticipation of reaching a discussion of whose opinion should be followed in ethical matters. In preparation for drawing an analogy between body and soul, Socrates brings up the matter of treating bodily disease:

SOCRATES: Well then, if through yielding to the opinion of the ignorant we ruin that which is benefited by health and injured by disease, is life worth living for us when that is ruined? And that is the body, is it not?

CRITO: Yes.

SOCRATES: Then is life worth living when the body is worthless and ruined?

CRITO: Certainly not.

(47d-e)

As is so often the case when Socrates is dominating a dialogue, Crito's answer here is merely obligatory. There seems to have been no question in either man's mind of the proper response.

Socrates makes a similar point in the *Gorgias,* where he compares the art of rhetoric and the art of piloting. Piloting, he says, is straightforward and does not make grand or extravagant claims of performing some transcendental feat; it simply offers a service for a fee. The pilot of a ship takes passengers and their goods from one point to another and makes no claim to benefit them in any other way. For he knows how great the uncertainty is which of the passengers he has benefited by not allowing them to be lost at sea. Depending on their individual circumstances, some might have been better off had they been so lost. As an example of the complexity of this calculus, Socrates points to the person who is "a victim of severe and incurable diseases of the body." Should such a person escape drowning, he would be "miserable in not having died" (512a). Predictably, Socrates then extends the analogy to individuals who have diseases of the soul. Here again, the opinion that persons with certain incurable diseases are better off dead is presented as self-evident.

The plight of the institutionalized terminally ill is described in *Love's Labour's Lost.* Near the end of the play, the three women protagonists agree to marry their three respective suitors after a one-year period of mourning for the king of France, who has just died. Rosaline makes a special condition for marrying her suitor Biron, however: because of his incessantly mocking wit, he must spend the entire year in a hospital trying to make the dying patients smile:

ROSALINE: You shall this twelvemonth term from day to day
            Visit the speechless sick and still converse
            With groaning wretches; and your task shall be,
            With all the fierce endeavor of your wit
            To enforce the pained impotent to smile.

BIRON: To move wild laughter in the throat of death?
            It cannot be; it is impossible:
            Mirth cannot move a soul in agony.

ROSALINE: ... Then, if sickly ears,
             Deafed with the clamours of their own dear groans,
             Will hear your idle scorns, continue then,
             And I will have you and that fault withal.

                                      (5.2.860-867, 873-876)

While Shakespeare does not go so far as to say that death would be preferable to the state in which these patients are described, this is certainly implied. Their unrelieved suffering from excruciating pain constitutes one compelling argument in favor of the right of the incurably ill to die. Whether this argument holds today, in light of modern advances in pain control, is a matter in dispute.[21]

Bodily Impairment

Far more controversial than cases involving the terminally ill are cases involving the disabled, especially paraplegics and quadriplegics. Such persons may be sufficiently healthy to live for many years, but entrapped in a condition of almost total dependency on others that some find humiliating. In *Final Exit,* Derek Humphry recognizes the sensitivity of this subject: "There is no more controversial aspect of euthanasia than that involving the handicapped. Merely to mention it causes my critics to refer to me as a Nazi, wanting to get rid of 'burdens on society.' That is not my wish."[22]

The sentiment from which Humphry wishes to disassociate himself was first pronounced by Plato, who suggested it as a policy of the ideal state depicted in the *Republic.* In book 3, Socrates is conversing with Glaucon about the art of medicine that will be practiced in the ideal state to be established. Socrates says that this art will care for such of the citizens as are truly well born. However, those who are not well born, "such as are defective in body," will be allowed to die. Glaucon responds, "This certainly has been shown to be the best thing for the sufferers themselves and for the state" (410a). This attitude is voiced again in book 5, where Socrates is describing the state's system of "eugenics," or selective breeding. The offspring of the good will be raised, but the offspring of the inferior, and any of the offspring of the good who are born defective, will be disposed of in secret, "so that no one will know what has become of them." This time Glaucon does not even allude to the best interests of the sufferer; he says chillingly, "That is the condition of preserving the purity of the guardians' breed" (460c).

The notion that a physical disability renders one's life unbearable can be seen as early as Homer. In the *Odyssey,* the god Hephaestus has just learned that a trap he set has worked: his wife Aphrodite and her lover Ares have been ensnared in a net during a tryst while he was away. Hephaestus goes home with a heavy heart, but upon reaching the gateway he is seized by fierce anger. "And terribly he cried out and called to all the gods," saying:

> "Father Zeus, and ye other blessed gods that are forever, come hither that ye may see a laughable matter and a monstrous, even how Aphrodite, daughter of Zeus, scorns me for that I am lame and loves destructive Ares because he is comely and strong of limb, whereas I was born misshapen. Yet for this is none other to blame but my two parents —would they had never begotten me!" (8.305-312)

Perhaps the only thing an immortal could do was to wish that he had never been begotten, since death was not an available remedy for those who dwelt on Mount Olympus.

Hephaestus's disability was from birth. In *Titus Andronicus,* as the result of a horrible crime, a character becomes disabled as an adult. Lavinia, a young woman who is the daughter of the Roman general Titus Andronicus, has been raped and mutilated by Chiron and Demetrius, the two evil sons of Tamora the Goth. The nature of her mutilation is especially shocking: her attackers cut off both of her hands and her tongue to prevent her from revealing their identity. Immediately after the attack, Chiron and Demetrius joke about what they have done: when Chiron says that if he were Lavinia he would go hang himself, Demetrius responds, "If thou hadst hands to help thee knit the cord" (2.4.10). In a similar vein, when Lavinia's father, Titus, and her uncle, Marcus, are commiserating about her condition, Titus makes a metaphorical reference to carving a hole in her breast to receive all of the tears flowing down her chest. Marcus scolds his brother for his insensitivity, but in so doing demonstrates his own thoughtlessness:

> MARCUS: Fie, brother, fie! teach her not thus to lay
>   Such violent hands upon her tender life.
>
> TITUS: How now! has sorrow made thee dote already?
>   Why, Marcus, no man should be mad but I.
>   What violent hands can she lay on her life?
>
>   (3.2.21-25)

Lavinia is in a situation very similar to that of quadriplegics today. In a chapter entitled "The Dilemma of Quadriplegics" in *Final Exit,* Derek Humphry states that it is virtually impossible for such persons to carry out their "self-deliverance" unassisted.[23] A highly publicized example of a person in this predicament was Elizabeth Bouvia, a young woman who had been paralyzed by cerebral palsy from birth. Elizabeth, whose movement was restricted to partial use of one hand, had no family ties, no close personal relationships, and no likelihood of employment. Having decided in 1983 that she did not wish to continue living, she checked herself into a California hospital, which she asked to provide any necessary pain control and other personal care while she starved herself to death. A legal battle and media circus ensued as the hospital took measures to force-feed Elizabeth, who combatively asserted that her right to die should not be denied simply because she lacked the physical ability to carry out the act alone.[24]

A common theme among persons with significant bodily impairment is the desire not to continue in a condition of almost total dependency on others for life's every need. In such cases, the availability of close relatives or friends who can provide assistance, which Elizabeth Bouvia lacked, makes some difference. Titus Andronicus makes a touching pledge to learn to communicate with his tongueless and handless daughter Lavinia:

> TITUS: Come, let's fall to; and, gentle girl, eat this:
> Here is no drink! Hark, Marcus, what she says;
> I can interpret all her martyred signs;
> She says she drinks no other drink but tears,
> Brew'd with her sorrow, mesh'd upon her cheeks:
> Speechless complainer, I will learn thy thought;
> In thy dumb action will I be as perfect
> As begging hermits in their holy prayers:
> Thou shalt not sigh, nor hold thy stumps to heaven,
> Nor wink, nor nod, nor kneel, nor make a sign,
> But I of these will wrest an alphabet
> And by still practice learn to know thy meaning.
>
> (3.2.34-45)

Titus here seems genuinely committed to caring for his daughter, and he shows no preoccupation with the shame that Roman culture attached to being a rape victim. Later in the play, emulating the Roman hero Virginius, he kills Lavinia, allegedly in order to put an end to her shame and his sorrow. His real motivation may have had nothing to do with shame, however: he may have killed Lavinia as an act of mercy and simply used the legend of Virginius as a publicly acceptable explanation.

Mental Anguish

Even persons who support the right to die in cases of incurable disease or debilitating bodily impairment often balk at the prospect of extending the concept to persons who suffer from mental anguish, however painful. Perhaps the reason for this reluctance lies in the perception that mental anguish, unlike the physical conditions discussed, is likely temporary or can be relieved with proper treatment. In any event, mental anguish and consequent suicide threats abound in the Canon. This section will address two instances of characters who express a desire to die because of continuing pain and misery, the source of which happens to be mental rather than physical. In one case, the role of the will in overcoming death wishes is discussed. In the other, the protagonist feels impelled to defend her rationality, which her expressed desire to die draws into question.

The will's capacity to ward off bouts of suicidal depression is described in *Othello*. Near the beginning of the play, Roderigo is distraught because Desdemona, the object of his affections, has eloped with Othello. When he threatens to drown himself, his friend Iago responds that this is mere silliness. Roderigo counters, "It is silliness to live when to live is torment; and then have we a prescription to die when death is our physician" (1.3.309-311). Iago proceeds to ridicule Roderigo's suffering such torment merely because of a love interest. When Roderigo claims that it is not within his power to do anything about it, Iago launches into a disquisition about the power of the will to overcome life's stings:

IAGO: 'Tis in ourselves that we are thus or thus. Our bodies are our gardens, to the which our wills are gardeners; so that if we will plant nettles, or sow lettuce, set hyssop and weed up thyme, supply it with one gender of herbs, or distract it with many, either to have it sterile with idleness, or manured with industry, why, the power and corrigible authority of this lies in our wills.

(1.3.322-330)

In *King John,* young Arthur is the nephew of King John and his rival for the throne. When John's forces capture Arthur in battle, his mother, Constance, fears for his life and is distraught. King Philip of France tries to comfort her, but she refuses to take solace and in extravagant terms proclaims her desire for death: "Death, death; O amiable lovely death!/Thou odiferous stench! sound rottenness!" (3.4.25-26). King Philip's efforts fail to calm her down, Cardinal Pandulph interjects that she is uttering madness, not sorrow. Constance takes offense at this characterization of her mental state and seeks to demonstrate her rationality:

CONST.:   Thou art not holy to belie me so;
          I am not mad: this hair I tear is mine;
          My name is Constance; I was Geoffrey's wife;
          Young Arthur is my son, and he is lost:
          I am not mad: I would to heaven I were!
          For then, 'tis like I should forget myself:
          O, if I could, what grief should I forget!

                                                    (3.4.44-50)

She then proceeds to explain that it is precisely her rational awareness of her son's plight that impels her to suicide:

CONST.:   Preach some philosophy to make me mad,
          And thou shalt be canonized, cardinal;
          For being not mad but sensible of grief,
          My reasonable part produces reason
          How I may be delivered of these woes,
          And teaches me to kill or hang myself:
          If I were mad, I should forget my son,
          Or madly think a babe of clouts were he:
          I am not mad; too well, too well I feel
          The different plague of each calamity.

                                                    (3.4.51-60)

Constance's position is weakened somewhat by the fact that young Arthur has merely been captured, and it is not yet known what his fate will be. When she exits the scene still raving, King Philip follows her, saying that he fears "some outrage" (3.4.106).

The conflict between the cardinal and Constance demonstrates the disagreement still current over whether suicide can ever be the product of a rational mind not subject to any pathological disorders. Jack Kevorkian adamantly maintains that sometimes suicide can be a rational choice by a mentally competent person who is suffering emotionally.[25] But the preponderance of medical opinion is to the contrary. Noting that more than ninety percent of suicides are preceded by a major depression, one medical professor has written, "To suggest self-determination can apply to the decision to commit suicide is to assume incorrectly that a rational decision can be made to end one's life."[26] And the author of a book on this subject has concluded that virtually every study undertaken has found a relationship between suicide and mental illness, "with its attendant distortions of perception, cognition, and will."[27]

Old Age

The largest contingent of persons who might wish to exercise their right to die are the elderly who are afflicted with neither a terminal illness nor a severe mental or physical impairment but simply face the prospect of gradual deterioration of their bodies and consequently of their quality of life. Derek Humphry refers to persons in the more advanced stages of such deterioration as suffering from "terminal old age."[28] While the proportion of the general population that survives other diseases and vicissitudes to succumb to mere "old age" has increased, there have always been enough such cases for this aspect of human experience to be well represented in the Canon.

One of the earliest examples of the miseries of old age is found in the *Odyssey*. Odysseus, having been gone from his home in Ithaca for twenty years (ten fighting in the Trojan War and ten wandering in his attempt to return), is naturally apprehensive about the fate of the family members he left behind. When, in book 11, he goes to the underworld and encounters the shade of his mother, Anticleia, he has the first opportunity in two decades to get news from home. Naturally he asks about his wife, his son, and his father. All are still alive, but the report on his father, Laertes, is not encouraging. Laertes stays out in the fields and no longer goes to town, Odysseus is told; he dresses in rags and sleeps in the ashes before the hearth in the winter and outdoors on a pile of leaves in the summer. "There he lies sorrowing, and nurses his great grief on his heart, in longing for thy return, and heavy old age has come upon him" (11.195-196). The shade of Anticleia then proceeds to tell Odysseus of her own death from a broken heart over the loss of her son.

When Odysseus reaches Ithaca, he disguises himself as a tattered beggar and visits the family farm, where he questions the swineherd Eumaeus about his father. The report this time is even worse. Eumaeus tells Odysseus that Laertes has been praying for death:

> "Then verily, stranger, will I frankly tell thee. Laertes still lives, but ever prays to Zeus that his life may waste away from his limbs within his halls. For wondrously does he grieve for his son that is gone, and for the wise lady, his wedded wife, whose death troubled him most of all, and brought him to untimely old age. But she died of grief for her glorious son by a miserable death, as I would that no man may die who dwells here as my friend and does me kindness." (15.352-360)

One might question whether Laertes' old age is really "untimely." After all, his grandson Telemachus must be over twenty, and his son Odysseus was already a well-established leader of Ithaca when he left for the Trojan War two decades earlier. In any event, whether because of advanced chronological age or because of the suffering he has endured, Laertes obviously feels that the time has arrived for him to die. Others seem to have similar inklings: when his daughter-in-law Penelope formulated her scheme of weaving by day and unweaving by night to delay answering the suitors, her explanation was that she was making a shroud for Laertes "against the time when the fell fate of grievous death shall strike him down" (19.144-145).

A combination of advanced years and extreme grief has also taken its toll on the Duchess of York in *Richard III*. The Duchess's grief stems from the fact that she gave birth to the monstrous Richard. She shares her misery with several others whose lives have been destroyed by murders her son committed. When the group breaks up, the Duchess directs each person to a place of good fortune. As for herself, she says, "I to my grave, where peace and rest lie with me!" She then allows that she has seen "eighty odd years of sorrow," and for every hour of joy there has been a week of grief (4.1.95-96). She sees no source of earthly peace under the circumstances and therefore longs for the peace that only death can provide.

The ending of *King Lear* provides another passage in which an elderly person has reached a point at which death seems the most desirable outcome. At the end of the scene in which Lear raves madly over the hanged body of his only faithful daughter, Cordelia, he collapses in a frenzy. Edgar and Kent rush to his side. When Edgar observes that he has fainted and tries to revive him, Lear's loyal friend Kent advises against it:

KENT: Vex not his ghost: O, let him pass! he hates him much
That would upon the rack of this tough world
Stretch him out longer.

EDGAR: He is gone, indeed.

KENT: The wonder is, he hath endured so long:
He but usurp'd his life.

(5.3.313-317)

Kent's advice against reviving Lear is obviously motivated by compassion for his dying friend, who has already lived beyond ("usurped") his allotted term of years. This advice might be summed up by the modern notation DNR (do not resuscitate), which is frequently used on hospital medical charts to indicate the wishes of dying patients or their families.[29]

To be sure, all three of these passages involve elderly persons who have overwhelming sources of personal grief in addition to the ordinary physical ailments of old age. Laertes has endured twenty years of waiting for the return of his son, who is missing and unaccounted for after a distant war; the Duchess of York has witnessed a series of grotesque crimes committed by her deranged and monstrous son; and Lear has suffered cruel abuse at the hands of two of his daughters and guilt over the death of the third. Still, each one reaches a point at which there seems to be no reason to carry on further. Only Laertes is clearly mistaken.

The Timing and Manner of Death

Not only are there certain categories of people who are most likely to assert a right to die; there are also certain types of desires that are most often expressed concerning the timing and manner of death. Unfortunately, there is widespread and not unsubstantiated fear today that hospitals and the medical profession will not follow individuals' wishes on the manner of their death.[30] As a recent note in the *Harvard Law Review* stated, "[Patients] want control over when they die, where they die, and their physical and mental state at the time of their deaths."[31] As the courts become more involved in questions of this nature, the works of the Canon can provide guidance concerning how

Western culture has viewed them in the past. Commonly expressed in these works are the desire not to live beyond one's usefulness to society; to have a quick rather than a lingering death; and to die at a time when one is prepared psychologically and emotionally to do so.

Beyond Usefulness

In *All's Well That Ends Well,* the king of France, who is terminally ill, has just met young Bertram, whose late father had been his friend and confidant. Reminiscing, the king recalls conversations he used to have with Bertram's father about how long one should want to live:

KING: "Let me not live," quoth he
       "After my flame lacks oil, to be the snuff
       Of younger spirits, whose apprehensive senses
       All but new things disdain; whose judgments are
       Mere fathers of their garments; whose constancies
       Expire before their fashions." This he wish'd:
       I after him do after him wish too,
       Since I nor wax nor honey can bring home,
       I quickly were dissolved from my hive
       To give some labourers room.

                                           (1.2.58-67)

Bertram's father's comments reveal his fear of being out of fashion, while the king is more concerned about his inability to be productive and useful to society. In any event, a lord immediately speaks up to change the direction of the king's thoughts: "You are loved, sir; /They that least lend it you shall lack you first" (1.2.67-68). The king concedes that he does "fill a place," and then gives a sign of hopefulness by commenting that, if a certain famous physician who had served Bertram's family were still alive, he would consult him.

A direct and almost ruthless statement of the view that people should not outlive their usefulness to society is found in the *Republic.* Socrates is criticizing the medical profession in his era for using various new medications to keep people alive, albeit in a struggling and unproductive state, for too long. He contrasts this approach with that of Asclepius, the god of healing, who, he asserts, could have used such medications but chose not to:

It was not from ignorance or inacquaintance with this type of medicine that [Asclepius] did not discover it to his descendants, but because he knew that for all well-governed peoples there is a work assigned to each man in the city which he must perform, and no one has leisure to be sick and doctor himself all his days. (406c)

Socrates goes on to praise the art of Asclepius in dealing with minor and curable ailments. But when bodies were diseased "inwardly and throughout," he did not attempt to "prolong a wretched existence":

> But if a man was incapable of living in the established round and order of life, he did not think it worth while to treat him, since such a fellow is of no use either to himself or to the state. (407e)

In the modern world, Western societies have rejected assessments of the worth of individuals' lives based on their ability to contribute to society in a narrowly utilitarian sense. However, as the rationing of health care becomes an economic necessity, economists have devised a scale to rank treatments; called QALYs (quality-adjusted life years), it "measures the all but unmeasurable, the true value of treatments in terms of not just prolonged life but quality of life."[32] It is likely that this scale attempts to measure much of what Plato had in mind when he referred to the need for a fellow to be of use "either to himself or to the state."

A final point concerning Plato's treatment of this issue in the *Republic* relates to the role and motivation of physicians. Socrates realizes that the standard for treatment that he has been describing (the ability of the patient to resume a productive life) will have no meaning when applied to a rich man, who has no appointed tasks and whose only object in living is "to practice virtue" (407a). He believes that an excessive preoccupation with the health of a failing body usually constitutes an impediment even to practicing virtue. Therefore, "the art of medicine should not be for such nor should they be given treatment even if they were richer than Midas" (408b). Still, Socrates is wary enough to note that, according to legend, Asclepius was bribed with gold to heal a man already at the point of death. This wariness is as common today as ever. As a recent article in *Time* magazine put it, "Some are cynical about doctors' motives. 'The longer I am on a machine,' one patient said, 'the more money they make.'"[33]

Make It Quick

Perhaps the most universal wish concerning the circumstances of death is that it be quick and painless. Much of what has often passed as fear of death is in fact fear of the process of dying. The desire for a quick death was clearly expressed even in the heroic culture portrayed by Homer, in which valiant warriors rarely expressed their fears openly.

In the *Iliad,* the Trojan prince Paris is engaged in furious fighting against the Greeks following the death of an ally who had once been his host. In wrath, he flings a bronze-tipped arrow that strikes Euchenor under the ear, ending his life. Homer diverts our attention from the bloody battle long enough to tell us Euchenor's story. He was the son of the Corinthian seer Polyidus, who had often told his son of the fate that awaited him at Troy: he must either perish of a dire disease at home or be slain by the Trojans in the war. An additional consideration was that a heavy fine would have been assessed against him had he chosen not to serve in the army. The choice was clear: "wherefore he avoided at the same time the heavy fine of the Achaeans and the hateful disease, that he might not suffer woes at heart" (13.669-670). At least the arrow of Paris brought him a quick death; the woes at heart caused by a lingering disease were dreaded even by a courageous warrior.

A similar sentiment is expressed in the *Odyssey* by a disobedient crew member who causes Odysseus much grief. In the course of his travels, Odysseus arrives on the island of the sun god Helios. The sorceress Circe has forewarned him that he must under no circumstances kill the sacred cattle belonging to Helios. He repeats this warning to his crew, but when they are stranded on the island for a whole month and their food supply is exhausted, Eurylochus stirs up some trouble: "Hear my words, comrades, for all your evil plight. All forms of death are hateful to wretched mortals, but to die of hunger, and so meet one's doom, is the most pitiful" (12.340-342). He then proposes that they kill the sacred cattle; should Helios be angry and destroy their ships, "rather would I lose my life once for all with a gulp at the wave, than pine slowly away in a desert isle" (12.350-351). Others apparently shared this view, because Eurylochus succeeded in persuading them to disobey Odysseus.

The Readiness Is All

Most people would prefer to die at a point at which they feel psychologically and emotionally that the time is right. This sense of preparedness might hinge upon the happening of some last, longed-for event of personal significance (for example, the birth of a grandchild or one last visit to a revered site). It might also hinge upon making final preparations of a worldly nature. Both kinds of readiness are found in the works of the Canon.

At the end of the *Iliad,* the city of Troy is in flames, and most of the royal family have been slain. King Priam resolves to go alone to the Greek camp to seek to ransom the body of his son Hector, whom Achilles has slain in battle. Priam's wife Hecuba pleads with him not to go, for he will surely not return. Priam responds that he is merely obeying instructions from Zeus. Then he adds, "And what though Achilles should murder me? Once my arms have clasped Hector's corpse, and my tears have wetted it, I too am ready to die" (24.226-227).[34] Priam's response acknowledges that he no longer has anything to live for and that, to be ready to die, he needs only the emotional satisfaction of saying farewell to his beloved son.

In *Timon of Athens,* the Athenian general Timon has become a misanthrope and is living alone in the woods. He is visited by his loyal steward Flavius and a delegation of senators, who try to persuade him to return to Athens and lead the defense of the city against an attack by Alcibiades, who has been banished. Timon rejects their pleas because he has other plans:

> TIMON: Why, I was writing of my epitaph:
> It will be seen to-morrow: my long sickness
> Of health and living now begins to mend,
> And nothing [oblivion] brings me all things. Go, live still;
> Be Alcibiades your plague, you his,
> And last so long enough!
>
>   (5.1.188-193)

When the senators keep trying in vain to change his mind, Flavius finally intercedes and asks them to trouble him no further, for clearly his mind is made up. Timon then delivers his parting shot, announcing his intention to die on the seashore:

> TIMON: Come not to me again: but say to Athens,
> Timon hath made his everlasting mansion
> Upon the beached verge of the salt flood;
> Who once a day with his embossed froth
> The turbulent surge shall cover: thither come,
> And let my grave-stone be your oracle.
> . . . .
> Graves only be men's works and death their gain!

Sun, hide thy beams! Timon hath done his reign.

(5.1.217-222, 225-226)

Later Timon's epitaph is discovered on the seashore, exactly as he intended. He had meticulously prepared every detail of his death, and those who knew of his plans respected his wishes enough not to try to interfere.

Requests for Assistance

As in Elizabeth Bouvia's case, persons with significant bodily impairment often require assistance to exercise their right to die. Even able-bodied persons sometimes need assistance in bringing about their own death. The authors of a book on the right to die introduce a chapter entitled "Helping Another to Die" as follows: "Helping another to die is probably the most intensely personal test of individual conscience known to mankind. Most of us are shocked and revolted by murder, suicide, or genocide, but when someone we know cries out with justification for help in dying, who among us dares to respond? If we help accelerate death in these circumstances, are we being ruthless or humane?"[35]

These are precisely the questions that must have been in the minds of those surrounding the king in *King John*. Near the end of the play, attendants enter, carrying the king on a chair. He is in excruciating pain, having been poisoned by a monk. When Prince Henry asks him how he fares, he responds:

KING JOHN: Poison'd, – ill fare – dead, forsook, cast off:
            And none of you will bid the winter come
            To thrust his icy fingers in my maw,
            Nor let my kingdom's rivers take their course
            Through my burn'd bosom, nor entreat the north
            To make his bleak winds kiss my parched lips
            And comfort me with cold. I do not ask you much,
            I beg cold comfort; and you are so strait
            And so ingrateful, you deny me that.

(5.7.35-43)

Thus the king castigates those around him for refusing to put an end to his misery. Still, he must have understood that, in a king's court filled with murderous intrigues, to participate in the death of the king – however humane one's purpose - would have been risky indeed.

The type of assistance most people would seek in an effort to end their own lives would be that of the pharmacist or physician. Lethal drugs and poisons have been "controlled substances" for centuries, and even in Shakespeare's time special efforts were needed to get access to them. In *Romeo and Juliet*, Romeo has been banished to Mantua, and Friar Laurence is helping Juliet with a plot to reunite the young lovers. The friar gives Juliet a potion that puts her into a deep sleep simulating death. News of Juliet's supposed death reaches Romeo in Mantua before the friar's messenger can get there. Grief-stricken, he goes to an apothecary to procure a lethal drug for himself, intending to drink it and die at Juliet's side. Romeo tries to negotiate with the apothecary, who responds:

> APO.:   Such mortal drugs I have; but Mantua's law
> Is death to any he that utters [dispenses] them.
>
> (5.1.66-67)

Romeo reminds the apothecary of the obvious poverty in which he lives and persuades him to accept a bribe:

> ROMEO: There is thy gold, worse poison to men's souls,
> Doing more murders in this loathsome world,
> Than these poor compounds that thou mayst not sell.
> I sell thee poison; thou hast sold me none.
>
> (5.1.80-83)

Of course, the law against dispensing lethal drugs might have been intended as a guard more against murder than against suicide.

An apothecary also figures in another Shakespearean death, that of the cardinal in *II Henry VI*. The cardinal has been suffering the pangs of a guilty conscience for his role in planning the murder of Gloucester. He is taken deathly ill and lies in bed, delirious and in great agony. The king and his party discover him there and try to converse with him. In his raving, he calls out, "Give me some drink; and bid the apothecary/Bring the strong poison that I bought of him" (3.3.17-18). The exact cause of the cardinal's physical ailment is not revealed, and he might have already consumed some of the poison alluded to. In any event, those present realize that he is beyond saving and heed Salisbury's advice, "Disturb him not; let him pass peaceably" (3.3.25).

In *Antony and Cleopatra*, Cleopatra has resolved to kill herself, and she lets her servants know of her intent. At one point, when Proculeius brings falsely optimistic greetings from Caesar, she is not fooled; she tries to stab herself but is restrained. Later a rustic clown delivers a basket of figs containing the poisonous "worms" (aspic), the means she uses to commit suicide. At the end of the play, Caesar arrives and, observing Cleopatra's body, tries to figure out how she died. When a guard points out the aspic's trail on the fig leaves in the basket, Caesar says:

CAESAR: Most probable
        That so she died; for her physician tells me
        She hath pursued conclusions infinite
        Of easy ways to die.

(5.2.356-359)

No question arising out of the right-to-die movement has been more controversial than the proper role of physicians in giving advice and/or assistance to patients who want to die. People who generally support the idea of self-determination concerning refusal of unwanted medical treatment sometimes balk at the idea of physicians' actually administering fatal injections or writing prescriptions with knowledge of their intended use.

There is a wide variety in the approaches of physicians who favor some form of assisted suicide. The celebrated Dr. Jack Kevorkian has gone so far as to propose a new medical specialty for those with expertise in helping patients die (obitiatry); he would establish a chain of clinics (obitoria) where patients would go to die (medicide).[36] At the other end of the spectrum are the more conventional physicians like Dr. Timothy Quill, who attracted national attention when he admitted in an article in the *New England Journal of Medicine* that he wrote a prescription for a lethal dose of barbituates for a patient dying of leukemia.[37] The concept of a legal right to die with assistance from a physician has been defended in major legal journals such as the *Harvard Law Review*.[38] Clearly this is a matter that will be highly controversial as society becomes increasingly receptive to some measure of self-determination regarding the timing and manner of death.

Who Should Decide?

Modern cases involving the right to die often arise when someone is unable to make critical personal health-care decisions because he or she is either comatose or suffering from some form of dementia. In such cases, a quandary arises over who should make the necessary decisions about initiating or suspending life support systems, for example. In her concurring opinion in the Cruzan case, Justice Sandra Day O'Connor concentrated on strategies for protecting an incompetent individual's right to refuse medical treatment. She wrote that "no national consensus has yet emerged on the best solution for this difficult and sensitive problem."[39] Among the parties often called upon to make decisions of this kind are family members, physicians, the state, and the gods, and passages from the Canon shed light on the appropriateness of each.

Family Members

Ordinarily the next of kin is presumed to be the proper party to make any necessary decisions concerning medical treatment in cases in which the patient is incompetent. And yet, as the Supreme Court's opinion in the *Cruzan* case clearly states, no one, no matter how closely related, can presume to know exactly what decision a patient would have made for himself or herself.[40] In addition, the possibility of self-serving motivation cannot be overlooked. As Chief Justice William Rehnquist stated in that case, "Not all incompetent patients will have loved ones available to serve as surrogate decision-makers. And even where family members are present, 'there will, of course, be some unfortunate situations in which family members will not act to protect a patient.'"[citations omitted].[41] This point is made less delicately by the author of a book on the concept of privacy: "There are evil families, greedy families, and disturbed families. Not all of us are safe in life, or near death, with the decisions our families might make for us."[42]

As far back as Genesis, greed has engendered deceit within families when old age incapacitates a senior member. In chapter 27, the elderly Isaac's eyesight is failing. His wife Rebekah conspires with Jacob, their younger son, to take advantage of Isaac's blindness to cheat the elder son Esau out of his blessing. When Rebekah overhears Isaac asking Esau to go out hunting and bring him some venison to eat, she prepares some savory goat meat for him instead. She dresses Jacob in Esau's clothing and covers Jacob's smooth skin with the goat's hairy skin because Esau is hairy. Jacob then carries the meat to his father and impersonates his older brother, even lying in response to direct questioning about his identity. As a result, Jacob secures his father's blessing in addition to the birthright, both of which rightfully belonged to Esau.

Scheming by untrustworthy offspring is one of the primary themes of *King Lear*. In the first scene of the play, Lear's two selfish daughters,

Regan and Goneril, conspire to put their own interests ahead of their father's. They justify this by referring to his increasing senility, which Regan calls "the infirmity of his age" (1.1.296) and Goneril "the unruly waywardness that infirm and choleric years bring with them" (1.1.301-303). In the next scene, the Earl of Gloucester is said to be having problems with his own children. His illegitimate son Edmund has planted a letter for Gloucester to find, in which his legitimate son Edgar supposedly urges Edmund to join him in a conspiracy to kill their father for his property. The letter reads in part, "If our father would sleep till I waked him, you should enjoy half his revenue for ever, and live the beloved of your brother" (1.2.55-57). Later in the play, when Lear refuses to come in from a violent storm and his friend Kent questions his sanity, Gloucester can empathize:

GLOUCESTER: Canst thou blame him?
    His daughters seek his death: ah, that good Kent!
    He said it would be thus, poor banish'd man!
    Thou say'st the king grows mad; I'll tell thee, friend,
    I am almost mad myself: I had a son,
    Now outlaw'd from my blood; he sought my life,
    But lately, very late: I loved him, friend:
    No father his son dearer: truth to tell thee,
    The grief hath crazed my wits. What a night's this!

                                                (3.4.167-175)

The audience knows, although Gloucester does not, that his legitimate son Edgar is innocent of the supposed plot against his life. The important point here, however, is that the existence of the plot, paralleling an actual plot by Lear's two daughters, was credible to Gloucester. Where matters of inheritance are concerned, even the bonds between parents and their children can be strained.

Another example of this jaundiced view of human nature is found in *II Henry IV*. King Henry has taken deathly ill, and his son Prince Hal arrives and keeps watch at his sleeping father's bedside. The king's crown lies nearby, and the prince addresses it, saying that the stresses and strains it represents have killed his father. Assuming that his father has died, the prince distractedly puts the crown on his own head and wanders from the room. The king awakens and, missing his crown, jumps to the conclusion that the prince has exhibited impatience for him to die:

KING: See, sons, what things you are!
         How quickly nature falls into revolt
         When gold becomes her object!
         . . . .
         Thou hast stolen that which after some few hours
         Were thine without offence; and at my death
         Thou hast seal'd up my expectation:
         . . . .
         Thou hidest a thousand daggers in thy thoughts,
         Which thou hast whetted on thy stony heart,
         To stab at half an hour of my life.
         What! canst thou not forbear me half an hour?
         Then get thee gone and dig my grave thyself,
         And bid the merry bells ring to thine ear
         That thou art crowned, not that I am dead.
                              (4.5.65-67, 102-104, 107-113)

The prince's tears ultimately convince the king that he was wrong about his son; still, the king was all too ready to jump to a false conclusion because that conclusion was so credible a reflection of human nature.

Obviously there are great pitfalls in giving family members the power to make life-and-death decisions for another. As a practical matter, however, physicians and hospitals often rely on the family as the primary decision maker on medical treatment for an incompetent patient. One reason for this is fear of litigation. A medical professor has pointed out, a bit perversely, that there has never been a successful lawsuit against a physician who gave treatment in accordance with the family's wishes and against the patient's wishes. "That's because the patients aren't there. They are either incompetent or they have already died."43

Physicians

In the past, physicians had almost total control over treatment of their patients. Especially where incompetent patients were concerned, unless family members actively interceded, a physician could virtually play God. It is unknown how many life-and-death decisions were quietly made by physicians, after consultation with family members, before the case of Karen Ann Quinlan catapulted the right-to-die issue into the glare of public attention. In the current climate, most physi-

THE RIGHT TO DIE 203

cians are unwilling to make such decisions, preferring to serve in an advisory role.[44]

An example of a physician making unilateral life-and-death decisions is found in *Richard II*. King Richard has been told that John of Gaunt, having been poisoned by a monk, is on his deathbed. Richard is delighted, because he anticipates confiscating John's property to finance his military campaign in Ireland. He therefore responds to the bearer of the news concerning John, "Now put it, God, in the physician's mind/To help him to his grave immediately!" (1.4.59-60). It is unclear whether this is a prayer that the physician be merciful (in putting John out of the misery he is suffering from the poison's effect) or corrupt (in making John's resources available for the military campaign).

When it comes to matters of life and death, there are limits even to the understanding of physicians. In the dialogue *Laches,* Socrates is discussing the definition of courage with two generals, Nicias and Laches. Courage is said to be knowledge of what is to be dreaded and what is to be dared. Nicias asserts that doctors know about what is healthy and what diseased. But this is all they know. They do not know whether health is sometimes to be dreaded rather than sickness. For some people, there are times when it is better for them not to rise from their sickbed. Sometimes it is even preferable to be dead. Laches offers the possibility that it is a seer rather than a doctor who knows such things. However, Nicias rejects this possibility, because a seer's business is only to judge the signs of what is to come, not to know what is better or worse for a person to suffer or not to suffer. In frustration, Laches says that he does not see what Nicias is driving at, "for he points out that neither a seer nor a doctor nor anybody else is the man he refers to as the courageous, unless perchance he means it is some god" (196a). This passage clearly articulates the distinction between the type of knowledge a physician has and the type only higher wisdom can encompass.

The State's Interest

Yet another party that is often involved in decisions about life and death is the state. Precisely what the state's role should be was hotly disputed in the *Cruzan* case. The Court's opinion stated that the due process clause did not require Missouri to repose judgment on these matters with anyone but the patient herself; in the absence of clear and convincing evidence of what the patient herself would have decided, Missouri's interest in the protection of human life was allowed to prevail.[45] In his dissenting opinion, Justice William Brennan wrote, "I cannot agree with the majority that where it is not possible to determine what choice an incompetent patient would make, a State's role as *parens patriae* permits the State automatically to make that choice itself.... A State's legitimate interest in safeguarding a patient's choice cannot be furthered by simply appropriating it."[46] Brennan's view seems to have been that, if the standard of proof required were not so strict, there would be very few cases in which it would be impossible for a court to determine what choice an individual would have made.

This clashing of individual interests with those of the state in choices made by dying persons can be seen in the *Laws,* although in a passage where Plato is discussing wills and the succession of property rights rather than the right to die. The Athenian begins this part of his conversation with the Spartan Clinias by casting doubt upon the mental state of persons near death:

ATHENIAN: For most of us are more or less in a dull and enfeebled state of mind, when we imagine that we are nearly at the point of death.

CLINIAS: What do you mean by this, Stranger?

ATHENIAN: A man at the point of death, Clinias, is a difficult subject, and overflowing with speech that is alarming and vexatious to a lawgiver.

(922c)

The Athenian goes on to explain that such a man will insist that only he should decide how to dispose of his own property. In the past, lawgivers have deferred to such insistence because they feared incurring the anger of men in this situation. However, he proposes a different approach:

ATHENIAN: O friends, we will say, for you, who are literally but creatures of a day, it is hard at present to know your own possessions and, as the Pythian oracle declares, your own selves, to boot. So I, as lawgiver, make this ruling: ... rather will I legislate with a general view to what is best for your whole race and State, justly accounting of minor importance the interests of the individual.

(923a-b)

The Athenian's view of the primacy of the state's interest where property is concerned is not unlike that of Justice Scalia where human life is concerned. Scalia argued in the *Cruzan* case that the state's interest in the protection of human life is so compelling that it may override an individual's (alleged) constitutional right to die.[47]

Only the Gods

Notwithstanding all of the above discussions about the claims of family members, physicians, and the state to participate in life-and-death decisions for incompetent persons, there is still a strong current in the Western tradition that favors leaving such decisions to divine powers. The Canon provides many instances of explicit deference to the will of the gods in such cases. For example, in the *Odyssey*, Odysseus has returned to Ithaca disguised as a tattered beggar. He visits his family farm and is given a meal by the swineherd Eumaeus, whom he asks about his background. Eumaeus responds with a lengthy story, beginning on the island of Syria:

> There is an isle called Syria, if haply thou hast heard thereof, above Ortygia, where are the turning-places of the sun. It is not very thickly settled, but it is a good land, rich in herds, rich in flocks, full of wine, abounding in wheat. Famine never comes into the land, nor does any hateful sickness besides fall on wretched mortals; but when the tribes of men grow old throughout the city, Apollo, of the silver bow, comes with Artemis, and assails them with his gentle shafts, and slays them. (15.403-411)

This vignette gives an idealized depiction of how the elderly would like their deaths to be: quick, painless, and determined by benevolent deities.

Although she is neither elderly nor terminally ill, Penelope has suffered such travails that, in despair, she wishes for the end of her life. She refers to the same myth that Eumaeus related when she begs Artemis prematurely to shoot her with one of those gentle shafts:

> Artemis, mighty goddess, daughter of Zeus, would that now thou wouldest fix thy arrow in my breast and take away my life even in this hour.... Would that even so those who have dwelling on Olympus would blot me from sight, or that fair-tressed Artemis would smite me, so that with Odysseus before my mind I might even pass beneath the hateful earth, and never gladden in any wise the heart of a baser man. (20.61-63, 79-82)

One might expect that a person so desirous of death would take matters into her own hands; however, there is a clear presumption that the timing of death is a matter for the gods to decide.

A similar attitude prevails in the Hebrew scriptures. There, rather than contemplating suicide, even men who are suffering mightily ask divine authority to end their lives. For example, in the book of Jonah the Lord has instructed Jonah to prophesy against the city of Nineveh, and Jonah has duly warned that city that it will be destroyed within forty days because of its evil ways. However, when the city mends its ways and the Lord decides not to destroy it, Jonah is demoralized. He prays to the Lord to end his life: "Therefore now, O Lord, take, I beseech thee, my life from me; for it is better for me to die than to live" (4.3).

In a similar vein, as a result of the series of catastrophes that have plagued him, Job wonders why death is denied to those who long for it:

> Wherefore is light given to him that is in misery, and life unto the bitter in soul;
> Which long for death, but it cometh not; and dig for it more than for hid treasures;
> Which rejoice exceedingly, and are glad, when they can find the grave? (3.20-22)

He wishes that God would end his life:

> Oh that I might have my request; and that God would grant me the thing that I long for!
> Even that it would please God to destroy me; that he would let loose his hand, and cut me off! (6.8-9)

Still, Job does not actively consider suicide. When his wife earlier suggested that he curse God and die, he reproached her for speaking "as one of the foolish women speaketh" (2.9-10).

Deference to divine authority concerning when to die can also be seen in Shakespeare. For example, in *III Henry VI,* the weak King Henry is lamenting the burdens of kingship and longing for a simpler existence. He says in a soliloquy, "Would I were dead! if God's good will were so: /For what is in this world but grief and woe?" (2.5.19-20). While Henry would prefer death, since that is apparently not God's will, he goes on to wish for the pastoral life of a shepherd as the next best choice. The reluctance of many Shakespearean characters even to consider suicide is based upon a taboo with a primarily (but not exclusively) religious rationale.

Reasons for the Taboo

People have been shown to defer to the gods for a decision as to the timing of their death, often in circumstances where suicide might have seemed a rational choice. Such deference seems to be based on a clear but largely unarticulated taboo against taking one's own life. Certain passages in the Canon reveal the actual bases for this taboo, which include religious strictures, social pressures, and simple fear of the unknown.

Religious Strictures

Plato's *Phaedo* contains one of the foremost passages in which a religious objection is given to taking one's own life. Socrates is in prison, conversing with his friends Simmias and Cebes as he awaits execution at sunset. Cebes asks Socrates why people say one is not permitted to take one's own life. Socrates admits that he has often heard that opinion expressed. He adds that if death is always and without exception better than life (as he has taught), "it will perhaps seem strange to you that these human beings for whom it is better to die cannot without impiety do good to themselves, but must wait for some other benefactor" (62a). Socrates admits that it does sound strange when put this way but suggests that there may be a good justification nevertheless. He goes on to offer his own opinion:

> "But this at least, Cebes, I do believe is sound, that the gods are our guardians and that we men are one of the chattels of the gods. Do you not believe this?"
>
> "Yes," said Cebes, "I do."
>
> "Well then," said he, "if one of your chattels should kill itself when you had not indicated that you wished it to die, would you be angry with it and punish it if you could?"
>
> "Certainly," he replied. (62b-c)

Socrates concludes that from this point of view, it is not at all unreasonable to say that a person should not kill himself until the gods visit some necessity upon him. This conclusion comports with what is said in the *Republic:* at 615c, the character Er, who had a near-death experience in which he got a glimpse of the afterlife, is said to have reported that in the afterlife the souls of those who are guilty of self-slaughter are singled out for special requitals.

And yet Plato also had a practical side. As was discussed earlier, in the same work in which the Tale of Er is recounted, Plato has Socrates criticize the medical profession for keeping people alive when they can no longer be useful to society. And in the *Laws* he seems amenable to at least some justifications for suicide. There, after a long discussion of all kinds of murder, he has the Athenian say:

> Now he that slays the person who is, as men say, nearest and dearest of all, – what penalty should he suffer? I mean the man that slays himself, – violently robbing himself of his Fate-given share of life, when this is not legally ordered by the State, and when he is not compelled to it by the occurrence of some intolerable and inevitable misfortune, nor by falling into some disgrace that is beyond remedy or endurance. (873c)

The Athenian does not spell out what kinds of "misfortune" or "disgrace" he is referring to. As is so often the case, the older Plato of the *Laws* has a very different outlook from that of the more fervid and idealistic Plato of the earlier dialogues.

As was pointed out in the preceding section, there is an implicit presumption in the Hebrew scriptures that only God should decide when a healthy person's life should end. However, both the Hebrew and Christian scriptures are silent on the issue of mercy-killing. Arguments have been attempted based upon the sixth commandment (thou shalt not kill), but this prohibition is better translated "thou shalt not murder" and has not generally been viewed as prohibiting all killing of human beings.[48] Reference is sometimes made to passages in I Corinthians in which St. Paul refers to the sanctity of the body as the temple of the Holy Spirit, which should not be defiled or destroyed.[49] However, the use of plural pronouns and verb forms in these passages clearly shows that Paul is referring to the congregation of believers as the "body" and not to any individual's corporeal existence.[50]

Even though there is no scriptural authority for this position, Church tradition has historically condemned both suicide and euthanasia.[51] Thus, in Shakespeare's plays set in the Christian era, one finds reference to this doctrine as absolute authority.[52] For example, in *Cymbeline,* Pisanio, Posthumus's servant, has followed his master's instructions to accompany Imogen, Posthumus's wife, to a remote seashore so he can kill her as punishment for her supposed adultery. When Pisanio tells Imogen of his purpose by showing her the written instructions from Posthumus, her first impulse is to kill herself. She cannot do it, however, because "against self-slaughter/There is a prohibition so divine/That cravens my weak hand" (3.4.78-80). She therefore implores Pisanio to hurry up and carry out the deed for which he was dispatched.

One of the best-known aspects of Hamlet's complex personality is his proneness to death wishes and suicidal impulses. In a soliloquy early in the play, he voices his wish for death but also the reason for his hesitance:

> HAMLET: O, that this too too solid flesh would melt,
> Thaw and resolve itself into a dew!
> Or that the Everlasting had not fix'd
> His canon 'gainst self-slaughter! O God! God!
> How weary, stale, flat, and unprofitable
> Seem to me all the uses of this world!
>
> (1.2.129-134)

Hamlet is tormented by the demon of his father's ghost but perceives himself as too weak to exact the vengeance required of him. His later, more famous soliloquy ("To be or not to be") brings into question whether Hamlet's unwillingness to commit suicide was really based on his religiosity or on some other inhibition.

Religious strictures in the Canon against suicide and euthanasia are thus seen to be not nearly as clear or unambiguous as one might have expected. What little authority there is in these works is susceptible of various interpretations. Concerning a recent right-to-die initiative in Washington state, one journalist concluded, "Protestants, Catholics, and Jews all describe life as 'a gift from God' over which humans only have 'stewardship.' But they differ over how that stewardship can be exercised: whether people have the right to choose when and how to die, or whether the choice must be left to God."[53] And philosopher James Rachels has pointed out that, to be consistent, those who believe that only God should make this choice would have to reject all life-prolonging measures, for "we alter the length of a person's life when we save it just as much as when we take it."[54] By logic, leaving such matters entirely to divine authority would entail abolishing the practice of medicine.

Social Pressures

In addition to religious strictures, social pressures of one kind or another have contributed to the taboo against suicide. These pressures include the stigma of cowardice, concern about the effects of one's suicide on those left behind, and the awkwardness of one's funeral and burial under such circumstances.

Even for a person fighting a terminal illness, there may seem to be a certain heroism in "never giving up" and a certain cowardice in "taking the easy way out." Especially for a person who is not in excruciating pain or other unendurable condition, there is a significant risk that the choice to end his or her life will be interpreted by others as an indication of weak character. In the passage from the *Laws* quoted above, in which the Athenian indicated that there might be some "misfortune" or "disgrace" that would make suicide a compelling choice, a contrast is drawn with other circumstances in which a person is "merely inflicting upon himself this iniquitous penalty owing to sloth and unmanly cowardice" (873c).

Another source of social pressure against suicide is the effect it might have on the welfare of loved ones left behind. Even when the circumstances surrounding the choice to die are compelling, family and friends may suffer a feeling of abandonment. This would be even more true in cases in which others relied on the decedent economically or psychologically. In Sonnet 66, the despairing poet first states his disillusion with life ("Tired with all these, for restful death I cry") and then lists all the aspects of life that he finds wearisome. In the rhymed couplet at the end, however, he gives one countervailing factor that overrides all that has gone before: "Tired with all these, from these would I be gone,/Save that, to die, I leave my love alone."

Social pressure against suicide also derives from concern over how the funeral and burial will be handled under the circumstances. Of course, people are less apt to be concerned about such matters today than in the past, when there were strict rules requiring that suicides be denied certain customary rites because of the manner of their death. Following the discussion of suicide in the *Laws* cited above, the Athenian prescribes the allowable circumstances of burial:

> But for those thus destroyed the tombs shall be, first, in an isolated position with not even one adjacent, and, secondly, they shall be buried in those borders of the twelve districts which are barren and

nameless, without note, and with neither headstone nor name to indicate the tombs. (873d)

Similar customs prevailed in the Christian era, following the
Church tradition that strongly condemned all suicide. In *Hamlet,* much
attention is devoted to the kind of funeral rites and burial that will be
allowed for Ophelia, Hamlet's former girlfriend who has drowned sus-
piciously. At the opening of the funeral scene, two rustic gravediggers
are discussing what kind of burial Ophelia will be given. One asks the
other, "Is she to be buried in Christian burial that willfully seeks her
own salvation?" (5.1.1-2). Later in the scene, when the funeral party
enters, the clergyman discusses the ceremony with Ophelia's brother
Laertes:

DOCTOR: Her obsequies have been as far enlarged
          As we have warranty: her death was doubtful:
          And, but that great command o'ersways the order,
          She should in ground unsanctified have lodged
          Till the last trumpet.
          . . . .

LAERTES: Must there no more be done?

DOCTOR: No more be done:
          We should profane the service of the dead
          To sing a requiem and such rest to her
          As to peace-parted souls.

                              (5.1.249-253, 258-261)

Such rigidity might seem almost barbaric to modern temperaments
accustomed to regard suicide as sad or even tragic, but not heinous.
However, in his concurring opinion in the *Cruzan* case, Justice Antonin
Scalia vehemently defended a state's interest in protecting human life,
including its right to outlaw and attempt to prevent (by force if necessary) all suicides, even suicide by refusing to take appropriate measures
necessary to preserve one's life.[55] Noting that at common law in England a suicide was criminally liable for his offense, Scalia stated,
"Although the States abolished the penalties imposed by the common
law (*i.e.,* forfeiture and ignominious burial), they did so to spare the innocent family, and not to legitimize the act."[56] One almost senses that,
if he had his way, Scalia would favor continuing to impose those penalties on people who dare to take their own lives.

Fear of the Unknown

The taboo against suicide, like all taboos, is based on a primal fear and dread of the unknown, and death — by its nature unknown and unknowable — is a prime subject for taboos of all sorts. This innate fear is likely to have stayed more hands from suicide than either religious strictures or social pressures. The works of the Canon contain a number of famous expressions of and reflections about the fear of death; of these, only two are cited here.

In the *Apology,* Socrates is convicted of crimes against the state (corrupting the young and teaching contrary to the official state religion). When he is sentenced to die, he faces the prospect of death with an equanimity that contrasts sharply to the chagrin of his friends and followers. In explaining to the court why he would prefer to accept the death penalty rather than change his customary ways of teaching, he says:

> For to fear death, gentlemen, is nothing else than to think one is wise when one is not; for it is thinking one knows what one does not know. For no one knows whether death be not even the greatest of all blessings to man, but they fear it as if they knew that it is the greatest of evils. And is not this the most reprehensible form of ignorance, that of thinking one knows what one does not know? (29a-b)

Of course, the response might be made that *not* to fear death is also presumptuous, because one is again presuming to know something that one does not. The point should be that one does not know whether to fear death or not, because nothing is known about the hereafter.

Perhaps the most famous expression of the fear of death in all of Western literature is from Hamlet's "To be or not to be" soliloquy. Hamlet expresses a desire for a kind of sleep that will end "the heartache and the thousand natural shocks that flesh is heir to," but then he has second thoughts:

HAMLET: To die, to sleep;
    To sleep: perchance to dream: ay, there's the rub;
    When we have shuffled off this mortal coil,
    Must give us pause:
    . . . .
                            Who would fardels bear,
    To grunt and sweat under a weary life,
    But that the dread of something after death,
    The undiscovered country, from whose bourn

No traveller returns, puzzles the will
And makes us rather bear those ills we have
Than fly to others that we know not of?

(3.1.64-68, 76-82)

In Hamlet's view, one's conditions of life would have to be bad indeed for one to overcome these misgivings and choose to encounter the unknown. The choice to do so is an intensely personal one and is fraught with religious and spiritual dimensions that seem to make interference by the state inappropriate. As was the case with abortion, this is an area in which one's constitutional right to freedom of religion might well be asserted. Further legal developments concerning the constitutional basis for the right to die are likely.

Man's confrontation with the certainty of death and reflections on his own mortality are at the core of the Western humanistic tradition. The works of the Canon are at their richest in providing glimpses of people with various physical and mental ailments wrestling with such fundamental questions as whether or not their lives are worth living and, if not, what their consciences will allow them (or others) to do about it. These works clearly show that quality-of-life considerations have always been a factor in making life-and-death decisions. It is not accurate to say that modern society is abandoning a traditional view of the sanctity of human life and departing into an unknown gray area (the slippery slope) when such qualitative judgments are made, at least by the individuals themselves.

What is new is the fact that the medical profession is now having to deal with these questions on a much larger scale than ever before and in a context in which advances in medical technology have made it possible to prolong individual lives longer than ever before. In previous eras, most people died at home; now about eighty percent of all deaths occur in a hospital or other institutionalized setting.[57] This means that the problems involved for physicians and health-care institutions in making end-of-life decisions are both more common and more visible than ever before. In addition, as people have become more attentive to their legal rights and more willing to assert them, a climate of caution has resulted, and lawyers and judges are far more likely to be involved.

Another new aspect of this issue is the fact that the right-to-die movement has become highly politicized. Pro-life advocates have become increasingly aggressive in pressing their demands that life-prolonging treatments be given even to severely defective newborns and to the comatose who have no hope of ever resuming a meaningful life. Proponents of the right to die, on the other hand, have placed initiatives on the ballot in several states seeking to legalize physician-assisted suicide. While such efforts have so far been rejected at the ballot box in this country, in 1993 the Netherlands became the first Western country to legally countenance the right to die with the assistance of a physician, a move that has drawn strong criticism from the medical establishment in the United States.[58]

Students now in our colleges and universities will face these and other questions resulting from advances in the life sciences and attendant technology, questions that cannot even be framed at the present time. To be able to answer them, they will need both a command of the technologies employed and an understanding of the complex moral and religious implications of their use. The human dimension of these problems should never be overlooked, and the works of the Canon provide profound insight into that dimension of decision making. To entrust such decisions to persons unfamiliar with the rich cultural tradition that preceded them would be a frightening prospect indeed.

Notes

1. Thus the popularity of Sherwin B. Nuland's recent book *How We Die: Reflections on Life's Final Chapter* (New York: Alfred A. Knopf, 1994).

2. Peter Steinfels, "At Crossroads, U.S. Ponders Ethics of Helping Others Die," *New York Times,* October 28, 1991, p. A1.

3. Alida Brill, *Nobody's Business: Paradoxes of Privacy* (Reading, Mass.: Addison-Wesley, 1990), p. 161.

4. Derek Humphry, *Final Exit: The Practicalities of Self-Deliverance and Assisted Suicide for the Dying* (New York: Dell, 1991).

5. Leon R. Kass, "Suicide Made Easy: The Evil of 'Rational' Humaneness," *Commentary,* vol. 92, no. 6 (December 1991), p. 19.

6. Quoted on the frontispiece of Humphry, *Final Exit.*

7. See Joseph P. Shapiro, "Death on Trial," *U.S. News & World Report,* April 25, 1994, pp. 31-39.

8. Timothy E. Quill, *Death and Dignity: Making Choices and Taking Charge* (New York: Norton, 1993), pp. 151-154.

9. See Jane Gross, "At AIDS Epicenter, Seeking Swift, Sure Death," *New York Times,* June 20, 1993, sec. 1, p. 10; and Lisa Belkin, "There's No Simple Suicide," *New York Times Magazine,* November 14, 1993, pp. 48 ff.

10. Henry R. Glick, *The Right to Die: Policy Innovation and Its Consequences* (New York: Columbia University Press, 1992), p. 90.

11. *In re Quinlan,* 70 N.J. 10, 355 A. 2d 647, cert denied *sub nom., Garger v. New Jersey,* 429 U.S. 922, 97 S. Ct. 319, 50 L. Ed. 2d 289 (1976).

12. Richard Sherlock, *Preserving Life: Public Policy and the Life Not Worth Living* (Chicago: Loyola University Press, 1987), pp. 118-119.

13. *Cruzan v. Director, Missouri Department of Health,* 497 U.S. 261, 110 S. Ct. 2841, 111 L. Ed. 2d 224 (1990).

14. The Court's splintered decision makes it difficult to be sure of the precise holding. Eminent legal scholar Ronald Dworkin, noting that even Justice Scalia seemed to be confused about the effect of the Court's judgment in *Cruzan,* states, "Most commentators have concluded, after studying all the opinions the various justices wrote in the case, that its effect was to affirm some constitutional right to die, even though the actual ruling upheld the power of a state to impose severe restrictions on the way in which that right must be exercised." *Life's Dominion: An Argument about Abortion, Euthanasia, and Individual Freedom* (New York: Alfred A. Knopf, 1993), p. 198.

15. 497 U.S. at 293.

16. 497 U.S. at 310-311 and 330.

17. 497 U.S. at 356-357.

18. Glick, *The Right to Die,* p. 4.

19. Dworkin, *Life's Dominion,* p. 193.

20. Ibid., p. 184.

21. In a recent survey of 1400 doctors and nurses at five major hospitals, eighty-one percent said they agreed that "the most common form of narcotic abuse in caring for dying patients is undertreatment of pain" (cited by Dworkin, *Life's Dominion,* p. 183). A professor at the Boston University School of Medicine estimates that up to ninety percent of patients die in too much pain (quoted by Nancy Gibbs, "Rx for Death," *Time,* May 31, 1993, p. 36). However, the director of the Pain Control Center of the Bowman Gray School of Medicine argues that no one should want to die today because of pain. Richard L. Rauck, "Pain Is Not Good Reason to Die," *Winston-Salem Journal,* February 27, 1993, p. 15.

22. Humphry, *Final Exit,* p. 46.

23. Ibid., p. 49.

24. See Derek Humphry and Ann Wickett, *The Right to Die: Understanding Euthanasia* (New York: Harper & Row, 1986), pp. 149-155.

25. Gibbs, "Rx for Death," p. 39.

26. Nicholas A. Pace, "We Should Treat Depression, Not Assist Suicide," letter to the editor of the *New York Times,* February 4, 1993, p. A14.

27. Sherlock, *Preserving Life,* pp. 178-179.

28. Humphry, *Final Exit,* p. 53.

29. Quill, *Death and Dignity,* pp. 197-198.

30. See Jane E. Brody, "The Rights of a Dying Patient Are Often Misunderstood, Even by Medical Professionals," *New York Times,* January 27, 1993, p. B7; and Katrine Ames, "Last Rights," *Newsweek,* August 26, 1991, p. 41.

31. "Physician-Assisted Suicide and the Right to Die with Assistance," *Harvard Law Review,* vol. 105 (June, 1992), p. 2026.

32. Gina Kolata, "Ethicists Struggle with Judgment of the 'Value' of Life," *New York Times,* November 24, 1992, p. B5.

33. Gibbs, "Rx for Death," p. 37.

34. Translated by Robert Graves (London: Cassell , 1960).

35. Humphry and Wickett, *The Right to Die,* p. 296.

36. See Jack Kevorkian, *Prescription: Medicide — The Goodness of Planned Death* (Buffalo, N.Y.: Prometheus Books, 1991), pp. 202-203.

37. See Quill, *Death and Dignity,* pp. 9-16, reprinted from the *New England Journal of Medicine,* vol. 324, March 7, 1991, pp. 691-694.

38. See note 31 above.

39. 497 U.S. at 292.

40. 497 U.S. at 286.

41. 497 U.S. at 281.

42. Brill, *Nobody's Business,* pp. 163-164.

43. Dr. John Ely, a professor at the University of Iowa College of Medicine, quoted by Gibbs, "Rx for Death," p. 37.

44. Dr. Timothy E. Quill points out that even playing an advisory role can be tricky: "It is legally safer for a physician to turn his back on a suffering patient who wants to die than to thoughtfully discuss his options with him." See "On Trial – How We Die," op-ed piece in the *New York Times,* September 27, 1993, p. A11.

45. 497 U.S. at 286.

46. 497 U.S. at 327.

47. 479 U.S. at 299-300.

48. See James Rachels, *The End of Life: Euthanasia and Morality* (Oxford: Oxford University Press, 1986), pp. 161-162.

49. The passages are I Corinthians 3.16-17 and 6.19-20.

50. See William F. Orr and James A. Walther, *The Anchor Bible: I Corinthians* (Garden City, N.Y.: Doubleday, 1976), pp. 174 and 203.

51. See Rachels, *The End of Life,* p. 162.

52. Two notable Shakespearean suicides involve non-Christians. Cleopatra's suicide takes place in a play set in the pre-Christian era: "Let's do it after the high Roman fashion,/And make death proud to take us." *Antony and Cleopatra* 4.15.87-88. Although he appears in a play set in the Christian era, Othello is a Moor: "This did I fear, but thought he had no weapon;/For he was great of heart." *Othello* 5.2.360-361.

53. Steinfels, "At Crossroads, U.S. Ponders Ethics of Helping Others Die," p. A15.

54. Rachels, *The End of Life,* p. 163.

55. 497 U.S. at 293.

56. 497 U.S. at 294.

57. 497 U.S. at 302.

58. See Marlise Simons, "Dutch Move to Enact Law Making Euthanasia Easier," *New York Times,* February 9, 1993, pp. A1 and A7; and Walter

Reich, "Shame on the Dutch," op-ed piece in the *New York Times,* February 27, 1993, p.15.

6: The Death Penalty

CAPITAL PUNISHMENT EXISTED in all of the cultures represented by the works of the Canon, and the practice figures prominently in all of those works. Still, in spite of its wide prevalence, infliction of the death penalty has been disquieting to people's consciences throughout all those eras and remains so now. Columnist George Will has written, "Capital punishment, perhaps more than any other perennial issue of public argument, teaches intellectual humility. No matter which side of the issue you are on, if you do not feel the weakness of your position and see the strengths of the other side, you fully understand neither your position nor the other side's."[1] The moral uncertainties that have always surrounded this issue have made it a primary subject for dramatization by the great literary artists of the Western tradition.

The author of a 1987 book on the death penalty debate described it as "the epitome of the unresolvable issue, the question which people answer on the basis of gut reactions rather than logical arguments."[2] While most people would probably agree that abortion has displaced capital punishment as the epitome of the unresolvable issue, at least as the focus of recent public attention, the death penalty remains a subject with which American society has never come to terms. When hearings were held before the Senate Judiciary Committee in July 1993 on the nomination of Ruth Bader Ginsburg to the Supreme Court, more sparks were generated in questioning about the death penalty than any other issue (perhaps because Judge Ginsburg's views on abortion were already well known).[3]

The ambivalence of American society about the death penalty is reflected in several oddities about the resulting political alignments. For example, those who are pro-life, who oppose abortion and the right to die, are generally in favor of capital punishment. On the other hand, those who are pro-choice, who favor abortion rights and the right to die, generally oppose capital punishment.[4] If the sanctity of life were the only concern, one would expect the pro-life movement to oppose capital punishment. And if the ending of life were an acceptable means of furthering utilitarian ends, one would expect the pro-choice movement to favor retaining capital punishment as an option available to the state for appropriate cases. The failure of these alignments to maintain a consistent pattern points to a fundamental dissonance within our political system over this issue.

Capital punishment seems to bring out inconsistencies in all who come into contact with it. For example, lawyers for the American Civil Liberties Union have been criticized for defending the right of persons in a persistent vegetative state to refuse life-preserving medical treatment; at the same time, they have attempted to press appeals on behalf of condemned prisoners who prefer to die.[5] Even the execution process is riddled with illogicalities. Helen Prejean, a nun who wrote a recent book giving an eyewitness account of executions in Louisiana, has observed, "There is an elaborate ruse going on here, a pitiful disguise. Killing is disguised as a medicinal act. The attendant will even swab the 'patient's' arm with alcohol before inserting the needle — *to prevent infection.*" [emphasis in original].[6]

A public policy that is so obviously disturbing to the psyche of the nation might be expected to have had a troubled constitutional past, and such is indeed the case. After a brief recounting of that past, passages from the Canon will vividly reveal the human dimension of trials in capital cases and subsequent executions. These passages demonstrate why capital punishment is an issue that has never been laid to rest, and possibly never will be.

Constitutionality of the Death Penalty

The Eighth Amendment provides, in stark simplicity, that "cruel and unusual punishments" shall not be inflicted. That provision has never been interpreted to mean that the death penalty is per se a cruel or unusual punishment. Two other constitutional provisions come into play to buttress the view that the death penalty is constitutional. The Fifth and Fourteenth Amendments both provide that no person shall be deprived of "life, liberty, or property, without due process of law," thereby implying that *with* due process of law a person *may* be deprived of life. The Fifth Amendment also provides that no person shall be held for "a capital, or otherwise infamous crime" unless on a presentment or indictment of a grand jury, thus explicitly recognizing the existence of capital punishment.

The closest that the U.S. Supreme Court has ever come to declaring the death penalty unconstitutional was in the 1972 case *Furman v. Georgia.* [7] That case, which was decided only a few months before *Roe v. Wade,* came at a time when the nation's political climate and the court's ideological makeup were most receptive to arguments for abolishing the death penalty. In a 5 to 4 decision, with each of the nine justices filing a separate opinion, the Court held that the death penalty *as applied* was so arbitrary, capricious, and discriminatory as to constitute cruel and unusual punishment. Two of the five justices in the majority (William Brennan and Thurgood Marshall) regarded the death penalty as unconstitutional no matter how it was administered. As a consequence of the *Furman* decision, the death sentences of all prisoners then awaiting execution were commuted, and a moratorium on executions was extended until state legislatures could reform their statutes to meet the Court's new criteria.[8]

By 1976 the tide had turned and the opportunity for abolishing the death penalty was lost. As a result of the nation's shifting political climate and change in the Court's makeup, in *Gregg v. Georgia* the Court held by a vote of 7 to 2 that the death penalty does not inherently constitute cruel and unusual punishment in violation of the Eighth Amendment.[9] After *Gregg,* more state legislatures began to reinstate the death penalty, and at this writing thirty-seven states and two federal jurisdictions have done so.[10] Most polls indicate that the American public favors retention of the death penalty for murder, by substantial margins.[11] President Clinton, the most liberal president in recent years, supports the death penalty and even advocates extension of the number of federal offenses for which it may be imposed.[12] The position of the American public seems not to have been affected by the increasing pace of executions, as many prisoners long on death row have begun to exhaust their possibilities for appeal.

In spite of the fact that the death penalty seems to be firmly entrenched in the current political climate, occasional flareups occur when the U.S. Supreme Court is required to decide cases that tug at the public's conscience in especially provocative ways. The most recent such case was *Herrera v. Collins,* decided in January 1993, in which the Court was confronted with the seemingly simplistic question of whether the constitution forbids the execution of a person who is actually innocent of the charges against him.[13] The question is in fact a complex one, going to the heart of our federalist system, in which the individual states have plenary authority over most crimes. The role of the federal courts historically has been to ensure that the accused's constitutional rights are not violated by the procedures the states use in their criminal justice systems, and the means of making such determinations is the writ of *habeas corpus*. The factual question of guilt or innocence is a matter for determination by the state courts, and the judgment of state courts is final unless the accused's constitutional rights have been violated. Thus the question arose: would execution of a person for a crime of which he or she is actually innocent violate any recognized constitutional right?

In *Herrera,* a convicted murderer claimed that new evidence, which came to light eight years after his conviction, would prove his innocence. The state of Texas required that requests for a new trial based on newly discovered evidence be made within thirty days after sentencing. Herrera's attorneys therefore sought a stay of his scheduled execution from the U.S. Supreme Court, alleging only that he was actually innocent and claiming no other constitutional basis for the requested stay. The Court, by a 6 to 3 vote, refused to stay the execution. The majority's reasoning was that, in this case, the state of Texas had provided an appropriate avenue for a "fail-safe" appeal, namely an appeal to the governor for clemency.[14] The Court was obviously swayed by its perception that Herrera was in fact guilty. It held open for another day what it might do in a case in which it was convinced that the defendant was actually innocent, and no avenues for further consideration by the state existed.[15] Less than four months after the Supreme Court's decision was announced, Governor Ann Richards having denied clemency, Herrera was executed.[16]

In a pattern that became familiar to Court watchers, Justice Antonin Scalia and Justice Harry Blackmun exchanged barbs in the *Herrera* decision. Blackmun, joined by Justices Stevens and Souter, wrote in his dissent that "Nothing could be more contrary to contemporary standards of decency or more shocking to the conscience than to execute a person who is actually innocent" [citations omitted].[17] In his concurring opinion, Scalia observed that there is nothing in the "text, tradition, or even in contemporary practice (if that were enough)" to support a constitutional right to demand judicial consideration of newly discovered evidence under the circumstances. Scalia added, "If the system that has been in place for 200 years (and remains widely approved) 'shocks' the dissenters' consciences, perhaps they should doubt the callibration of their consciences, or, better still, the usefulness of 'conscience-shocking' as a legal test."[18] Blackmun responded in kind: "Just as an execution without adequate safeguards is unacceptable, so too is an execution when the condemned prisoner can prove that he is innocent. The execution of a person who can show that he is innocent comes perilously close to simple murder."[19]

One lesson of the *Herrera* case is that, in the American constitutional system, no one wants to assume the final responsibility for executions. Some members of the Court seem to have been motivated in recent capital cases by a desire for relief from the burden of acting as the place of last resort for every prisoner facing execution. Henry Schwarzschild has described the prevailing majority on the Court as having become "impatient, even surly" at being compelled to rule on each case and as being "acutely discomforted by such constant reminders that their decisions 'place the hangman's noose around some person's neck.'"[20] The effect of the *Herrera* decision was to shift that responsibility to the governor for consideration of executive clemency. However, governors are no more eager for this burden than the judiciary. The comments by Governor Edwin Edwards of Louisiana are typical: "I tried to get the legislature to remove the whole process from the governor, but I recognize that in the final analysis some one person has to have the authority to stop an execution.... The whole process is in the judicial system; then, all of a sudden, in the last thirty days to have it sitting on the heart and mind and soul of one man is a very difficult position to be in."[21]

After the *Herrera* decision, tensions escalated within the Supreme Court over this issue. In February 1994, in an emotional solitary dissent to a Court order refusing to hear the appeal of a death-row inmate, Justice Blackmun, soon to retire, declared, "From this day forward, I no longer shall tinker with the machinery of death.... Rather than continue to coddle the Court's delusion that the desired level of fairness has been achieved and the need for regulation eviscerated, I feel morally and intellectually obligated simply to concede that the death penalty experiment has failed."[22] And, in its 1994-95 term, the Court is scheduled to hear argument of another "actual innocence" case, this time involving a Missouri prisoner who is said to have strong evidence that he did not commit the murder for which he has been sentenced to die.[23] This case could require the Court to examine more closely the extent of its own responsibility to review cases of this nature.

Human Aspects of Trials in Capital Cases

One is led to wonder why a governmental policy that seems so favored by the public is at the same time so bereft of hands willing to carry it out. Illumination of this puzzle is provided by the works of the Canon, which offer insights into the human dimension of capital punishment that only literary artists with supreme dramatic powers could provide. They show that the nature of the law is to be inflexible and to refuse to allow exceptions. Against this backdrop, pleas for mercy by the family of the accused and demands for justice by the family of the victim are depicted. Finally, the unavoidable possibility of human error — always a primary argument against capital punishment — is raised.

The Law Makes No Exceptions

The first reference to capital punishment in the Hebrew scriptures is in Genesis, where it is written, "Whoso sheddeth man's blood, by man shall his blood be shed: for in the image of God made he man" (9.6). Shedding of another's blood, or murder, is considered a capital offense because of the unique value of human life, which was created in the image of God. This unique value is still honored today in that murder is the only crime for which people are regularly executed in America. The Hebrew law, on the other hand, considered a host of other crimes capital, including such lesser offenses as working on the Sabbath and keeping an ox known to be dangerous.[24] Justice is depicted in the Hebrew scriptures as swift, sure, and unrelenting. The overwhelming majesty of the law gave people no choice but to obey, and once commission of a capital crime was established, there appeared to be no reason for further talk.

A good example of this approach is found in chapter 7 of Joshua. When the Israelites fail to take Ai during the assault on Jericho, their leader Joshua is distraught and prostrates himself before the Lord, begging to know the reason for this misfortune. The Lord responds that Israel has sinned and broken the Lord's covenant, for someone in their midst has violated a sacred ban by stealing and hiding away property taken during the assault. The Lord further instructs that the person responsible "and all that he hath" be burned with fire (7.15). Joshua proceeds to investigate by use of the sacred lot, which was employed to evoke confessions of guilt (though not to determine guilt without interrogation).[25]

When the lot implicates Achan, Joshua says to him, "Achan, My son, give, I pray thee, glory to the Lord God of Israel, and make confession unto him; and tell me now what thou hast done; hide it not from me." Achan immediately offers a full confession, admitting his guilt and showing apparent remorse:

> Indeed I have sinned against the Lord God of Israel, and thus and thus have I done:
> When I saw among the spoils a goodly Babylonish garment, and two hundred shekels of silver, and a wedge of gold of fifty shekels weight, then I coveted them, and took them; and, behold, they are hid in the earth in the midst of my tent, and the silver under it. (7.20-21)

Joshua sends his aides to Achan's tent, and they locate the goods exactly where he said they were. Joshua takes swift action, transporting Achan and his property and family to the valley of Achor. There, Joshua pronounces final judgment:

> Why hast thou troubled us? the Lord shall trouble thee this day. And all Israel stoned him with stones, and burned them with fire, after they had stoned them with stones.
> And they raised over him a great heap of stones unto this day. So the Lord turned from the fierceness of his anger. (7.25-26)

Joshua clearly saw himself as an agent of the Lord, acting in obedience to his direct command. That removed from him the onus of determining the relevance of confession and remorse and of deciding whether or not to spare Achan's life.[26]

Capital punishment was also well accepted in Greek culture, and a stern justice is described in the dialogues of Plato. In the *Euthyphro*, Socrates and Euthyphro have a chance encounter with each other while conducting some personal business in the halls of justice. Socrates asks Euthyphro what has brought him there, and he replies that he has come to file murder charges against his own father, who was responsible for the death of a hired servant on the family farm. This situation of intense moral conflict leads to a conversation about the nature of holiness. Socrates observes that what is loved or hated by the gods might vary, depending on which of the gods one is talking about. Euthyphro answers that the gods seem to be unanimous on this point: none of them would argue that a person who kills someone wrongfully ought not to pay the penalty.

Socrates suggests that the conversation focus on the view of human beings, and he reiterates the question within that context. Has Euthyphro ever heard anyone argue that a person who has killed someone wrongfully — or, for that matter, who has done anything else wrongfully — ought not to pay the penalty? Euthyphro equivocates before conceding the point:

EUTH.:   Why, they are always arguing these points, especially in the law courts. For they do very many wrong things; and then there is nothing they will not do or say, in defending themselves, to avoid the penalty.

SOCRATES: Yes, but do they acknowledge, Euthyphro, that they have done wrong and, although they acknowledge it, nevertheless say that they ought not to pay the penalty?

EUTH.:   Oh, no, they don't do that.

(8c)

As was the case in Joshua, there is no recognition here of the possible relevance of confession, remorse, pardon, or clemency. A rational system of justice, "a government of laws and not of men," simply leaves no room for arguments why one should not pay the prescribed penalty once guilt has been established.

Several Shakespearean plays portray officials who rely on their understanding that the criminal law in capital cases leaves no room for pity. In *Timon of Athens,* three senators have just pronounced a sentence of death upon a man who has killed someone in a hot-blooded quarrel. In justifying the sentence, one senator remarks to the others, "Nothing emboldens sin so much as mercy" (3.5.3). Alcibiades, the brilliant but unstable military leader, enters and wishes the senators "honour, health, and compassion." He has come to speak on behalf of the accused, who is his friend: "I am an humble suitor to your virtues;/For pity is the virtue of the law,/And none but tyrants use it cruelly" (3.5.5-9). Alcibiades attributes his friend's misdeed to excessive spirit and beseeches the senators, "O my lords,/As you are great, be pitifully good" (3.5.51-52). When the senators refuse to relent, Alcibiades reminds them of his friend's record of distinguished military service and urges that he be released back into that service:

ALCIB.:   If by this crime he owes the law his life,
           Why, let the war receive 't in valiant gore;
           For law is strict, and war is nothing more.

1 SENATOR: We are for law: he dies; urge it no more,
           On height of our displeasure: friend or brother,
           He forfeits his own blood that spills another.

(3.5.83-88)

As Alcibiades continues to protest, the senators become irritated and decree immediate execution for the friend and perpetual banishment for Alcibiades. They clearly resent Alcibiades' attempt to force them to consider penal possibilities other than the obvious one set forth by the law, which they may safely rely upon.

A different scenario is presented in *The Comedy of Errors*. Egeon, a merchant from Syracuse, appears before the Duke of Ephesus to answer the charge that he has violated the Ephesian law forbidding Syracusians to come to marketplaces in Ephesus. The penalty is death unless a ransom of one thousand marks can be raised. The duke instructs Egeon to plead no more, because his hands are tied by the "rigorous statutes" that have been enacted in the wake of a trade dispute between Syracuse and Ephesus, a situation that "excludes all pity from our threatening looks" (1.1.9-10). Nevertheless, he invites Egeon to tell his story, and Egeon's account of the loss of his wife and infant son at sea many years before moves the duke so deeply that, when Egeon pauses at one point, he interjects, "Nay, forward, old man; do not break off so;/For we may pity, though not pardon thee" (1.1.97-98). When Egeon finishes recounting the story of his unflagging search for his lost family members, the duke feels powerless to modify the sentence that has been pronounced:

DUKE: Hapless Egeon, whom the Fates have mark'd
           To bear the extremity of dire mishap!
           Now, trust me, were it not against our laws,
           Against my crown, my oath, my dignity,
           Which princes, would they, may not disannul,
           My soul should sue as advocate for thee.
           But, though thou art adjudged to the death
           And passed sentence may not be recall'd
           But to our honour's great disparagement,
           Yet will I favor thee in what I can.

(1.1.141-150)

Another example of the stringency of the law is found in *Henry V*. King Henry is leading the English forces against the French in one of literature's most famous displays of bravado and courage in battle. The king has only recently come into his own as a strong leader after a period during his young adulthood when he associated with disreputable sorts and conducted himself irresponsibly. Among his drinking buddies from former days was one Bardolph, an unscrupulous character with whom the prince had uproarious fun. During the military campaign, the Welsh lieutenant Fluellen reports to the king that one of the men has been caught robbing a church and will likely be executed. When the man's name is revealed to be Bardolph, the king unflinchingly commands, "We should have all such offenders so cut off" (3.6.113-114). He then sets forth the rules of conduct that the fighting men must observe, thus dramatically demonstrating that Prince Hal has been transformed into King Henry V.

The difficulties involved in maintaining a system of mandatory capital punishment inviolate are apparent. Not only will passionate appeals and cunning devices be used to undermine such a system; those responsible for administering the system will be tempted to allow their own feelings to interfere with its administration. Over history, the practice of mandatory capital punishment has proved virtually impossible to achieve.[27] Nevertheless, the rationale of "a government of laws and not of men" is a necessary fiction, and the law's inflexible requirements have always been invoked by persons in the uncomfortable position of having to enforce it.

Pleas for Mercy by the Family of the Accused

In the American judicial system, there are two principal points in handling capital cases where consideration is given to the accused's personal character and individual circumstances other than his or her guilt or innocence. The first is at the postconviction sentencing hearing. According to one trial lawyer experienced in such cases, "That's when you want to try to get family, friends, employers, clergy, who know your client, to speak for him. If the jury can see your client as a human being, no matter what terrible crime he or she may have done, your client has a chance to live."[28] Such a courtroom strategy was also used by Athenians in the time of Plato. In the *Apology,* as Socrates is offering his defense in his own capital trial, he alludes to practices that were common in trials in his day:

> Perhaps some among you may be offended when he remembers his own conduct, if he, even in a case of less importance than this, begged and besought the judges with many tears, and brought for-

ward his children to arouse compassion, and many other friends and relatives; whereas I will do none of these things, though I am, apparently, in the very greatest danger. (34c)

Socrates felt that displays of this kind were demeaning, and he was unwilling to resort to them even to save his life. He advises the court against being swayed by them: "You should make it clear that you will be much more ready to condemn a man who puts before you such pitiable scenes and makes the city ridiculous than one who keeps quiet" (35b).

The second point at which matters of this kind may be raised today is in an appeal for pardon or executive clemency, usually made either to the state's governor or to a special board established for this purpose. This is the avenue for relief to which the Supreme Court pointed in the *Herrera* case, in which Chief Justice William Rehnquist quoted Blackstone's Commentaries on the advantage of having a magistrate "who has it in his power to extend mercy, wherever he thinks that it is deserved; holding a court of equity in his own breast, to soften the rigour of the general law, in such criminal cases as merit an exemption from punishment."[29] The possibility of clemency, which exists throughout many years of appeals and extends all the way to the moment of execution, is a source of continual hope for condemned prisoners and their families. But this possibility also places a great burden on family members to do everything possible to prevent a scheduled execution.[30]

A good example of dramatically excessive pleading is found in *Titus Andronicus*. Quintus and Martius, two sons of Titus, have been condemned to death for a murder they did not commit. When the official party passes, escorting Titus's two bound sons to the place of execution, Titus pleads with them on the basis of both his sons' innocence and his own service to the state in many military campaigns. When his pleas are ignored, the proud general even prostrates himself, continuing to beg long after the official party has exited:

TITUS: O reverend tribunes! O gentle, aged men!
           Unbind my sons, reverse the doom of death;
           And let me say, that never wept before,
           My tears are now prevailing orators.

                                                    (3.1.23-26)

His son Lucius arrives and tells Titus that nobody is there to hear his pleas. Titus responds that he has a duty to plead nevertheless:

TITUS: Why, 'tis no matter, man: if they did hear,
     They would not mark me, or if they did mark,
     They would not pity me, yet plead I must;
     And bootless unto them.

                 (3.1.33-36)

Another play in which pleas for pardon figure prominently is *Richard III*. King Edward is filled with remorse that his warrant to have his brother Clarence killed for treason was not countermanded by a later cancellation. As he grieves, Lord Stanley arrives to request a pardon for a servant who committed a murder during a drunken brawl. The king is appalled that his subjects come to ask for pardons for people who have committed all kinds of outrages, but also that he himself routinely grants them ("And I, unjustly too, must grant it you.") He then refers to the death of his brother Clarence: "But for my brother not a man would speak,/Nor I, ungracious, speak unto myself/For him, poor soul" (2.1.125-128). The king voices the guilt he feels over his failure to plead his brother's cause (to himself) rather than over having issued the original death warrant.

Familial responsibility to plead for a condemned brother is also seen in *Measure for Measure*. Lord Angelo, who is substituting as ruler of Vienna while the duke takes a brief leave from his onerous responsibilities, has decided to enforce the law against fornication more strictly than has been the recent custom and places a death sentence on Claudio, a young man whose only offense is having impregnated his girlfriend. Lucio, a friend in whom Claudio has confided, visits Claudio's sister Isabella in the convent where she lives to tell her of her brother's plight. Isabella is at a loss as to how she can help: "Alas! what poor ability's in me/To do him good?" (1.4.75-76). Her reaction is not unlike that of families of condemned prisoners today. A researcher who has studied such families has noted the sense of helplessness and frustration they experience. The sister of a condemned man is quoted as having said, "It hurts you can't do anything. There's nothing you can do. It's like we're a million miles away and there's nothing we can do. Every day, I wish I could do something, but I can't."[31]

Lucio suggests that Isabella go to Angelo to plead for her brother's life, hinting that he might be swayed by a maiden's suit. Isabella follows Lucio's suggestion and goes to Angelo's house to make her plea. She begins on a low-key note, simply begging that mercy be shown to her brother in spite of his offense: "I do think that you might pardon

him and neither heaven nor man grieve at the mercy." (2.2.49-50).
When Angelo dismisses her out of hand, Isabella (at Lucio's urging)
steps up the intensity of her pitch. She suggests that Angelo, too, could
have committed an offense such as her brother's, although, if the roles
were reversed, her brother would certainly have been less stern and
more merciful. She then asks Angelo whether he would like to be
judged by God as sternly as her brother was being judged. She alludes
to the fact that many have committed the same offense as Claudio with
impunity and again asks for pity. Angelo responds:

> ANGELO: I show it most of all when I show justice;
> For then I pity those I do not know,
> Which a dismissed offence would after gall;
> And do him right that, answering one foul wrong,
> Lives not to act another. Be satisfied;
> Your brother dies to-morrow; be content.
>
> (2.2.100-105)

Isabella accuses Angelo of abuse of his authority and notes that even
Jove uses his unlimited power only as needed, calibrating his response
to correspond to the severity of an offense. This divine restraint is
compared with that of humans:

> ISABELLA: But man, proud man,
> Drest in a little brief authority,
> Most ignorant of what he's most assured,
> His glassy essence, like an angry ape,
> Plays such fantastic tricks before high heaven
> As makes the angels weep.
>
> (2.2.117-123)

Struck by Isabella's impassioned pleas on behalf of her brother, Angelo relents to the extent of asking her to come back the next day. He
has been smitten by her, so he plots to seduce her: he will offer clemency for her brother in exchange for sex. A significant part of the play
is taken up by Isabella's quandary over what to do. With the help of
Friar Lodowick (who is in fact the duke in disguise), she formulates a
scheme of her own: she will appear to go along with Angelo's bargain
but will arrange for Mariana, Angelo's spurned fiancée, to substitute
for her in the dark.

The point made here is that Isabella, a virgin who has just entered a
convent, might plausibly have been expected to surrender what in her
culture was most precious — her virginity — to save the life of her con-

demned brother. In modern society, virginity is not nearly so prized, but housing is becoming less and less affordable: one researcher has recorded the desperation of two sisters who felt compelled to put up the deed to their house to pay lawyers for further appeals after their brother's execution date was set.[32]

Demands for Justice by the Family of the Victim

Of course, pleas for mercy by the family of the accused must be balanced against demands for justice by the family of the victim. The American judicial system has sometimes been accused of paying too much attention to protecting the rights of the defendant in criminal cases and not enough to vindicating the rights of the victim (if he or she is alive) or the victim's family. Victims' families have made demands of the legal system since the beginning of Western civilization; a family that has surrendered its primitive right to seek vengeance on its own will naturally expect to be able to rely on the state to fulfill this responsibility.

In the *Iliad,* the god Hephaestus is forging a new shield for the Greek hero Achilles, whose armor was borrowed by his friend Patroclus while Achilles was sulking in his tent. (After Patroclus was killed in battle, the Trojan warrior Hector stole the armor, leaving Achilles in need of new equipment.) Homer describes in great detail the scenes that are engraved on the shield. Two prosperous towns are depicted: one is peaceful and law-abiding, and the other is preparing for war. Scenes from the first town are mainly concerned with weddings and festivals, although a different theme is also presented:[33]

> But citizens also thronged the market-place, to witness a bitter legal conflict. A man had been murdered, and though the murderer was volunteering to pay the highest blood-price sanctioned, the next-of-kin demanded his death. The crowd being by no means unanimous in its sympathies, heralds kept order, and provided white wands for the city elders, who sat on smooth marble benches in the holy circle of justice. (18.497-505)

Because the families of homicide victims have a very clear focus for their rage, they often become obsessed with hatred of the killer and preoccupied with judgment and retribution.[34] When family members confront the accused in a courtroom, outbursts are not unusual. Typical was that of the father of one of three eight-year-old boys who were murdered by three teenage boys in West Memphis, Arkansas, in May

1993: a newspaper report of the arraignment stated, "Inside the court-room, Steven Branch, the father of one of the victims, lunged at a defendant, screaming, 'I'll chase you all the way to hell.' Court officers subdued Mr. Branch and led him out of the room."[35] A crowd of about two hundred observers outside the courthouse shouted as the teenagers were taken away.

The Possibility of Human Error

Because execution is an irrevocable penalty, the possibility — some would say the inevitability — of human error is the basis for one perennial argument against capital punishment. Chief Justice William Rehnquist acknowledged this point in his opinion in the *Herrera* case, in which he wrote, "It is an unalterable fact that our judicial system, like the human beings who administer it, is fallible."[36] At the same time, Rehnquist emphasized that the constitutional requirement of due process does not require that every conceivable step be taken, at whatever cost, to eliminate the possibility of convicting an innocent person: "To conclude otherwise would all but paralyze our system for enforcement of the criminal law."[37] As a practical matter, therefore, the question becomes what percentage of erroneous executions society is willing to tolerate to keep the costs of administering justice within reason.

In a 1992 book based on years of cumulative research, the authors identified 416 cases in which the wrong person was convicted of a capital offense in the United States in this century; of these, 23 were actually executed.[38] As if to answer that book's assertion that "no court, chief executive, or other official body has ever acknowledged that an innocent person has been executed in this century," both the majority and the dissenters in the *Herrera* case expressly cited it.[39] The dissenters called it "impressive," while the majority observed that other scholars "have taken issue with this study."[40] Quibbles about this particular study notwithstanding, the public acknowledgment in this case of the possibility of wrongful executions in the American criminal justice system was unprecedented.

The need for special protections to minimize the possibility of human error in capital cases has been recognized from the beginning of Western civilization. For example, Deuteronomy records that, in the Hebrew law, a penalty of death by stoning was imposed upon a person who violated the law against worshipping other gods. In such cases, "at the mouth of two witnesses, or three witnesses, shall he that is worthy of death be put to death; but at the mouth of one witness he shall not be put to death" (17.6). Similarly, in the *Apology,* Socrates reveals that some of the Greek states had special requirements for proof in capital cases. In defending himself against a capital charge, he observes that, unlike those states, Athens allows such cases to be concluded in one day:

> The truth is rather that I am convinced that I never intentionally wronged any one; but I cannot convince you of this, for we have conversed with each other only a little while. I believe that if you had a law, as some other people have, that capital cases should not be decided in one day, but only after several days, you would be convinced; but now it is not easy to rid you of great prejudices in a short time. (37a-b)

Socrates is arguing for the wisdom of sleeping on a decision to impose the death penalty. Given the lengthy delays and multiple appeals allowed in the American criminal justice system, the danger of overly hasty decisions is not one normally incurred.

In the *Crito,* Plato acknowledged the possibility that the state could make mistakes in spite of all precautions. In that dialogue, Socrates is in prison awaiting execution when he is visited by his friend Crito, who offers to help him escape by paying a few well-placed bribes. Socrates rejects this offer, saying that he is indebted to the laws of Athens for the institutions that have nurtured and sustained him all his life. Therefore, he owes them a contractual duty to obey their dictates, even though that means both refusing to escape and facing execution. In making his point, Socrates imagines a conversation with the laws in which, if he tried to escape, they would ask him why he is trying to destroy them:

SOCRATES: What shall we say, Crito, in reply to this question and others of the same kind? For one might say many things, especially if one were an orator, about the destruction of that law which provides that the decisions reached by the courts shall be valid. Or shall we say to them, "The state wronged me and did not judge the case rightly"? Shall we say that, or what?

CRITO: That is what we shall say, by Zeus, Socrates.

SOCRATES: What then if the laws should say, "Socrates, is this the agreement you made with us, or did you agree to abide by the verdicts pronounced by the state?"

(50b-c)

Socrates' point is that a citizen's agreement with the state is that he or she will abide by the state's verdicts, right or wrong. Later in the *Crito*, the laws are envisioned as saying about the possibility of escape, "Now, however, you will go away wronged, if you do go away, not by us, the laws, but by men" (54c). Because Socrates recognized the power of this argument, he declined his friend's offer to help him escape.

Socrates's sublime vision made him one of the great martyrs and inspirational leaders of the Western tradition. One would not expect ordinary people, then or now, to exhibit such moral courage in the face of imminent execution. Today, death-row prisoners who maintain that they have been erroneously convicted and their supporters wage large-scale media campaigns to gain public sympathy for their plight. Typical of several such prisoners in recent years was Roger Keith Coleman, who was convicted of murdering his sister-in-law in Grundy, Virginia. In the days before his execution in May 1992, Coleman appeared on television talk shows and on the cover of *Time* magazine, which proclaimed "This Man Might Be Innocent, This Man is Due to Die." The article inside opined, "If, in essence, Coleman's supporters have sought to stage a new trial through the press, the tactic is understandable: the courts have so far failed Coleman miserably."[41]

One is led to wonder how Socrates would react to such unapologetic disavowals of trust in public institutions, which everyone acknowledges to be fallible. Given widely held perceptions like the foregoing, the question becomes whether society's gain by retaining capital punishment can possibly outweigh the consequent losses in confidence in the American judicial system whenever there is lingering doubt about the guilt of a condemned person.

Penalties Worse Than Death

Some of the traditional arguments for capital punishment, such as the deterrence argument, implicitly assume that death is the worst possible punishment that can be inflicted upon someone. The works of the Canon provide ample evidence that such is not always the case: torture, banishment, life imprisonment, and enduring a guilty conscience are sometimes said to be worse.

Torture

When people reflect upon what the Eighth Amendment's ban on "cruel and unusual punishments" was meant to forbid, forms of torture most often come to mind. One authority on capital punishment, Hugo Bedau, has written, "Some punishments seem clearly and incontestably cruel and unusual. Boiling in oil, death by a thousand cuts, impalement, and burying alive are all acts that have been authorized by governments in the past as punishment. Unquestionably, imposing any of them in our society today would be cruel and unusual, no matter who the offender or what the crime."[42] Because torture has long been regarded as inconsistent with minimal standards of human decency, the works of the Canon contain very few instances of such behavior officially imposed by a state as punishment. Of course, the most obvious exception is crucifixion as described in the Christian gospels, a practice too familiar to require elaboration here.

Another form of state-imposed torture was the practice of burning alleged witches at the stake, which figures in the plot of *I Henry VI.* Joan la Pucelle (Joan of Arc), the maiden warrior for the French, has been captured by the English and condemned to burn at the stake as a sorceress. (The validity of the charges against her is established in the preceding scene, in which she is portrayed as conversing with Fiends.) In impassioned tones, Joan defends herself as virtuous and as having been sent on a special mission by "inspiration of celestial grace,/To work exceeding miracles on earth" (5.4.40-41). Her captors, York and Warwick, are not impressed:

YORK: Ay, ay: away with her to execution!

WARWICK: And hark ye, sirs; because she is a maid,
         Spare for no faggots, let there be enow:
         Place barrels of pitch upon the fatal stake,
         That so her torture may be shortened.

                                                    (5.4.54-58)

Joan then takes a calculated risk: she feigns pregnancy to avoid execution, saying, "Murder not then the fruit within my womb,/Although ye hale me to a violent death" (5.4.63-64). This attempt backfires, however, when her captors show no inclination to spare the claimed fetus and focus instead on Joan's admission that she is not a virgin: "Strumpet, thy words condemn thy brat and thee:/Use no entreaty, for it is in vain" (5.4.84-85).

An even more torturous punishment is described in Shakespeare's early and macabre tragedy *Titus Andronicus*. Aaron the Moor has been having an adulterous affair with Tamora the Goth and conspires with her and her two grown sons to get revenge against Titus Andronicus for the death of another of Tamora's sons. The conspirators commit several horrible crimes. At the end of the play, Titus's son Lucius captures Aaron and, before deciding what to do with him, asks him if he is not sorry for his heinous deeds. Aaron is defiant and unrepentant. Saying that his only regret is not having done more evil, he recounts some of what he has been able to accomplish in his lifetime: in addition to many murders and rapes, he has set deadly enmity between friends, made poor men's cattle break their necks, and set fire to barns and haystalks in the night. Often he would dig up corpses from the earth and set them upright at their dear friends' door ("Even when their sorrows almost was forgot"), having carved into the corpse's skin, as on the bark of a tree, the words "Let not your sorrow die, though I am dead" (5.1.137,140).

What manner of punishment would be appropriate retribution for a criminal like Aaron? Shakespeare has clearly pulled out all stops in portraying him as the most thoroughly evil, unrepentant character imaginable. Mere death by one of the usual means does not seem commensurate with the extremity of his malevolence, so Lucius is called upon to be creative:

> LUCIUS: Set him breast-deep in earth, and famish him;
> There let him stand, and rave, and cry for food:
> If anyone relieves or pities him,
> For the offence he dies. This is our doom:
> Some stay, to see him fasten'd in the earth.

> (5.3.179-183)

Aaron continues to defy the authorities by wishing that he could have accomplished even more evil. Even as his character is depicted with dramatic excess, the manner in which he is tortured is both cruel and quite unusual.

Banishment

In Genesis, the first murderer is Cain, a son of Adam and Eve. Cain is a farmer, while his brother Abel is a shepherd. Both brothers bring an offering to the Lord, who accepts Abel's but rejects Cain's. As a result Cain becomes enraged and, when they are out in the field, slays his brother. The Lord questions Cain and then imposes punishment:

> And now art thou cursed from the earth, which hath opened her mouth to receive thy brother's blood from thy hand;
> When thou tillest the ground, it shall not henceforth yield unto thee her strength; a fugitive and a vagabond shalt thou be in the earth. (4.11-12)

Cain responds that his punishment is greater than he can bear, and he appeals to the Lord not to banish him:

> Behold, thou hast driven me out this day from the face of the earth; and from thy face shall I be hid; and I shall be a fugitive and a vagabond in the earth; and it shall come to pass, that every one that findeth me shall slay me. (4.14)

The Lord meets this objection by proclaiming that whoever slays Cain will suffer vengeance sevenfold, and he places a mark on Cain as a warning to anyone who might try to kill him.

Shakespeare uses the theme of Cain's banishment in *Richard II*. At the end of the play, Exton has murdered King Richard II, thinking that this is what Henry Bolingbroke (who aspires to the throne) wanted him to do. Bolingbroke expresses dismay and anger at Exton. He says that, although he did wish Richard dead, he did not intend for him to be murdered. He then consigns Exton to a double punishment. Not only must he endure the affliction his conscience was presumed to engender ("The guilt of conscience take thou for thy labor"). In addition, he is sentenced to the banishment endured by Cain: "With Cain go wander thorough shades of night,/And never show thy head by day nor light" (5.6.41, 43-44). Banishment is the perfect remedy from Bolingbroke's perspective. It removes Exton from the scene, where his presence would serve as a constant reminder to Bolingbroke of what has been done. At the same time, because Exton is not put to death, it prevents Bolingbroke from having to assume the burden of responsibility for any further deaths.

In book 9 of the *Laws,* the Athenian describes the system of criminal justice that he believes would be best for an ideal state. He says that there are some crimes – such as doing violence to one's parents – for which a penalty more severe than death is needed:

> Death is not a most severe penalty; and the punishments we are told of in Hades for such offences, although more severe than death

and described most truly, yet fail to prove any deterrent to souls such as these, – else we should never find cases of matricide and of impiously audacious assaults upon other progenitors. Consequently, the punishments inflicted upon these men here in their lifetime for crimes of this kind must, so far as possible, fall in no way short of the punishments in Hades. (881a-b)

The Athenian goes on to suggest that banishment most closely fits the bill he has described. The accused would be banished for life from the city and all sacred places. Further, he would be denied all personal contact with people from his home city. If anyone should so much as eat or drink with him, or even greet him in passing, that person would have to purify himself because he would have incurred a share of contagious guilt. (The severity of this punishment is approximated in modern times by the use of solitary confinement in prisons for the disruptive prisoners who cannot be handled in any other way.)

The psychological pain of banishment is intensified when a person has strong emotional bonds with people from whom he or she is thereby separated. This is most dramatically portrayed in *Romeo and Juliet,* where Romeo is banished as punishment for having killed Juliet's kinsman Tybalt in a street brawl. Romeo's banishment comes at a time when the young couple are about to be married, and for both of them the prospect of separation is unendurable. When the nurse tells Juliet that Romeo is banished, she repeats the words and cries, "There is no end, no limit, measure, bound,/In that word's death; no words can that woe sound" (3.2.125-126). Romeo is delivered news of the prince's judgment while he is in Friar Lawrence's cell, and he is equally distraught:

FRIAR: A gentler judgment vanished [escaped] from his lips,
            Not body's death, but body's banishment.

ROMEO: Ha, banishment! be merciful, say 'death;'
            For exile hath more terror in his look,
            Much more than death: do not say 'banishment.'

FRIAR: O deadly sin! O rude unthankfulness!
            Thy fault our law calls death; but the kind prince,
            Taking thy part, hath rush'd aside the law,
            And turn'd that black word death to banishment.
            This is dear mercy, and thou seest it not.

                                        (3.3.10-14, 24-28)

The difference between Romeo's viewpoint and the friar's on the relative undesirability of death and banishment underscores how personal the perception of punishment is.

Today banishment and expatriation are regarded as cruel and unusual forms of punishment prohibited by the Eighth Amendment. This interpretation was made only in the late 1950s. (Torture, on the other hand, has been held to violate the Eighth Amendment since the nineteenth century.[43]) Americans may voluntarily renounce their citizenship, but it is not constitutionally permissible to take it away from them as a form of punishment. According to former Chief Justice Earl Warren, citizenship is the right to have rights, and no citizen may be deprived of that right, regardless of what crimes he or she may have committed.[44]

Life Imprisonment

Unlike torture and banishment, life imprisonment is constitutional, and as a consequence it is the principal alternative to execution for persons convicted of murder today. The possibility of life imprisonment for committing a capital offense is largely a modern phenomenon; in bygone eras, it would have seemed odd for a state to commit significant financial resources to maintain an able-bodied person in prison for life. Even today, a frequent argument against life imprisonment is the significant drain on the state's resources it entails.[45]

One case in which imprisonment is mentioned as an option is that of Socrates. In the *Apology*, after Socrates has been found guilty of the charges against him, both he and his accuser are allowed to propose an appropriate penalty, with the jury to decide between them. The accuser proposes death, and Socrates discusses the relative merits of imprisonment, fine, and banishment as alternatives:

> What penalty shall I propose? Imprisonment? And why should I live in prison a slave to those who may be in authority? Or shall I propose a fine, with imprisonment until it is paid? But that is the same as what I said just now, for I have no money to pay with. Shall I then propose exile as my penalty? Perhaps you would accept that. I must indeed be possessed of a great love of life if I am so irrational as not to know that if you, who are my fellow citizens, could not endure my conversations and my words,... others will not be willing to endure them. (37c-d)

It is unclear from the context exactly what "imprisonment" would have entailed. Socrates alludes to being compelled to be a slave to those in authority, so it appears that some kind of physical labor was involved. If it were just a matter of being locked up in a cell, one might well imagine that Socrates would feel perfectly comfortable, notwithstanding the imprisonment of his body, as long as his mind was free. He seemed to be adept at finding people from all walks of life to engage in conversation, so fellow prisoners might have been no exception. But if imprisonment meant hard labor, Socrates might well have preferred death. In any event, his proposal to pay a fine of thirty minae (a modest sum) virtually ensured that he would be put to death.

Enduring a Guilty Conscience

Without question the most virulent form of punishment for murder in the works of the Canon is enduring a guilty conscience. Ironically, this form of punishment is noticeably lacking from the contemporary scene, in which very few criminals charged with capital offenses seem to show evidence of genuine remorse. One might speculate concerning the reason for this; possibly it is because of loss of the fear of damnation, which in the past was deeply ingrained. Whatever the reason, the dramatic power of the literary artists who produced these works is put to its highest use in portraying human personalities wracked and twisted by pangs of guilt and by fear of retribution for their crime, whether here or in the hereafter.

The argument of punishment by a burdened conscience was put forward by Socrates in the *Gorgias*. He claims that the worst possible evil is "to do wrong and not pay the penalty" and that the wrongdoer who pays no penalty is "peculiarly and pre-eminently wretched among men" (479d-e). He then concludes logically, if ironically, that the worst thing that can be done to a wrongdoer is for him not to be permitted to be punished in other ways, because he would thereby be relieved of the burden of the injustice he has committed:

> Supposing our enemy has wronged some one else, we must make every exertion of act and word to prevent him from being punished or coming to trial, or if he does, we must contrive that our enemy shall escape and not be punished;... or if he has committed crimes that deserve death, that he shall not die; if possible, never die, but be deathless in his villainy, or failing that, live as long a time as may be in that condition. (481a)

Socrates' interlocutor, Callicles, is so astounded by this argument that he asks a companion whether Socrates is in earnest or joking, since, if he is indeed serious, the life of humans has been turned upside down, and everyone does the exact opposite of what he ought to do.

Shakespeare adopts a similar theme in his long poem *The Rape of Lucrece*. The virtuous Roman matron Lucrece has been raped in her own bed by Tarquin, a prince who was her houseguest, while her husband was away on a military campaign. While Lucrece lies in bed after Tarquin's escape, thoughts revolve in her mind as she seeks to come to terms with what has happened. She prays to Time to assist in ensuring that Tarquin receives punishment commensurate with his crime: "Disturb his hours of rest with restless trances,/Afflict him in his bed with bedrid groans" (974-975). Rather than wishing for Tarquin's life to be cut short because of his crime, Lucrece wishes for him a surfeit of time in which to suffer the presumed psychological consequences of what he has done:

> Let him have time to tear his curled hair,
> Let him have time against himself to rave,
> Let him have time of Time's help to despair,
> Let him have time to live a loathed slave,
> Let him have time a beggar's orts to crave.

(981-985)

Lucrece wants Tarquin's future to be much more intimidating than the prospect of a swift, sure death.

Perhaps the most famous statement of a guilty conscience by a murderer in Shakespeare is that of Macbeth, who has been manipulated by his wife into murdering the visiting king, Duncan. Macbeth has killed Duncan and stabbed two attendants to death in their beds as they slept, in order to implicate them in the king's murder. He suffers mightily as a result and hears a voice crying "Macbeth shall sleep no more!" (2.2.43). He tells Lady Macbeth he is afraid to think of what he has done:

> MACBETH: Whence is that knocking?
> How is't with me, when every noise appals me?
> What hands are here? ha! they pluck out mine eyes.
> Will all great Neptune's ocean wash this blood
> Clean from my hand? No, this my hand will rather
> The multitudinous seas incarnadine,

Making the green one red.

(2.2.57-63)

Lady Macbeth says that her hands are the same color, but that she would be ashamed to wear a heart as white as her husband's. Her eventual suicide, however, belies the steely nonchalance she affects.

In *Cymbeline,* a guilty character raises the question of whether death would not be preferable to enduring the burden of his conscience. Posthumus, a banished Englishman, is serving in the Roman army during its campaign against England. While clad in the tattered garments of a peasant, he has fought secretly for the English. In the battle's aftermath, he is captured by the forces of the English king Cymbeline and sent to jail, where he awaits execution as a prisoner of war. In jail, Posthumus has time to reflect upon his situation, and he demonstrates a guilty conscience over his role in his wife Imogen's presumed death. (He had directed his servant Pisanio to take Imogen to a remote seashore and kill her because of her alleged adultery with Iachimo, an unscrupulous Italian.) He compares his plight favorably to that of someone who suffers constantly from a disease rather than be cured by the sure physician, Death. He then exhibits his repentance by praying:

POST.:   My conscience, thou art fetter'd
            More than my shanks and wrists: you good gods, give me
            The penitent instrument to pick that bolt,
            Then, free for ever! Is't enough I am sorry?
            So children temporal fathers do appease;
            Gods are more full of mercy.

(5.4.8-13)

Posthumus clearly considers death a liberation from the pain he is suffering because of his guilty conscience. He then offers his life as reparation for Imogen's:

POST.:   For Imogen's dear life take mine; and though
            'Tis not so dear, yet 'tis a life; you coined it:
            . . . .
                                And so, great powers,
            If you will take this audit, take this life,
            And cancel these cold bonds [shackles].

(5.4.22-23, 26-28)

In the modern world there are condemned prisoners who express a firm preference for death over the mental anguish their continuing existence causes them. The principal difference is that such suffering to-day is not usually described in terms of a guilty conscience. More likely, it is described in terms of the person's pathological mental state (which is usually said to have caused, rather than resulted from, the crimes that have been committed). A good example is Gary Gilmore, the convicted murderer whose execution by firing squad in Utah in 1977 marked the resumption of executions in this country after a hiatus of several years. Gilmore had twice attempted suicide and was firm in his rejection of further appeals and his desire to die. In describing this resolve, one author wrote, "Gary Gilmore, the criminal who could be sensitive and poetic, was also a cold-hearted killer who had blasted innocent people into kingdom come. He could show remorse over what he had done. But now he had but one goal: to end a life that had been burdensome, had somehow been stacked against him, and had nothing left to offer him. Enough was enough!"[46]

The Effect of Executions

Whether or not society benefits from a system of capital punish-ment is debated. Regardless of one's position on that question, how-ever, it is indisputable that capital punishment exacts an extraordinary toll on everyone affected. The various parties who participate in bring-ing about an execution have always asked themselves, sometimes in-tensely and privately, whether or not they are doing the right thing. Those who face execution do so with a wide variety of emotions and reactions. And the effect of executions on the general public, for whose benefit they are carried out, cannot be overlooked. Passages from the Canon reveal the effect of executions on all these parties.

On the Sentencer

In the American judicial system, a sentence of death may be deliv-ered only by a jury of peers of the accused who have heard all the evi-dence of the case. In the judicial systems depicted in the works of the Canon, the sentencer could be a jury, or it could be an individual act-ing in an official capacity. In the latter case, the burden of making such decisions is all the more heavy.

In the *Gorgias,* Socrates puts forward one of his most exalted moral arguments − that it is better to suffer wrong than to do it. He says that the wrongdoer is more injured by his own conduct than is the person he wrongs. Thus the wrongdoer is to be pitied, for he will suffer much misery because of his ill deeds. Socrates tells Polus that this is true even if the person suffering the wrong is put to death:

POLUS: I suppose, at any rate, the man who is put to death unjustly is both pitiable and wretched.

SOCRATES: Less so than he who puts him to death, Polus, and less so than he who is put to death justly.

POLUS: In what way can that be, Socrates?

SOCRATES: In this, that to do wrong is the greatest of evils.

(469b)

Thus, according to Socrates' moral order, those who pass judgment in capital cases are in a hazardous position. Any mistakes they make will ultimately work to their own detriment, and knowledge of this should make all sentencers most uncomfortable at the prospect of an execution.

Socrates' argument in the *Gorgias* is abstract and theoretical. In the *Apology,* he has a chance to apply that argument to a real-life situation, ironically his own defense against a capital charge. He says to the jury of Athenian citizens:

Now I am going to say some things to you at which you will perhaps cry out; but do not do so by any means. For know that if you kill me, I being such a man as I say I am, you will not injure me so much as yourselves.... And so, men of Athens, I am now making my defence not for my own sake, as one might imagine, but far more for yours, that you may not by condemning me err in your treatment of the gift the God gave you. (30c-d)

Socrates views himself as a special gift to Athens from God, because he has served as a gadfly, stinging and arousing the city whenever it becomes sluggish or inattentive to moral issues. However, the argument as made in the *Gorgias* would apply whether or not the person who is unjustly condemned has special talents; members of a jury that unjustly convicted anyone would be doing a much greater injury to themselves than to the person convicted.

A different system of justice prevailed in Jerusalem during the time of Christ. A single public official, the Roman procurator or "governor" of Judaea, had full powers of life and death and could reverse capital sentences passed by the highest tribunal of the Jews. There was also a custom that during festivals, when the governor took up residence in

Jerusalem, he would release to the people a prisoner of their choice. According to the account in Matthew, when Jesus was brought before the governor Pontius Pilate, Pilate questioned him and marveled at his reticence. Pilate realized that Jesus had been brought before him because of envy, and his opinion was bolstered by a dream of his wife, who urged him to have nothing to do with "that just man" (27.19).

When Pilate asked the multitude whether he should hand over Jesus or the notorious outlaw Barabbas, the chief priests and elders persuaded the multitude to demand Barabbas. Pilate then asked what he should do with Jesus, and the multitude responded, "Let him be crucified." Pilate, obviously troubled by this prospect, said, "Why, what evil hath he done?" But the crowd insisted that he be crucified:[47]

> When Pilate saw that he could prevail nothing, but that rather a tumult was made, he took water, and washed his hands before the multitude, saying, I am innocent of the blood of this just person: see ye to it.
>
> Then answered all the people, and said, His blood be on us, and on our children. (27.23-25)

Pilate's washing his hands of the matter represents the failure of people in positions of authority to assume responsibility for what takes place on their watch, especially when that includes sentencing a possibly innocent person to death at the insistence of an unruly crowd. Describing another governor (Edwin Edwards of Louisiana) almost two thousand years later, Helen Prejean wrote, "I realize that the governor has found a moral niche in this process, a position from which he can make decisions and still lay his head on the pillow at night and go to sleep. He is a public official. His job is to carry out the law. He subordinates his conscience to the 'will of the people.'"[48]

One of the sources of discomfort which some sentencers feel in carrying out the law is intense awareness of their own capacity for wrongdoing. This is a principal theme of *Measure for Measure,* in which, as has been discussed, Lord Angelo enforces the law against fornication by sentencing Claudio to die but then offers to spare his life in exchange for sex with Claudio's sister Isabella. Before Angelo hears Isabella's plea and becomes enamored of her, his deputy Escalus tries to persuade him to be merciful to Claudio. Escalus's argument is based on the possibility that − given the right circumstances − Angelo himself could have committed the same sin as Claudio, a possibility that Angelo dismisses:

ESCALUS: Whether you had not sometime in your life
              Err'd in this point which now you censure him,
              And pull'd the law upon you.

ANGELO: 'Tis one thing to be tempted, Escalus,
              Another thing to fall.
              . . . .
              You may not so extenuate his offence
              For I have had such faults; but rather tell me,
              When I, that censure him, do so offend,
              Let mine own judgement pattern out my death,
              And nothing come in partial. Sir, he must die.

                                      (2.1.14-18, 27-31)

Only later, after he has become infatuated with Isabella, does Angelo admit (and then only in a soliloquy) the truth of what Escalus has suggested: "What dost thou, or what art thou, Angelo?.... Thieves for their robbery have authority/When judges steal themselves" (2.2.173, 176-177).

The moral dilemmas that sentencers face are not limited to cases in which they themselves have committed similar offenses. Rather, a general notion of one's own fallibility and susceptibility to emotions, biases, and other distortions of perception must give one pause when the decision at hand might end another's life. This difficulty is captured in Justice Harry Blackmun's poignant words from a 1972 capital punishment case: "Cases such as these provide for me an excruciating agony of the spirit. I yield to no one in the depth of my distaste, antipathy, and, indeed, abhorrence, for the death penalty, with all its aspects of physical distress and fear and of moral judgment exercised by finite minds.... For me, it violates childhood's training and life's experiences, and is not compatible with the philosophical convictions I have been able to develop. It is antagonistic to any sense of 'reverence for life.'"[49] Blackmun would eventually renounce the death penalty altogether a few months before his retirement from the Court.

On the Executioner

If the sentencer bears the greatest burden of moral responsibility for an execution, it is the executioner who is most directly involved in what is euphemistically called by prison bureaucracies "the final process."[50] Today executions are usually carried out by employees of the prison, although sometimes volunteers are used.[51] Physicians have generally refused to be involved; many regard this as "an impossible and unwanted burden and contrary to their essential task."[52] In depictions of executioners in the works of the Canon, two of the themes that emerge are the kindness of the compassionate executioner who tries to make the condemned prisoner as comfortable as possible under the circumstances and the dilemma of the executioner who has doubts about whether the execution is justified but is only "following orders."

In the *Phaedo,* Socrates is in prison surrounded by a few friends, awaiting his execution at sunset. The official death decree is delivered by a servant of "the eleven," who were the rulers of Athens at the time. He enters and says to Socrates:

> "Socrates, I shall not find fault with you, as I do with others, for being angry and cursing me, when at the behest of the authorities, I tell them to drink the poison. No, I have found you in all this time in every way the noblest and gentlest and best man who has ever come here, and now I know your anger is directed against others, not against me, for you know who are to blame. Now, for you know the message I came to bring you, farewell and try to bear what you must as easily as you can." (116c)

Bursting into tears, the messenger departs, and Socrates comments to his friends how charming the man has been during his regular visits and how nobly he has wept for him. The messenger obviously disagrees with the death sentence given to Socrates and makes it as clear as he can that he is not personally responsible.

Socrates also has good rapport with the attendant who administers the cup of poison. When he enters with the cup already prepared, Socrates says to him, "Well, my good man, you know about these things; what must I do?" The attendant replies, "Nothing, except drink the poison and walk about till your legs feel heavy; then lie down, and the poison will take effect of itself" (117a-b). Joe Ferreti, a longtime "death watch officer" for executions at San Quentin in California, told one researcher that, when he strapped a certain woman prisoner into the gas chamber and said his usual words, "Now take a deep breath and it won't bother you," she retorted "How in the hell would you know?"[53] While Socrates did not utter this sentiment, certainly the question is one deserving of his method.

Another compassionate executioner is portrayed in *Cymbeline.* After his capture by the forces of King Cymbeline during a battle against the Romans, Posthumus is in jail awaiting execution as a prisoner of war when he feels the pangs of a guilty conscience for his role in his wife Imogen's presumed death. He is remorseful and wishes for death to release him from his misery. When the jailer enters to escort him to his execution, the jailer tries to engage him in some lighthearted banter. He points out that there are advantages to going to the gallows: "But the comfort is, you shall be called to no more payments, fear no more tavern bills.... O, the charity of a penny cord!" (5.4.160-161, 169-170). Amused by the jailer's wit, Posthumus observes wryly, "I am merrier to die than thou art to live" (5.4.175-176). The two men continue to joke in a way that seems to belie the seriousness of Posthumus's situation. However, such attempts at levity may not be all that unusual: Helen Prejean reports that when Tim Baldwin was executed in Louisiana in 1984, a guard in the death house whispered to him, "You gotta understand, Tim, this is nothing personal."[54]

A related theme found in the Canon is the dilemma of the executioner who has doubts about whether an execution is justified but believes he must follow orders. In *Measure for Measure,* Lord Angelo has, with unprecedented severity, sentenced Claudio to death for having violated the law against fornication. The provost, whose job it is to carry out the ruler's directions, has qualms about the sentence: "All sects, all ages smack of this vice; and he/To die for't!" (2.2.5-6). Hoping for a change of mind, he approaches Angelo yet again and asks whether or not Claudio shall die the next day:

ANGELO: Did not I tell thee yea? hadst thou not order?
           Why dost thou ask again?

PROVOST: Lest I might be too rash:
           Under your good correction, I have seen,
           When, after execution, judgment hath
           Repented o'er his doom.

                                              (2.2.8-12)

Angelo responds that this is his concern, not the provost's, and that he should mind his own business.

The provost's qualms are based on the horror one might feel if, after an execution, one discovers that it was wrongful after all. (He implies that excessive haste has resulted in some such executions during Angelo's rule.) This sense of horror may be seen in the accounts of the crucifixion in the synoptic gospels. A Roman centurion was keeping watch at the site. It is unclear exactly what his role in the execution was; he may have been overseeing the attendants who actually carried out the acts that were directed. According to the version in Luke, there was a darkness over all the earth, and as the moment of his death approached, the veil of the temple was rent in the middle. Jesus cried out his final words in a loud voice and gave up the ghost. The reaction of the centurion to these events is described at 23.47 in the King James Version as follows: "Now when the centurion saw what was done, he glorified God, saying, Certainly this was a righteous man."[55] However, several more recent translations (including the Revised Standard Version) render the centurion's words as "Indeed, this man was innocent."[56] From the centurion's perspective, that realization came tragically too late.

One of the most famous executions in Shakespeare is in *Richard III*, where two men have been hired by the malevolent Richard to kill his brother Clarence, who is imprisoned in the Tower of London. Clarence has committed no crime, and Richard's motivation to have him killed is to secure his own position as inheritor of the throne. Richard has tricked his brother King Edward into issuing a death warrant for Clarence under false pretenses, and the killing that is ordered is a murder thinly veiled as a lawful execution. The two hired men (whom Shakespeare calls the First and Second Murderers) sense this ambiguity. Even as they stand over the sleeping Clarence, they discuss their own responsibility for an execution when they are acting under the mantle of state authority. The second murderer fears that he will be held answerable to higher authority:

2ND M.:   The urging of that word "judgment" hath bred a kind of re-
           morse in me.

1ST M.:   What, art thou afraid?

2ND M.:   Not to kill him, having a warrant for it; but to be damned
           for killing him, from which no warrant can defend us.

                                                          (1.4.109-114)

The first murderer reminds the second of the reward Richard has promised them, and this serves to ward off the pangs of conscience, at least momentarily. As the murderers continue their discussion, Clarence awakens. Having guessed the purpose of their visit, he declares his innocence and asks the legal basis for any alleged sentence of death against him:

1ST M.:   What we will do, we do upon command.

2ND M.:   And he that hath commanded is the king.

CLARENCE: Erroneous vassal! The great King of kings
           Hath in the table of his law commanded
           That thou shalt do no murder: and wilt thou, then,
           Spurn at his edict and fulfil a man's?
           Take heed; for he holds vengeance in his hands
           To hurl upon their heads that break his law.

                                                  (1.4.198-205)

After further conversation about Clarence's role in past political con-
spiracies and his relationship with his brothers, the murderers finally
summon the will to dispatch him. As they exit the tower, the second
murderer expresses instant remorse: "A bloody deed and desperately
dispatched!/How fain, like Pilate, would I wash my hands/Of this most
grievous murder done!" (1.4.278-280). As was stated earlier, Pilate was
a sentencing authority rather than an executioner. However, the second murderer is clearly unable to protect himself through the self-
defensive posture of many executioners, who tell themselves that they
are only following orders.

Those who have studied executioners today find some better able
to formulate psychological coping mechanisms than others. One executioner, Major Kendall Coody of Louisiana, has been quoted as saying,
"I'm not sure how long I'm going to be able to keep doing this.... I get
home from an execution about two-something in the morning and I
just sit up in a chair for the rest of the night. I can't shake it. I can't
square it with my conscience, putting them to death like that." Helen
Prejean wrote concerning Coody, "Major Coody is not like the governor, the head of the Department of Corrections, the warden, and most
of the other guards around here [the Louisiana state prison at Angola].
He can't persuade himself that he's just *doing his job.*" [emphasis in
original].[57] The psychological pressures on executioners are so intense
that the custom has persisted of providing an escape hatch by making it
impossible to determine which executioner actually effected a condemned person's death. Thus, when Gary Gilmore was executed, one
of the guns used by the firing squad contained blanks, and when lethal
injections are administered, three persons may be involved in opening
the valves, with none knowing which is releasing the fatal dose.[58]

On the Person Executed

Watt Espy, the principal historian of executions in the United States, has written, "Only one who has endured the experience can fully understand the thoughts and emotions of a person who has been condemned to die at the hands of the executioner. Such an individual is kept in close confinement, deprived of all the creature comforts of life, forced to contemplate a sudden and violent death by a means already ordained and known to him or her. It is a period during which the soul and spirit of any mortal is severely tested."[59]

It is precisely because of the severity of this test that the manner of the deaths of the two uncontested martyrs of the Western tradition, Socrates and Jesus, was an important factor in our interpretation of the meaning of their lives. In the *Phaedo,* Socrates is depicted as facing death serenely, even cheerfully. Phaedo, who witnessed Socrates' death, reported later that "he seemed to me to be happy, both in his bearing and his words, he was meeting death so fearlessly and nobly" (58e). When he received the cup of poison, he offered a prayer and then "raised the cup to his lips and very cheerfully and quietly drained it" (117c). Socrates's acceptance of death was completely in accord with his teaching that a true philosopher will not fear it.

While Plato's account is our only source for details of the execution of Socrates, there are several different accounts of the crucifixion of Jesus. All four gospels depict him as facing his execution with magnanimity of spirit and without anger or resistance. However, the precise nature of his last words on the cross is unclear. According to the accounts in Mark and Matthew, they were "My God, my God, why hast thou forsaken me?" According to the account in Luke, he cried in a loud voice, "Father, into thy hands I commend my spirit." And in the version in John, Jesus simply realized that all things had been accomplished to fulfill the scripture, so he said only, "It is finished."[60] Interpretation of these various accounts is far beyond the scope of this work; suffice it to say here that the manner of Jesus' death is a crucial factor in the meaning that is attached to his life and teachings.

Shakespearean characters facing imminent execution react in a wide variety of ways. The most Christlike is that of the Duke of Buckingham in *Henry VIII.* Buckingham has been unjustly framed by his enemy Cardinal Wolsey. King Henry VIII has bought Wolsey's argument, and in spite of his popularity, Buckingham has been tried for treason, found guilty, and sentenced to death. As Buckingham passes through the streets on his way to execution, he compares his fate to that of his father, who was also unjustly accused of treason but who was put to death without a trial. Buckingham magnanimously forgives everyone on his way to death:

BUCK.:   The law I bear no malice for my death;
'T has done, upon the premises, but justice:
But those that sought it I could wish more Christians:
Be what they will, I heartily forgive 'em:
. . . .
For further life in this world I ne'er hope,
Nor will I sue, although the king have mercies
More than I dare make faults.

(2.1.62-65, 69-71)

Buckingham's composure and grace under extreme pressure put him almost in a category with Socrates and Jesus. The reaction of most mortals is not nearly so saintly, however. (This is what the messenger from those in power meant at *Phaedo* 116c when he told Socrates that condemned persons were usually angry and cursed him when he delivered the order for them to drink the poison.) One common reaction is defiance, and two Shakespearean characters who face a torturous death react in this way. As was discussed in an earlier chapter, in *I Henry VI,* Joan la Pucelle tried to avoid execution by feigning pregnancy. When that did not work, she became defiant and cursed her captors:

JOAN: Then lead me hence; with whom I leave my curse:
May never glorious sun reflex his beams
Upon the country where you make abode;
But darkness and the gloomy shade of death
Environ you, till mischief and despair
Drive you to break your necks or hang yourselves!

(5.4.86-91)

She can think of no worse curse than that her captors suffer from guilty consciences ("the gloomy shade of death environ you") over having executed her, which may even lead them to suicide.

Another Shakespearean character who faces a torturous death is Aaron the Moor in *Titus Andronicus,* who has been sentenced to be buried chest-deep and starved to death. In continuing defiance, Aaron wishes that he could have done more evil:

AARON: O, why should wrath be mute, and fury dumb?
I am no baby, I, that with base prayers
I should repent the evils I have done:
Ten thousand worse than ever yet I did
Would I perform, if I might have my will:
If one good deed in all my life I did,
I do repent it from my very soul.

(5.3.184-190)

The unrepentant spirit Aaron exhibits is not unlike that often seen in hardened criminals today. For example, in January 1993 the state of Washington executed Wesley Allan Dodd, who was convicted of torturing, raping, and killing three young boys. Dodd waived all appeals and chose to be executed by hanging rather than lethal injection. He stated in a court brief intended to cut off all appeals by third parties on his behalf, "I must be executed before I have an opportunity to escape or kill someone else. If I do escape, I promise you I will kill and rape again, and I will enjoy every minute of it."[61]

Somewhere between the extremes of magnanimous forgiveness and unrepenting defiance lie the most common reactions of condemned persons who face imminent execution: fear and desperation. This is the reaction of Claudio in *Measure for Measure*. When he first learns that Lord Angelo has offered to spare his life in exchange for sex with his sister, Isabella, he is shocked and dismisses the possibility out of hand. Once he has had time to think about it, however, he begins to waver. Eventually he becomes desperate and pleads with his sister to accept Angelo's offer:

CLAUDIO: Ay, but to die and go we know not where;
To lie in cold obstruction and to rot;
This sensible warm motion to become
A kneaded clod;
. . . .
                'Tis too horrible!
The weariest and most loathed worldly life
That age, ache, penury, and imprisonment
Can lay on nature is a paradise
To what we fear of death.

(3.1.118-121, 128-132)

Claudio then begs Isabella to let him live: "What sin you do to save a brother's life,/Nature dispenses with the deed so far/That it becomes a virtue" (3.1.134-136). Isabella is not persuaded and calls her brother a beast for even suggesting such a thing. Rejecting his pitiful pleas, she angrily proclaims that it is better for him to die quickly. (Later, through some complicated maneuvers carried out with the help of the duke, she is able to save her brother after all.)

While one cannot imagine an inmate on death row today articulating his dread at the prospect of death as Claudio does, the sentiment expressed is one that must be shared by many. A former warden in California has recounted the story of the execution of one prisoner who had to be carried to the gas chamber and who managed to get out of the straps three times. To get through the execution, the warden had to rely on rote: "The fact that the fellow is crying and baying like a dog ... you just can't deal with it at that point. You've got to carry out the job at hand. A grown man afraid to go to his death — as all of us are, to some degree — makes you sad. You feel sympathy for him, but you have to put those feelings aside."[62] Accounts such as this make one wonder how society's attitude towards capital punishment would be affected if executions were made public.

On the Public

The effect of executions on the public has long been debated. Supporters of capital punishment claim that public awareness of executions contributes to the desired deterrent effect. Opponents of capital punishment argue just as vehemently that executions have a brutalizing effect on society and tend to make killing acceptable as a means of handling difficult problems. With assistance from the American Civil Liberties Union, some prisoners have recently sought to have their executions by gas videotaped for later use in others' appeals. In the 1992 execution of Robert Alton Harris in California, such a tape was actually made, but it was destroyed by court order in January 1994 without ever having been shown publicly.[63] As a practical matter, our society has struck a compromise by holding executions in private in the middle of the night but allowing controlled press coverage. This coverage — which has expanded to include press conferences with death row inmates, television images of the ambulance bearing the body of the executed, and vigils outside the prison by both mourners and revelers — has been said "to transform a closely guarded, hidden expression of the ultimate power of the state into a very public ceremonial event."[64]

The secrecy surrounding executions is not a time-honored tradition. As recently as 1937, the last public hanging took place in Texas; the preceding one in Kentucky in 1936 drew a crowd of over twenty thousand people, some of whom climbed poles and stood on rooftops to get a good view.[65] Helen Prejean has written of such an execution, "It was awful to see, and fascinating. And visible. It was truthful.... And it was obviously punishment. It was death. Forcible, violent, premeditated death. And the people knew it, and the people came to watch because it was death, because death, when you can see it happening in front of your eyes, is always something to watch."[66] Prejean's description of the public's fascination with executions is very similar to a passage in the *Republic,* in which Socrates is discussing the conflict between desires (which are a function of the appetitive part of the soul) and anger (which is a function of the spirited part of the soul). Socrates tells the story of Leontius, who is on his way from the harbor area back to Athens and passes by the place under the city wall where the corpses from public executions lay:

> Leontius, ... becoming aware of dead bodies that lay at the place of public execution at the same time felt a desire to see them and a repugnance and aversion, and that for a time he resisted and veiled his head, but overpowered in despite of all by his desire, with wide staring eyes he rushed up to the corpses and cried, "There, ye wretches, take your fill of the fine spectacle!" (439e-440a)

One might well imagine opponents of capital punishment undergoing a similar struggle with the temptation to watch if executions were ever televised.

Some argue that televising executions – in full grisly detail – would carry the deterrence argument to its logical conclusion. Others argue that, if the public could actually see what is being done in its name, it would be horrified. Typical of the latter group is Millard Farmer, a lawyer who has represented death row inmates. Farmer commented after a recent execution, "Look how shamefully secret this whole thing is. A few select witnesses brought deep inside this prison in the dead of night to watch a man killed. If most people in Louisiana would see what the state did tonight, they would throw up."[67] Certainly the image of brutality by the state, in having its overpowering authority put a defenseless person to death, is to be avoided if at all possible. The state of Virginia faced a public relations nightmare in January 1993 when it executed a man who was confined to a wheelchair (as a result of an injury he sustained while he was on death row).[68] Although there was no legal reason to change the death sentence because the inmate had become physically impaired while awaiting execution, still the image of a disabled person being assisted from a wheelchair into the electric chair was disturbing to the public conscience, which has never come fully to terms with the death penalty.

Unlike the social issues that were the topics of the first five chapters of this book, the death penalty entails little that is new or subject to a different interpretation now than in previous generations. Rather, it is a perennial issue of public debate that has never been satisfactorily resolved and possibly never will be. Clearly the premeditated, intentional taking of a human life is an act so contrary to the moral and spiritual impulses of a civilized society that it is difficult for society to accept, even when it can be rationally defended and justified. Capital punishment evokes the primal fear and dread of an eventual higher authority beyond mankind's understanding, and this aspect of the issue is apparent to all who come into contact with it, even those whose sensibilities are ordinarily secular and bureaucratic.

The works of the Canon give capital punishment a fuller and more direct treatment than they give any of the other contemporary social issues discussed in this book. All of the cultures represented by these works practiced capital punishment. No considered argument for its abolition is offered anywhere in them. Still, the adverse human consequences of inflicting the death penalty are fully detailed. The toll – on sentencers, executioners, the persons executed, and the public alike – has always been substantial. One is led to ask whether the gains from retaining a system of capital punishment offset these well-documented costs.

In recent years, increased attention has been focused on the possibility that a person might be executed for a crime he or she did not commit. Judicial authorities have become more honest in admitting that, in the absence of a perfect system of criminal justice, some such executions are likely. From an economic perspective, society cannot afford a perfect judicial system, and the question becomes how many wrongful executions it is willing to accept in order to keep the costs of the criminal judicial system within reason. If it is admitted that there will inevitably be some wrongful executions, then who is responsible for them?

The problem of individual responsibility for executions carried out under state authority is a key one both now and in the works of the Canon. What is seen in both realms is a strong tendency for all those involved to want to place final responsibility in someone else's hands. One learns from the best of the Western tradition that the burden of making such decisions is simply too great for any individual to bear, and evidence of that truth persists today. When responsibility is diffused, however, the possibilities for human error and the likelihood of mismanagement increase significantly.

If the American people have never been able to square infliction of the death penalty with their public or private consciences, and if no one is willing — or should be expected — to take responsibility for executions, then why does society persist in retaining this social policy? The answer to this question probably lies in the prevalence of crime and violence in America and in the public's understandable fear. An unprecedented crime wave has overtaken the nation, immediately following a period in which the federal courts extended substantial new constitutional protections to criminal defendants. The public is outraged by repeated crimes committed by career criminals who obtain early release because of overcrowded prisons and return to their neighborhoods as virtual folk heroes.

It is difficult for strong intellectual principles and fine moral sensibilities to prevail in the face of problems of this magnitude. And yet today's students will be called upon to bring both to bear upon these and related problems in the future. The gravity of the situation demands that they have the advantage of the best preparation they can possibly be offered. They should not be denied a thorough grounding in the defining works of the Western tradition as an indispensable start. In addition to many other educational and cultural benefits, such a grounding will enable them to bring a broad perspective and seasoned humanity to problems as perennially intractable as capital punishment.

Notes

1. Quoted on back cover of Donald D. Hook and Lothar Kahn, *Death in the Balance: The Debate over Capital Punishment* (Lexington, Mass.: D. C. Heath, 1989).

2. Stephen Nathanson, *An Eye for an Eye? The Morality of Punishing by Death* (Totowa, N.J.: Rowman & Littlefield, 1987), p. ix.

3. Neil A. Lewis, "Ginsburg Deflects Pressure to Talk on Death Penalty," *New York Times,* July 23, 1993, pp. A1 and A8.

4. See Roger Rosenblatt, *Life Itself: Abortion in the American Mind* (New York: Random House, 1992), p. 119; and Hook and Kahn, *Death in the Balance,* pp. x-xi.

5. Walter Berns, *For Capital Punishment: Crime and the Morality of the Death Penalty* (New York: Basic Books, 1979), p. 9; and Hook and Kahn, *Death in the Balance,* pp. 99-100.

6. Helen Prejean, *Dead Man Walking: An Eyewitness Account of the Death Penalty in the United States* (New York: Random House, 1993), pp. 217-218.

7. *Furman v. Georgia,* 408 U.S. 238, 92 S. Ct. 2726, 33 L. Ed. 2d 346 (1972).

8. See generally Lee Epstein and Joseph F. Kobylka, *The Supreme Court and Legal Change: Abortion and the Death Penalty* (Chapel Hill: University of North Carolina Press, 1992), pp. 34-136.

9. *Gregg v. Georgia,* 428 U.S. 153, 96 S. Ct. 2909, 49 L. Ed. 2d 859 (1976).

10. Michael L. Radelet, "Introduction and Overview," *Facing the Death Penalty: Essays on a Cruel and Unusual Punishment,* ed. by Michael L. Radelet (Philadelphia: Temple University Press, 1989), pp. 4-5.

11. See polls cited by Elizabeth D. Purdum and J. Anthony Paredes, "Rituals of Death: Capital Punishment and Human Sacrifice," in *Facing the Death Penalty,* ed. by Michael L. Radelet, p. 139.

12. See Neil A. Lewis, "A New and Expanded Death Penalty Measure," *New York Times,* August 15, 1993, sec. 4, p. 4.

13. *Herrera v. Collins,* 113 S. Ct. 853, 122 L. Ed. 2d 203 (January 25, 1993).

14. 122 L. Ed. 2d at 226-227.

15. The Court stated, "We may assume, for the sake of argument in deciding this case, that in a capital case a truly persuasive demonstration of 'actual innocence' made after trial would render the execution of a defendant

unconstitutional, and warrant federal habeas relief if there were no state avenue open to process such a claim." 122 L. Ed. 2d at 227.

16. "Killer in Case on Curbing New Evidence Is Executed," *New York Times,* May 13, 1993, p. A8.

17. 122 L. Ed. 2d at 235.

18. 122 L. Ed. 2d at 234.

19. 122 L. Ed. 2d at 246.

20. Henry Schwarzschild, "Foreword," in *Facing the Death Penalty,* ed. by Michael L. Radelet, p. x.

21. Quoted by Prejean, *Dead Man Walking,* p. 57.

22. *Callins v. Collins,* No. 93-7054, 62 U.S.L.W. 3546, 3547 (February 22, 1994). See Linda Greenhouse, "Death Penalty Is Renounced by Blackmun," *New York Times,* February 23, 1994, pp. A1 and A10.

23. *Schlup v. Delo,* No. 93-7901, 62 U.S.L.W. 3640 (March 29, 1994). See Linda Greenhouse, "Justices to Rule on Inmates' 2d Appeals," *New York Times,* March 29, 1994, p. A8.

24. See, for example, Exodus 35.2 and 21.29.

25. See Robert G. Boling, *The Anchor Bible: Joshua* (Garden City, N.Y.: Doubleday, 1982), p. 226.

26. The story of Achan is complicated by the fact that the stolen property (and those who came into contact with it) might have carried a contagion that constituted a threat to public health. If so, this would tend to explain why Achan's family members were apparently stoned to death. However, Achan confessed only to having taken "booty," which does not necessarily imply contamination. See Boling, *The Anchor Bible: Joshua,* pp. 228-230.

27. Hugo A. Bedau, *Death Is Different: Studies in the Morality, Law, and Politics of Capital Punishment* (Boston: Northeastern University Press, 1987), p. 57.

28. Millard Farmer, quoted by Prejean, *Dead Man Walking,* p. 47.

29. 122 L. Ed. 2d at 224. The citation to Blackstone is Commentaries *397.

30. See Margaret Vandiver, "Coping with Death: Families of the Terminally Ill, Homicide Victims, and Condemned Prisoners," in *Facing the Death Penalty,* ed. by Michael L. Radelet, pp. 1127-1129.

31. John O. Smylka, "The Human Impact of Capital Punishment: Interviews with Families of Persons on Death Row," *Journal of Criminal Justice,* vol. 15 (1987), p. 343.

32. Smylka, "The Human Impact of Capital Punishment," p. 345.

33. Translated by Robert Graves (London: Cassell, 1960), p. 275. The meaning of a crucial part of this passage has been disputed; some scholars

have claimed that the only thing at issue was the factual question of whether or not the blood price had been paid. See the Loeb edition at p. 324, note 1.

34. Vandiver, "Coping with Death," p. 126.

35. "Three Teen-Agers Accused in the Killing of Three Boys," *New York Times,* June 6, 1993, sec. 1, p. 31.

36. 122 L. Ed. 2d at 226.

37. 122 L. Ed. 2d at 216.

38. Michael L. Radelet, Hugo A. Bedau, and Constance E. Putnam, *In Spite of Innocence: Erroneous Convictions in Capital Cases* (Boston: Northeastern University Press, 1992), pp. 17 and 271.

39. Ibid., p. 273.

40. 122 L. Ed. 2d at 236, n. 1 (Blackmun, dissenting), and 122 L. Ed. 2d at 226, n. 15 (Rehnquist, for majority).

41. Jill Smolowe, "Must This Man Die?" *Time,* May 18, 1992, p. 42.

42. Bedau, *Death Is Different,* p. 103.

43. See cases cited by Bedau, *Death Is Different,* p. 259, n. 30.

44. Berns, *For Capital Punishment,* p. 173 and p. 205, notes 24 and 25.

45. Opponents of the death penalty dispute these arguments with actual figures. Helen Prejean offers figures from Florida that show a cost of $3.18 million for each death sentence compared with a cost of life imprisonment (based on forty years) of about $516,000. *Dead Man Walking,* pp. 129-130 and 260, note 8.

46. Hook and Kahn, *Death in the Balance,* p. 100.

47. Cf. Luke 23.13-24 and John 18.31-32.

48. Prejean, *Dead Man Walking,* p. 57.

49. *Furman v. Georgia,* 408 U.S. 238, at 405-406 (Blackmun, dissenting).

50. Prejean, *Dead Man Walking,* p. 180.

51. A volunteer firing squad was used in the case of Gary Gilmore. See Schwarzschild, "Foreword," in *Facing the Death Penalty,* ed. by Michael L. Radelet, p. x.

52. Hook and Kahn, *Death in the Balance,* p. 58.

53. As reported by Michael A. Kroll, "The Fraternity of Death," in *Facing the Death Penalty,* ed. by Michael L. Radelet, p. 23.

54. Prejean, *Dead Man Walking,* p. 101.

55. The accounts in the other two synoptic gospels are different; both quote the centurion as having said that truly this man was "the Son of God." Cf. Mark 15.39 and Matthew 27.54.

56. In addition to the RSV, the Living Bible and the Anchor Bible translate *dikaios* as "innocent." The point is debated among scholars. See Joseph A. Fitzmyer, *The Anchor Bible: The Gospel According to Luke X-XXIV* (New York: Doubleday, 1985), p. 1520.

57. Prejean, *Dead Man Walking,* p. 180.

58. Hook and Kahn, *Death in the Balance,* pp. 100 and 66.

59. Watt Espy, "Facing the Death Penalty," in *Facing the Death Penalty,* ed. by Michael L. Radelet, p. 27.

60. Mark 15.34 ; Matthew 27.46 ; Luke 23.46 ; and John 19. 28-30.

61. Timothy Egan, "Child-Killer, Awaiting Noose, May Have Slain Illusions, Too," *New York Times,* December 29, 1992, p. A1.

62. Kroll, "The Fraternity of Death," p. 21.

63. Sabra Chartrand, "Given a Push, Maryland Alters Its Death Penalty," *New York Times,* March 25, 1994, p. B12.

64. Purdum and Paredes, "Rituals of Death," p. 141.

65. Hook and Kahn, *Death in the Balance,* p. 55.

66. Prejean, *Dead Man Walking,* p. 218.

67. Quoted by Prejean, *Dead Man Walking,* p. 94.

68. "Disabled Inmate Is Put to Death," *New York Times,* January 21, 1993 (L), p. A21.

Conclusion

SEVERAL YEARS AGO an investigative report on television focused on certain packaged tours of Europe that hit the high spots in such an intense and hurried fashion that the show was entitled "If This Is Wednesday, It Must Be Belgium." My readers must have some of the same feelings as tourists who took one of those whirlwind tours. This book has been a demonstration of what five great texts have to say about six complex and divisive social issues with which our society is wrestling. It has not been my purpose to contribute to our scholarly understanding of either the texts or the social issues. Rather, it has been my purpose to make a point, I hope dramatically and vividly, about the continuing relevance of these texts to the problems that face us today and about their special ability to speak in direct and meaningful ways to issues that vex the human spirit, even across centuries.

A part of me feels that it makes no sense even to have undertaken what I have tried to do here. It makes no sense for a book of this kind to have been needed. But then, we live in nonsensical times. Even as we face difficult and sometimes intractable social problems such as those discussed here, and even as commentators clamor for values to inform and guide public debate of those issues, we shun the most obvious resources our culture has provided and reject them as relics of antiquarian interest only. Our present-oriented media culture, which is so adept at spotting conflict and fanning its flames, has turned away from great literature, which has in the past served to provoke reflective thought and to guide the exploration of alternative approaches to critical human problems.

For those who are old enough to have learned through their own educational backgrounds what riches the great works of the Western tradition offer, this book will serve as a reminder of what may have become clouded by the passage of time or obscured by the current debate. For those who have not yet reached middle age and who therefore may be the products of a changed curriculum at all educational levels, this book may surprise; many may have had no idea that there is so much in these texts from bygone eras that speaks so compellingly to the needs and concerns of today.

In the Introduction, I stated that it was my intention to rebut the allegation of obsolescence implicit in the widely used acronym DWEMs (Dead White European Males). In light of the foregoing demonstration of these texts' vitality and continuing relevance, one must question how the notion of obsolescence came to be added to the other, more rampant criticisms of the traditional canon on the basis of racism, Eurocentrism, and sexism. No apparent rationale for their alleged demise, apart from the other, better known criticisms, has emerged. Does the argument run that *because* of objections on the grounds of racism, Eurocentrism, and sexism, these works are *therefore* dead? If so, is fairness in matters of race, gender, and class being made the *sole criterion* for judging the educational appropriateness of texts? Are the revisionists arguing that concern for such fairness should be so commanding as to override any presumption in favor of the traditional canon? I suspect that, upon reflection, very few educational leaders, even among those who genuinely favor social change, would go so far.

Much of recent scholarship has concentrated on pointing out the shortcomings of the traditional canon because of concerns related to race, gender, and class. There is no doubt validity to these arguments. There *is* much in the canon that does not meet today's standards of equity and fairness to all groups. However, after years of such criticisms, we need to ask now what is the consequence of the acknowledged existence of what are, by today's standards, shortcomings. It is by no means clear that we should automatically abandon these works or push them aside to make room for others that do meet contemporary standards of fairness to all. Rather, we need to focus again upon the counterweight of their undeniable strengths – aesthetic, moral and intellectual. As I hope this book has demonstrated, their strengths far outweigh their inadequacies. Thus the challenge we face is to learn how to use these works in the classroom in ways that will help students both to recognize the social inequities inherent in the texts for what they are and at the same time to appreciate the richness in other respects that only they can offer us.

It is probably not unrealistic for someone who writes a book on this particular subject to expect criticism from all sides. In anticipation thereof, I offer a few words to likely critics from both the revisionist and the traditionalist camps. To my colleagues in the revisionist camp,

I would say that students need not be put to a choice between reading literature that is aesthetically superior and reading literature that is socially relevant (and therefore, to some, educationally appropriate). The poetry of Homer and the plays of Shakespeare have never been surpassed in their almost universally recognized literary merit. At the same time, the brilliance of their insights into human motivation and the dynamics of social interaction renders much of what they composed directly relevant to the social issues with which we are struggling today. If one can learn about sexual harassment in various ways, including through literature of this caliber, why not learn about it in this way?

Another point that I would make to those on my left is that I am arguing for the centrality, not the exclusivity, of canonical texts as a basis for learning about the Western tradition. There are voices that are underrepresented or missing altogether from the works of the traditional canon, and those gaps should be filled. In filling them, however, we must bear in mind that one cannot begin to understand the perspectives of the underrepresented in any culture unless one first has a grasp of the majoritarian culture of the represented. Only then can differences be identified and appreciated, and only then can problems that result from "marginalization" be understood.

From my colleagues in the traditionalist camp, I would expect to encounter the criticism that I have somehow demeaned these great works of literature by turning them into mere instruments of social purpose. Some traditionalists maintain that literary works are self-justifying and must exist on a different plane — one of beauty, goodness, and truth. While I would agree that the greatness of these works does allow them to be treated on such a transcendental plane, I would argue that their centrality to Western culture as it is experienced today allows them also to be interpreted as speaking to present-day needs and concerns. If they are not so interpreted, they simply will not attract the interest of most students, who have grown up in a media-dominated culture very different from that of previous generations. To consign these works to a plane removed from the world we inhabit is to risk turning them into the museum relics that the rhetoric of the revisionists suggests.

One of my teachers of classical languages from a quarter of a century ago was adamantly opposed to his department's even considering teaching classical texts "in translation" (those were almost dirty words one did not speak in his presence). He maintained virtually as a moral principle that one could not understand the works of classical authors unless they were read in the original languages. His career fortunately ended just before enrollment in Latin and Greek courses nationwide plummeted. I have sometimes wondered how he would have coped with the situation we face today, in which classicists must be grateful for any enrollments at all, even "in translation." The resilience to understand – and even to share in – the outlook of today's students is a necessary characteristic for any teacher of the humanities, and in this realm, no less than in others, it is a case of survival of the fittest.

In the course of the current debate, the canon has been subjected to another onslaught of criticism based more on how traditional works are taught than on the choice of what texts should be taught. The traditionalist camp is sometimes accused of relying more on rote memorization and mastery of specific facts than on engendering genuine understanding. The answer to this criticism, of course, is that anything can be taught well, and anything can be taught poorly. I would posit that a teacher covering the topic of capital punishment, for example, who could not draw upon the passages cited in chapter six of this book to make the subject interesting to students probably could not make any other material interesting. Memorization of characters' names and plot outlines is actually antithetical to the questioning spirit that pervades these works and constitutes much of their appeal, and a teacher who relies on such an approach may not himself or herself embody that spirit. To attack the educational efficacy of the texts because of such failures seems misdirected.

This book contains a large amount of quoted material because only by presenting hundreds of specific passages could I even begin to convey an impression of the richness they offer. The primary difficulty in selecting these passages and weaving them into a coherent narrative was having to forego many other passages that might have shed additional light on the topics discussed. In concluding, I would make three specific points about what I have tried to show:

The Western tradition as represented in the works of the Canon is anything but monolithic. It should be abundantly apparent even to a reader whose only familiarity with the Canon is through reading this book that a wide array of outlooks, perspectives, and viewpoints on fundamental questions may be found in these five sources. Often one finds widely differing or even contradictory viewpoints within a single work. For example, the views of the younger Plato of the *Republic* and those of the older Plato of the *Laws* are fundamentally different on many important social issues. The Jesus of the New Testament radically transforms the Jewish law that originated with Moses in the Old Testament. Generations of scholars have debated whether the same poet who describes the fierce brutality of the male warrior culture of the *Iliad* could also have produced the elegant descriptions of the advanced, possibly matriarchal civilization of Phaeacia found in the *Odyssey*. And Shakespeare portrays with profound insight the motivations and innermost thoughts of kings and peasants, of men and women (with each gender sometimes exhibiting traits of the other), of oppressors and victims. To characterize the works of this tradition as presenting an elitist, or any other uniform, point of view is to misrepresent the unfathomable complexity and rich diversity of the human nature they so accurately portray. If some voices are missing from the chorus, that does not mean that the voices that are in the chorus are all singing in the same key.

The Western tradition as represented in the works of the Canon is anything but conservative. Quite to the contrary, true radicalness often prevails. In Plato we find a recommendation that, in the interest of full equality, women exercise naked alongside men in the palestra; he also gives a rationale for why the presence of homosexual couples contributes to the fighting effectiveness of an army. In a Christian gospel we see Jesus forgiving an adulteress and challenging her accusers to justify themselves. In Homer we encounter a common soldier scathingly denouncing the elite officers' privileges and seeking to persuade his peers to abandon the campaign against Troy. And in Shakespeare we hear the plaintive cries of an indigenous person who has been displaced by invaders from control of the island that was his native home; the prayers of a suffering king who would gladly trade his throne and all its perquisites for the simple life of a shepherd; and the rebellious cries of a revolutionary figure who incites a mob and urges that, as a first strategy in bringing about chaos, they kill all the lawyers.

To equate the great texts of the Western tradition with conservatism is to confuse the ideology of the texts themselves with the ideology of one group of recent advocates for the texts. All worthy causes attract some who support them for the wrong reasons. The great conversation, as the tradition is sometimes called, would have been a boring monologue rather than a riveting exchange if the full spectrum of views, from reactionary to radical, were not fully represented. As Nina

Auerbach has written concerning the prevalence of radical views in the canon, "The sedition that conservatives fear grows in their own backyard."*

The Western tradition as represented in the works of the Canon is anything but obsolete or irrelevant to the needs and concerns of today. This has been the primary focus of this book, which has necessarily concentrated on this one strand of the overall debate. If one is interested in the predicament of a young woman who has brought a charge of sexual harassment against a man in a position of power and whose character, motivation, and even mental stability are questioned as a result, one might think of either Anita Hill or Isabella in *Measure for Measure*. If one is concerned about the prevalence of date rape on campus and wants to know how the problem of when does "no" mean "yes" developed in our culture, one might turn to *The Two Gentlemen of Verona*. If recent research seeming to indicate that male homosexuality is genetically determined is confirmed, that would validate a mythical speculation found in Plato's *Symposium*. As the United States contemplates whether to allow RU486, the French "abortion pill," to be distributed, one might be surprised to learn from Plato's *Theaetetus* that midwives in ancient Greece knew how to use drugs as abortifacients. Supporters of Dr. Jack Kevorkian from the right-to-die movement would likely find it interesting that, in *Antony and Cleopatra,* Cleopatra's physician reported that she had long sought an easy way to die. And those who are concerned about whether the death penalty or some lesser penalty should be accepted by the family of a murder victim will find a town meeting considering just this question depicted on a shield forged by the god Hephaestus for Achilles in the *Iliad*. To add theoretical argument to bolster my conclusion here would be pointless; as I have done throughout this book, I shall let the texts speak for themselves.

I realize that those who are inclined to favor the great books philosophy of higher education will likely say that I have accomplished my purpose here; by the same token, those who are not so inclined will likely say that I have proved nothing. This may be the kind of book that is found convincing by those who are receptive to its point of view and unconvincing by those who are not. If there are readers whose receptivity is still malleable, I suppose that it is to them that I should make my appeal. Most importantly, if there are young readers who are

---

* *New York Times Book Review,* November 22, 1992, p. 11.

surprised by what they have read here and are thus drawn to become familiar with texts that previously seemed remote, then writing this book has been worthwhile.

Works Cited

Adler, Mortimer J. *How to Read A Book: The Art of Getting a Liberal Education.* New York: Simon & Schuster, 1940.

American Council of Learned Societies. "Speaking for the Humanites." Occasional Paper No. 7, reprinted in *Chronicle of Higher Education*, January 11, 1989, pp. A11-A22.

Ames, Katrine. "Last Rights." *Newsweek*, August 26, 1991, pp. 40-41.

Atlas, James. *Battle of the Books: The Curriculum Debate in America.* New York: Norton, 1992.

Auerbach, Nina. Book review in *New York Times Book Review*, November 22, 1992, p. 11.

Ayres, D. Drummond, Jr. "An Uproar over Comments by Republicans in Virginia." *New York Times*, March 19, 1993, p. A8.

Baehr v. Lewin, 852 P. 2d 44 (Supreme Court of Hawaii, May 5, 1993).

Barzun, Jacques. *Teacher in America.* Boston: Little, Brown, 1945.

Bedau, Hugo A. *Death Is Different: Studies in the Morality, Law, and Politics of Capital Punishment.* Boston: Northeastern University Press, 1987.

Belkin, Lisa. "There's No Simple Suicide." *New York Times Magazine*, November 14, 1993, pp. 48 ff.

Bennett, William J. *To Reclaim a Legacy.* Washington, D.C.: National Endowment for the Humanities, 1984, reprinted in *Chronicle of Higher Education*, November 28, 1984, pp. 16-21.

Berns, Walter. *For Capital Punishment: Crime and the Morality of the Death Penalty.* New York: Basic Books, 1979.

Bloom, Allan. *The Closing of the American Mind: How Higher Education Has Failed Democracy and Impoverished the Souls of Today's Students.* New York: Simon & Schuster, 1987

———. *Love and Friendship.* New York: Simon & Schuster, 1993.

Boling, Robert G. *The Anchor Bible: Joshua.* Garden City, N.Y.: Doubleday, 1982.

———. *The Anchor Bible: Judges.* Garden City, N.Y.: Doubleday, 1982.

Boswell, John. *Christianity, Social Tolerance, and Homosexuality.* Chicago: University of Chicago Press, 1980.

Bourque, Linda B. *Defining Rape.* Durham: Duke University Press, 1989.

Bowers v. Hardwick, 478 U.S. 186, 106 S. Ct. 2841, 92 L. Ed. 2d 140 (1986).

Brann, Eva T. H. "What Is a Book?" *St. John's Review,* vol. 41, no. 1 (1991-92), pp. 85-88.

Brill, Alida. *Nobody's Business: Paradoxes of Privacy.* Reading, Mass.: Addison-Wesley, 1990.

Brock, David. *The Real Anita Hill: The Untold Story.* New York: Free Press, 1993.

Brody, Jane E. "The Rights of a Dying Patient Are Often Misunderstood, Even by Medical Professionals." *New York Times,* January 27, 1993, p. B7.

Brownmiller, Susan. *Against Our Will: Men, Women, and Rape.* New York: Simon & Schuster, 1975.

Bryant, Anita. *The Anita Bryant Story: The Survival of Our Nation's Families and the Threat of Militant Homosexuality.* Old Tappan, N.J.: Revell, 1977.

Burgess, Ann W., ed. *Rape and Sexual Assault: A Research Handbook.* New York: Garland, 1985.

Burke, Carol. "Dames at Sea: Life in the Naval Academy." *New Republic,* August 17, 1992, pp. 16-20.

Callahan, Daniel. "The Abortion Debate: Is Progress Possible?" In *Abortion: Understanding Differences,* edited by Sidney Callahan and Daniel Callahan, pp. 309-324. New York: Plenum Press, 1984.

Callahan, Sidney. "Value Choices in Abortion." In *Abortion: Understanding Differences,* edited by Sidney Callahan and Daniel Callahan, pp. 285-301. New York: Plenum Press, 1984.

Callahan, Sidney, and Daniel Callahan, eds. *Abortion: Understanding Differences.* New York: Plenum Press, 1984.

Callins v. Collins, No. 93-7054, 62 U.S.L.W. 3546 (February 22, 1994).

Carnochan, W. B. *The Battleground of the Curriculum: Liberal Education and American Experience.* Stanford, Calif.: Stanford University Press, 1993.

Carrick, Paul. *Medical Ethics in Antiquity: Philosophical Perspectives on Abortion and Euthanasia.* Dordrecht: D. Reidel, 1985.

Carter, Bill. "Accuser in Rape Case Elects to Make Her Identity Public." *New York Times,* December 19, 1991 (L), p. B22.

"The Castration Option." Editorial in *New York Times,* March 10, 1992, p. A24.

Chartrand, Sabra. "Given a Push, Maryland Alters Its Death Penalty." *New York Times,* March 25, 1994, p. B12.

Cheney, Lynne V. *Humanities in America.* Washington, D.C.: National Endowment for the Humanities, 1988, reprinted in *Chronicle of Higher Education,* September 21, 1988, pp. A17-A23.

Cheney v. Pruitt, 963 F. 2d 1160 (9th Cir. 1991), *cert. denied* 113 S. Ct. 655, 121 L. Ed. 2d 581 (1992).

Cohen, David. "Notes on a Grecian Yearn." *New York Times,* March 31, 1993, p. A13.

Coker v. Georgia, 433 U.S. 584, 97 S. Ct. 2861, 58 L. Ed. 2d 207 (1977).

Corbett, Ken. "Between Fear and Fantasy." *New York Times,* February 3, 1993, p. A15.

Cox Broadcasting Corp. v. Cohn, 420 U.S. 469, 95 S. Ct. 1029, 105 L. Ed. 2d 443 (1975).

Crenshaw, Kimberle. "Whose Story Is It, Anyway? Feminist and Antiracist Appropriations of Anita Hill." In *Race-ing Justice, En-gendering Power: Essays on Anita Hill, Clarence Thomas, and the Construction of Social Reality,* edited by Toni Morrison, pp. 402-440. New York: Pantheon, 1992.

Cruzan v. Director, Missouri Department of Health, 497 U.S. 261, 110 S. Ct. 2841, 111 L. Ed. 2d 224 (1990).

Denniston, R. H. "Ambisexuality in Animals." In *Homosexual Behavior: A Modern Reappraisal,* edited by Judd Marmor, pp. 25-40. New York: Basic Books, 1980.

"Disabled Inmate Is Put to Death." *New York Times,* January 21, 1993 (L), p. A21.

Dover, Kenneth J. *Greek Homosexuality.* Cambridge, Mass.: Harvard University Press, 1989.

D'Souza, Dinesh. *Illiberal Education: The Politics of Race and Sex on Campus.* New York: Free Press, 1991.

Dworkin, Roger B. "Resistance Standard in Rape Legislation." *Stanford Law Review,* vol. 18, no. 4 (February 1966), pp. 680-689.

Dworkin, Ronald. *Life's Dominion: An Argument about Abortion, Euthanasia, and Individual Freedom.* New York: Alfred A. Knopf, 1993.

Egan, Timothy. "Oregon Measure Asks State to Repress Homosexuality." *New York Times,* August 16, 1992, pp. 1 and 17.

————. "Child-Killer, Awaiting Noose, May Have Slain Illusions, Too." *New York Times,* December 29, 1992, pp. A1 and A9.

Ellison v. Brady, 924 F. 2d 872 (9th Cir. 1991).

Epstein, Lee, and Joseph F. Kobylka. *The Supreme Court and Legal Change: Abortion and the Death Penalty.* Chapel Hill: University of North Carolina Press, 1992.

Erskine, John. *My Life as a Teacher.* Philadelphia: J. B. Lippincott, 1948.

Espy, Watt. "Facing the Death Penalty." In *Facing the Death Penalty: Essays on a Cruel and Unusual Punishment,* edited by Michael L. Radelet, pp. 27-37. Philadelphia: Temple University Press, 1989.

Estrich, Susan. "Rape." *Yale Law Journal,* vol. 95, no. 6 (May 1986), pp. 1087-1184.

————. *Real Rape.* Cambridge, Mass.: Harvard University Press, 1987.

Fairstein, Linda A. *Sexual Violence: Our War Against Rape.* New York: William Morrow, 1993.

Fish, Stanley. "The Common Touch, or, One Size Fits All." In *The Politics of Liberal Education,* edited by Darryl J. Gless and Barbara Herrnstein Smith, pp. 241-266. Durham: Duke University Press, 1992.

Fitzgerald, Louise F. "Sexual Harassment: The Definition and Measurement of a Construct." In *Ivory Power: Sexual Harassment on Campus,* edited by Michele A. Paludi, pp. 21-44. Albany: State University of New York Press, 1990.

Fitzmyer, Joseph A. *The Anchor Bible: The Gospel According to Luke X-XXIV.* New York: Doubleday, 1985.

The Florida Star v. B.J.F., 491 U.S. 524, 109 S. Ct. 2603, 105 L. Ed. 2d 443 (1989).

Fox-Genovese, Elizabeth. *Feminism Without Illusions: A Critique of Individualism.* Chapel Hill: University of North Carolina Press, 1991.

Furman v. Georgia, 408 U.S. 238, 92 S. Ct. 2726, 33 L. Ed. 2d 346 (1972).

Gabbard, Glen O. *Sexual Exploitation in Professional Relationships.* New York: American Psychiatric Association, 1989.

Gabriel, Trip. "The Trials of Bob Packwood." *New York Times Magazine,* August 29, 1993, pp. 30 ff.

Gates, Henry Louis, Jr. *Loose Canons: Notes on the Culture Wars.* New York: Oxford University Press, 1992.

Gelman, David. "The Mind of the Rapist." *Newsweek,* July 23, 1990, pp. 46-52.

Gibbs, Nancy. "Rx for Death." *Time,* May 31, 1993, pp. 35-44.

Giroux, Henry A. "Liberal Arts Education and the Struggle for Public Life: Dreaming about Democracy." In *The Politics of Liberal Education,* edited by Darryl J. Gless and Barbara Herrnstein Smith, pp. 119-144. Durham: Duke University Press, 1992.

Gless, Darryl J., and Barbara Herrnstein Smith, eds. *The Politics of Liberal Education.* Durham: Duke University Press, 1992.

Glick, Henry R. *The Right to Die: Policy Innovation and Its Consequences.* New York: Columbia University Press, 1992.

"Going 'Wilding' in the City." *Newsweek,* May 8, 1989, p. 65.

Goldman, Ari L. "Girl, 17, Accused of Killing Baby She Secretly Delivered." *New York Times,* June 3, 1993, p. A16.

Gomes, Peter J. "Homophobic? Re-Read Your Bible." *New York Times,* August 17, 1992, p. A19.

Goodman, Jill L. "Sexual Harassment: Some Observations on the Distance Travelled and the Distance Yet to Go." *Capital University Law Review*, vol. 10 (1981), pp. 445-463.

Graff, Gerald. *Beyond the Culture Wars: How Teaching the Conflicts Can Revitalize American Education*. New York: Norton, 1992.

Greenberg, David F. *The Construction of Homosexuality*. Chicago: University of Chicago Press, 1988.

Greenhouse, Linda. "On Privacy and Equality: Judge Ginsburg Still Voices Strong Doubts on Winning Strategy Behind Roe v. Wade." *New York Times*, June 16, 1993, pp. A1 and A11.

———. "Court, 9-0, Makes Sex Harassment Easier to Prove." *New York Times*, November 10, 1993, pp. A1 and A14.

———. "Death Penalty Is Renounced by Blackmun." *New York Times*, February 23, 1994, pp. A1 and A10.

———. "Justices to Rule on Inmates' 2d Appeals." *New York Times*, March 29, 1994, p. A8.

Gregg v. Georgia, 428 U.S. 153, 96 S. Ct. 2909, 49 L. Ed. 2d 859 (1976).

Griswold v. Connecticut, 381 U.S. 479, 85 S. Ct. 1678, 14 L. Ed. 2d 510 (1965).

Gross, Jane. "At AIDS Epicenter, Seeking Swift, Sure Death." *New York Times*, June 20, 1993, sec. 1, p. 10.

———. "After a Ruling, Hawaii Weighs Gay Marriages." *New York Times*, April 25, 1994, pp. A1 and C12.

Groth, A. Nicholas. *Men Who Rape: The Psychology of the Offender*. New York: Plenum Press, 1979.

Hadas, Moses. *Old Wine, New Bottles: A Humanist Teacher at Work*. New York: Trident Press, 1962.

Halperin, David M. *One Hundred Years of Homosexuality and Other Essays on Greek Love*. New York: Routledge, 1990.

Hanley, Robert. "Three Are Sentenced to Youth Center for Sexual Abuse of Retarded Girl." *New York Times*, April 24, 1993, pp. 1 and 8.

Harris v. Forklift Systems Inc., 114 S. Ct. 367, 126 L. Ed. 2d 295 (November 9, 1993).

Herrera v. Collins, 113 S. Ct. 853, 122 L. Ed. 2d 203 (January 25, 1993).

Highet, Gilbert. *The Art of Teaching*. New York: Vintage, 1950.

Hirsch, E. D., Jr. *Cultural Literacy: What Every American Needs to Know*. Boston: Houghton Mifflin, 1987.

Hiss, Tony. "The End of the Rainbow." *New Yorker*, April 12, 1993, pp. 43-54.

Hook, Donald D., and Lothar Kahn. *Death in the Balance: The Debate over Capital Punishment.* Lexington, Mass.: D. C. Heath, 1989.

Howe, Irving. "The Value of the Canon." *New Republic,* February 18, 1991, pp. 40-47.

Hudson, Rock, and Sara Davidson. *Rock Hudson: His Story.* New York: William Morrow, 1986.

Hughes, Robert. *Culture of Complaint: The Fraying of America.* New York: Oxford University Press, 1993.

Humphry, Derek. *Final Exit: The Practicalities of Self-Deliverance and Assisted Suicide for the Dying.* New York: Dell, 1991.

Humphry, Derek, and Ann Wickett. *The Right to Die: Understanding Euthanasia.* New York: Harper & Row, 1986.

Hutchins, Robert M. *The Higher Learning in America.* New Haven: Yale University Press, 1936.

In re Quinlan, 70 N.J. 10, 355 A. 2d 647, cert denied *sub nom., Garger v. New Jersey,* 429 U.S. 922, 97 S. Ct. 319, 50 L. Ed. 2d 289 (1976).

Isay, Richard A. "Removing the Stigma." Letter to the editor, *New York Times,* September 2, 1992, p. A18.

"The Jogger." Editorial in *New York Times,* December 2, 1989, sec. 1, p. 26.

Johnson, Dirk. "Colorado Ban on Gay Rights Laws Is Ruled Unconstitutional." *New York Times,* December 15, 1993, p. A11.

Kantrowitz, Barbara. "Naming Names." *Newsweek,* April 29, 1991, pp. 26-32.

Kaplan, David A. "Remove That Blue Dot." *Newsweek,* December 16, 1991, p. 26.

Kass, Leon R. "Suicide Made Easy: The Evil of 'Rational' Humaneness." *Commentary,* vol. 92, no. 6 (December, 1991), pp. 19-24.

Kennedy, George A. "Classics and Canons." In *The Politics of Liberal Education,* edited by Darryl J. Gless and Barbara Herrnstein Smith, pp. 222-231. Durham: Duke University Press, 1992.

Kevorkian, Jack. *Prescription: Medicide — The Goodness of Planned Death.* Buffalo, N.Y.: Prometheus Books, 1991.

"Killer in Case on Curbing New Evidence Is Executed," *New York Times,* May 13, 1993, p. A8.

Kimball, Roger. *Tenured Radicals: How Politics Has Corrupted Our Higher Education.* New York: Harper & Row, 1990.

King, Patricia. "The Senator, the Sex Stories." *Newsweek,* March 16, 1992, p. 64.

Kirk, Marshall and Hunter Madsen. *After the Ball: How America Will Conquer Its Hatred and Fear of Gays in the '90's.* New York: Doubleday, 1989.

Knight, Raymond A., Ruth Rosenberg, and Beth Schneider. "Classification of Sexual Offenders: Perspectives, Methods, and Validation." In *Rape and Sexual Assault: A Research Handbook,* edited by Ann W. Burgess, pp. 222-293. New York: Garland, 1985.

Knox, Bernard. *The Oldest Dead White European Males and Other Reflections on the Classics.* New York: Norton, 1993.

Kolata, Gina. "Ethicists Struggle with Judgment of the 'Value' of Life." *New York Times,* November 24, 1992, pp. B5 and B8.

Kroll, Michael A. "The Fraternity of Death." In *Facing the Death Penalty: Essays on a Cruel and Unusual Punishment,* edited by Michael L. Radelet, pp. 16-26. Philadelphia: Temple University Press, 1989.

Labaton, Stephen. "For Oklahoma, Anita Hill's Story Is Open Wound." *New York Times,* April 19, 1993, pp. A1 and A9.

Lewis, Neil A. "In Marshall Papers, Rare Glimpse at Court." *New York Times,* May 25, 1993, pp. A1 and A8.

———. "Ginsburg Deflects Pressure to Talk on Death Penalty." *New York Times,* July 23, 1993, pp. A1 and A8.

———. "A New and Expanded Death Penalty Measure." *New York Times,* August 15, 1993, sec. 4, p. 4.

L'Hommedieu, Elizabeth. "Walking Out on the Boys." *Time,* July 8, 1991, pp. 52-53.

Lippman, Theo, Jr. *Spiro Agnew's America.* New York: Norton, 1972.

Loving v. Virginia, 388 U.S. 1, 87 S. Ct. 1817, 18 L. Ed. 2d 1010 (1967).

Luker, Kristin. "Abortion and the Meaning of Life." In *Abortion: Understanding Differences,* edited by Sidney Callahan and Daniel Callahan, pp. 25-45. New York: Plenum Press, 1984.

MacKinnon, Catharine A. *Sexual Harassment of Working Women: A Case of Sex Discrimination.* New Haven: Yale University Press, 1979.

———. *Feminism Unmodified: Discourses on Life and Law.* Cambridge, Mass.: Harvard University Press, 1987.

———. "Reflections on Sex Equality under Law." *Yale Law Journal,* vol. 100, no. 5 (March 1991), pp. 1281-1328.

Majority Staff of the Senate Committee on the Judiciary. *The Response to Rape: Detours on the Road to Equal Justice.* Washington, D.C.: Senate Committee on the Judiciary, May, 1993.

"Man Is Convicted of Rape in Case Involving Condom." *New York Times,* May 14, 1993, p. A7.

"Man Trouble." Editorial in *National Review,* August 31, 1992, p. 18.

Manegold, Catherine S. "The Odd Place of Homosexuality in the Military." *New York Times*, April 18, 1993, sec. 4, pp. 1 and 3.

Marmor, Judd, ed. *Homosexual Behavior: A Modern Reappraisal.* New York: Basic Books, 1980.

Mayer, Jane and Jill Abramson. "The Surreal Anita Hill." *New Yorker*, May 24, 1993, pp. 90-96.

Meritor Savings Bank, FSB v. Vinson et al., 477 U.S. 57, 106 S. Ct. 2399, 91 L. Ed. 2d 49 (1986).

Michigan v. Lucas, 111 S. Ct. 1743, 114 L. Ed. 2d 205 (1991).

Mohr, Richard D. *Gays/Justice: A Study of Ethics, Society, and Law.* New York: Columbia University Press, 1988.

Morowitz, Harold J., and James S. Trefil. "Roe v. Wade Passes a Lab Test." *New York Times*, November 25, 1992, p. A21.

————. *The Facts of Life: Science and the Abortion Controversy.* New York: Oxford University Press, 1992.

Morrison, Toni, ed. *Race-ing Justice, En-gendering Power: Essays on Anita Hill, Clarence Thomas, and the Construction of Social Reality.* New York: Pantheon, 1992.

Nathanson, Stephen. *An Eye for an Eye: The Morality of Punishing by Death.* Totowa, N.J.: Rowman & Littlefield, 1987.

New York Times/CBS News Poll, reported in "How the Public Views Gay Issues." *New York Times*, March 5, 1993, p. A11.

"Not in My Town." *Newsweek*, June 1, 1987, p. 31.

Nuland, Sherwin B. *How We Die: Reflections on Life's Final Chapter.* New York: Alfred A. Knopf, 1994.

Nussbaum, Martha C. "The Softness of Reason: A Classical Case for Gay Studies." *New Republic*, July 13, 1992, pp. 26-35.

Oates, Joyce Carol. "Rape and the Boxing Ring." *Newsweek*, February 24, 1992, pp. 60-61.

Office of the Inspector General, Department of Defense. *The Tailhook Report: The Official Inquiry into the Events of Tailhook '91.* New York: St. Martin's Press, 1993.

Orr, William F., and James A. Walther, *The Anchor Bible: I Corinthians.* Garden City, N.Y.: Doubleday, 1976.

"The Other Minority." Editorial in *New Republic*, March 30, 1992, p. 7.

Pace, Nicholas A. "We Should Treat Depression, Not Assist Suicide." Letter to the editor of the *New York Times*, February 4, 1993, p. A14.

Paludi, Michele A., ed. *Ivory Power: Sexual Harassment on Campus.* Albany: State University of New York Press, 1990.

Paludi, Michele A., and Richard B. Barickman, eds. *Academic and Workplace Sexual Harassment: A Resource Manual.* Albany: State University of New York Press, 1991.

Petchesky, Rosalind P. *Abortion and Woman's Choice: The State, Sexuality, and Reproductive Freedom.* New York: Longman, 1984.

Pharr, Suzanne. *Homophobia: A Weapon of Sexism.* Inverness, Calif.: Chardon Press, 1988.

Phelps, Timothy M., and Helen Winternitz. *Capitol Games: Clarence Thomas, Anita Hill, and the Story of a Supreme Court Nomination.* New York: Hyperion, 1992.

"Physician-Assisted Suicide and the Right to Die with Assistance." *Harvard Law Review,* vol. 105 (June 1992), pp. 2021-2040.

Planned Parenthood v. Casey, 112 S. Ct. 2791, 120 L. Ed. 2d 674 (1992).

Prejean, Helen. *Dead Man Walking: An Eyewitness Account of the Death Penalty in the United States.* New York: Random House, 1993.

Purdum, Elizabeth D., and J. Anthony Paredes. "Rituals of Death: Capital Punishment and Human Sacrifice." In *Facing the Death Penalty: Essays on a Cruel and Unusual Punishment,* edited by Michael Radelet, pp. 139-155. Philadelphia: Temple University Press, 1989.

Quill, Timothy E. *Death and Dignity: Making Choices and Taking Charge.* New York: Norton, 1993.

———. "On Trial — How We Die." *New York Times,* September 27, 1993, p. A11.

Rachels, James. *The End of Life: Euthanasia and Morality.* Oxford: Oxford University Press, 1986.

Radelet, Michael L., ed. *Facing the Death Penalty: Essays on a Cruel and Unusual Punishment.* Philadelphia: Temple University Press, 1989.

Radelet, Michael L., Hugo A. Bedau, and Constance E. Putnam. *In Spite of Innocence: Erroneous Convictions in Capital Cases.* Boston: Northeastern University Press, 1992.

Rauck, Richard L. "Pain Is Not Good Reason to Die." *Winston-Salem Journal,* February 27, 1993, p. 15

Reich, Walter. "Shame on the Dutch." *New York Times,* February 27, 1993, p.15.

Rexroth, Kenneth. *Classics Revisited.* New York: New Directions, 1986.

Rhode, Deborah L. *Justice and Gender: Sex Discrimination and the Law.* Cambridge, Mass.: Harvard University Press, 1989.

Riddle, John M. *Contraception and Abortion from the Ancient World to the Renaissance.* Cambridge, Mass.: Harvard University Press, 1992.

Roberts, Sam. "Cardinal Reflects on Role as a Moral Lightning Rod." *New York Times,* June 2, 1993, pp. A1 and B12.

Roe v. Wade. 410 U.S. 113, 93 S. Ct. 705, 35 L. Ed. 2d 147 (1973).

Rohter, Larry. "Battle over Protests at Abortion Clinics Shifts to High Court." *New York Times,* April 28, 1994, pp. A1 and A8.

Roiphe, Katie. *The Morning After: Sex, Fear, and Feminism on Campus.* Boston: Little, Brown, 1993.

Rorty, Richard. "Two Cheers for the Cultural Left." In *The Politics of Liberal Education,* edited by Darryl J. Gless and Barbara Herrnstein Smith, pp. 233-240. Durham: Duke University Press, 1992.

Rosenblatt, Roger. *Life Itself: Abortion in the American Mind.* New York: Random House, 1992.

Rothstein, Mervyn. "At Columbia, Classics Are Attacked as Old Deities." *New York Times,* October 10, 1992, p. 10.

Rutter, Peter. *Sex in the Forbidden Zone: When Men in Power — Therapists, Doctors, Clergy, Teachers and Others — Betray Women's Trust.* Los Angeles, Calif.: Jeremy P. Tarcher, 1989.

Salholz, Eloise. "The Death of Dr. Gunn: A Physician Becomes a Casualty of the Abortion Wars." *Newsweek,* March 22, 1993, p. 34.

Schlup v. Delo, No. 93-7901, 62 U.S.L.W. 3640 (March 29, 1994).

Schwarzschild, Henry. "Foreword." In *Facing the Death Penalty: Essays on a Cruel and Unusual Punishment,* edited by Michael Radelet, pp. ix-xi. Philadelphia: Temple University Press, 1989.

Searle, John. "The Storm over the University." *New York Review of Books,* December 5, 1990, pp. 34-42.

Shapiro, Joseph P. "Death on Trial." *U.S. News & World Report,* April 25, 1994, pp. 31-39.

Shaw, Peter. *Recovering American Literature.* Chicago: Ivan R. Dee, 1994.

Sherlock, Richard. *Preserving Life: Public Policy and the Life Not Worth Living.* Chicago: Loyola University Press, 1987.

Shilts, Randy. *Conduct Unbecoming: Gays and Lesbians in the U.S. Military.*New York: St. Martin's Press, 1993.

Simon, Paul. *Advice & Consent: Clarence Thomas, Robert Bork, and the Intriguing History of the Supreme Court's Nomination Battles.* Washington, D.C.: National Press Books, 1992.

Simons, Marlise. "Dutch Move to Enact Law Making Euthanasia Easier." *New York Times,* February 9, 1993, pp. A1 and A7.

Smolowe, Jill. "Must This Man Die?" *Time,* May 18, 1992, pp. 41-44.

———. "The Abortion Pill: New, Improved, and Ready for Battle." *Time,* June 14, 1993, pp. 48-54.

Smylka, John O. "The Human Impact of Capital Punishment: Interviews with Families of Persons on Death Row." *Journal of Criminal Justice*, vol. 15 (1987), pp. 331-347.

Stanley v. Georgia, 394 U.S. 557, 89 S. Ct. 1243, 22 L. Ed. 2d 542 (1969).

State in Interest of M.T.S., 129 N.J. 422, 609 A. 2d 1266 (July 30, 1992).

Stearns, Peter N. *Meaning over Memory: Recasting the Teaching of Culture and History*. Chapel Hill: University of North Carolina Press, 1993.

Steinfels, Peter. "At Crossroads, U.S. Ponders Ethics of Helping Others Die." *New York Times*, October 28, 1991, pp. A1 and A15.

Summers, Anthony. *Official and Confidential: The Secret Life of J. Edgar Hoover*. New York: G. P. Putnam's Sons, 1993.

Sykes, Charles J. *The Hollow Men: Politics and Corruption in Higher Education*. Washington, D.C.: Regnery Gateway, 1990.

"The Tavern Rape: Cheers and No Help." *Newsweek*, March 21, 1983, p. 25.

"Text of Pentagon's New Policy Guidelines on Homosexuals in the Military," *New York Times*, July 20, 1993, p. A12.

Thomson, Judith Jarvis. "A Defense of Abortion." *Philosophy & Public Affairs*, vol. 1, no. 1 (1971), pp. 47-66.

Thornton, Agathe. *Homer's Iliad: Its Composition and the Motif of Supplication*. Göttingen: Vandenhoeck & Ruprecht, 1984.

"Three Teen-Agers Accused in the Killing of Three Boys." *New York Times*, June 6, 1993, sec. 1, p. 31.

Tribe, Laurence H. *Abortion: The Clash of Absolutes*. New York: Norton, 1992.

Turque, Bill. "Gays under Fire." *Newsweek*, September 14, 1992, pp. 34-40.

Vandiver, Margaret. "Coping with Death: Families of the Terminally Ill, Homicide Victims, and Condemned Prisoners." In *Facing the Death Penalty: Essays on a Cruel and Unusual Punishment*, edited by Michael L. Radelet, pp. 123-127. Philadelphia: Temple University Press, 1989.

Van Doren, Mark. *Liberal Education*. New York: Henry Holt, 1943.

"A Victim's Life Sentence." *People Weekly*, April 25, 1988, pp. 40-45.

Webster v. Reproductive Health Services, 492 U.S. 490, 109 S. Ct. 3040, 106 L. Ed. 2d 410 (1989).

Weddington, Sarah. *A Question of Choice*. New York: G. P. Putnam's Sons, 1992.

Weiss, Michael. "Crimes of the Head: Feminist Legal Theory Is Creating a Government Not of Laws but of Women." *Reason*, vol. 23, no. 8 (January, 1992), pp. 28-33.

Wells-Petry, Melissa. *Exclusion: Homosexuals and the Right to Serve.* Washington, D.C.: Regnery Gateway, 1993.

Wenz, Peter S. *Abortion Rights as Religious Freedom.* Philadelphia: Temple University Press, 1992.

Winders, James A. *Gender, Theory, and the Canon.* Madison: University of Wisconsin Press, 1991.

Woodward, Kenneth L. "Was It Real or Memories?" *Newsweek,* March 14, 1994, pp. 54-55.

Ziegenmeyer, Nancy. *Taking Back My Life.* New York: Summit Books, 1992.

Index

ABOUT THE AUTHOR

Laura Christian Ford is associate provost at Wake Forest University in Winston-Salem, North Carolina. She previously served on the legal staffs of Princeton University and the American Council on Education. She holds the J.D. from the University of Virginia School of Law and the Ph.D. in classics from Princeton University. She has also studied at Harvard University and the American School of Classical Studies at Athens.